A HANDBOOK OF TRAINING MANAGEMENT

REVISED SECOND EDITION

Kenneth R Robinson

Kogan Page

IMPORTANT – Every possible care has been taken to ensure that the factual information given in this handbook is accurate at the time of going to press. The publishers cannot accept responsibility for any errors or omissions, however caused.

First published in 1981 by Kogan Page Ltd
120 Pentonville Road, London N1 9JN

Revised second edition published 1988
Reprinted 1989, 1990

British Library Cataloguing in Publication Data

Robinson, Kenneth R.
A handbook of training management.—2nd ed.
1. Employees, Training of
I. Title
658.3′124 HF5549.5.T7

ISBN 1-85091-663-2

Printed and bound in Great Britain by
Biddles Ltd, Guildford and King's Lynn

Contents

Preface

Unlike the traditional callings of medicine, law and divinity, or business specializations such as financial or production management, training management cannot be said to have had a very long history as a recognized profession. Until a few years ago training in business was carried out on an *ad hoc* and highly selective basis, being confined mainly to the skills required by apprentices learning a trade. The idea that training was needed by everyone in employment from top management down, was not readily conceded because most people assumed that they learned what they were required to know from experience. In the years since the last war, however, there has been a growing awareness that there are more efficient means of acquiring knowledge and skill to do one's job. Many pressures have been brought to bear on managements to accelerate progress towards experienced worker standard for all employees. The complex nature of modern business, together with the increased streamlining of organizations to meet world competition and to counter inflation, calls for training policies which are professionally managed from an influential level. In the larger organizations, therefore, the arm of personnel management which specializes in training has emerged as a profession in its own right.

A Handbook of Training Management has been written with the purpose of providing present and prospective training managers with an operating guide to that profession. It does not claim to give comprehensive answers to all the questions that might be asked. It seeks to condense the more important practical issues of training management into one book, at the same time offering pointers to other sources of relevant information in the extensive and updated bibliography. It is hoped, therefore, that it will enable the reader to identify areas of importance and concern and provide routes to more detailed knowledge.

It should not be assumed that examples used in the book are proposed as the only means of achieving a particular end. As with all aspects of management, the approach to decision-making and problem-solving in training must always allow for alternative options and solutions.

Much of what has already appeared in this handbook about the training process is, of course, still valid. It is therefore retained here with only minor modifications. Not surprisingly over a period of years, however, national bodies such as the Manpower Services Commission, now renamed the Training Commission, have changed both in their structure and in their strategy. For the benefit of students of training management, the historical development of the training division of the Commission has been retained and the latest information on its forward plans added. There has also been evidence of changes in the approach to certain aspects of training, and new passages have been included which draw attention to such developments.

The author does not see the need to modify significantly his observations and predictions in the last section of the final chapter. The hoped-for improvements in the UK economy have been slow to materialize and some training departments find themselves in much the same situation as they were several years ago. Unhappily, when a business begins to make satisfactory profits again after struggling through a difficult period, there is always a long delay in restoring the investment in training. Often this is done in tantalizingly small stages. Budgets are still tight and there is a continuing reluctance in some quarters to face up to the need to prepare both management and workforce to cope with the up-turn when it eventually arrives. Opportunities are lost: the penalties will once more be paid when increasing demands for well-trained employees cannot be met.

Although the frequent use of the male gender in the text may convey the impression that training management is a man's world and the place of women is only in the lower strata of the training activity, no such implication is intended. In the author's view, the profession provides an ideal career for women, offering them the opportunity to make a significant contribution to organizational success. Regrettably, only a very small proportion of those who work in training seem to have the desire to move into the managerial echelons of the profession. It is hoped, however, that this book may help to encourage more women seriously to consider this aspect of business as one of their career goals.

KRR 1988

Chapter 1

The Development of the Training Profession

Training is a commonly used term which has a wide variety of connotations depending on one's experience and background. To the racing enthusiast it may conjure up visions of producing a Derby winner, to the circus proprietor of taming wild animals for public entertainment, to dog owners of animals being schooled for security duties, farm work or mere domestication. In employment, formal training is traditionally associated with the instruction of apprentices and craftsmen who at one time had to pay the employer for the privilege. Today most people have had the benefit of some training to enable them to carry out the requirements of their particular station in life. They may well have considered that they learned much of what they needed to know by experience and will not recognize that this in itself is a form of training, albeit with disadvantages as well as advantages over more formal methods of instruction.

We need to be clear about what we mean by training in the context of this book. Whilst we are concerned mainly with the business environment, this does not mean that the principles, concepts and methods cannot be equally applicable to other professions, such as local government or education. There is no reason at all why one profession should not adopt the most acceptable features of training expertise available in another. There is much common ground in all aspects of human work activity.

Unfortunately training is too often equated with courses of instruction, which may be either internal or external to the organization. This is far too restrictive. A good deal of training does in fact take place in a specially set-aside training room, but there are many other means of achieving learning, some of them generally more effective. Examples of alternative methods are: on-the-job practical instruction, job rotation, supervised project work, programmed learning, coaching, prescribed reading and language laboratories. As will be seen later in this book, the list is by no means exhaustive.

One of the objectives of an organization should be to provide opportunities for its employees to optimize their performance in pursuit of the organization's goals. With this end in view it may be profitable also to help employees to satisfy their own personal objectives. If they feel that the organization cares about them as people there is more likelihood of their responding willingly to satisfying the needs of the concern. When we consider training, therefore, we are seeking, by any instructional or experiential means, to develop a person's behaviour pattern, in the areas of knowledge, skill or attitude, in order to achieve a desired standard or level of performance. This is the definition we shall be using throughout this book.

Most people employed in a training activity, whether in industry, commerce, the services or the public sector, will say that learning is at the centre of their existence. They will accept that employees at all levels, including themselves, have to learn about the organization of which they form a part, its objectives and its place in the community, about the work-based activities in which they are involved, and for which they may be responsible, about the other people with whom they have to come into contact and co-operate, and so forth. Learning is an essential prerequisite for adequate performance in one's occupation, whatever the job may be.

Nevertheless, learning is such a natural and common phenomenon that it is frequently taken for granted. After all, it was of vital importance to early man, who speedily learned to acquire skills in order to survive in a hostile environment. If he did not learn the knowledge and skills necessary to make and to use weapons and tools he could not hunt for food and he starved. If he could not protect himself from enemies and predators, his life was cut short in untimely fashion. The young learned skills by watching more mature adults and copying them, and this technique has survived to the present day, although the idea of learning by 'sitting next to Nelly' has in recent years come in for a good deal of criticism from those who have committed themselves to more advanced and systematic methods and learning technologies.

The development of training as a profession has been interesting in the way in which it has been influenced by the behavioural scientists during the present century. When the researchers have proposed new routes to understanding human behaviour, trainers have not surprisingly seized the opportunity to modify their approaches to training in line with the new fashion. This has created a certain amount of confusion since fashions are constantly changing and, like economists, no two behaviourists seem to be able to agree. Nevertheless the overall trend has been significantly away from a didactic approach to one which is highly participative. Present day professional trainers see their role as the creation of a learning rather than a teaching situation. The ways of achieving this may to some suggest a *laissez-faire* approach, but the results which have been obtained when compared with 'chalk and talk' methods speak for themselves.

The first documented behavioural work of importance to the training profession was probably that of Taylor and the Gilbreths at about the turn of the century.[1] Their research into the nature of jobs and what constituted a fair day's work focused management's attention on the value of time and method study. Analysing the job scientifically made it possible for management to determine the most productive way of carrying it out.

Predictably a number of scientists and others took up the challenge to build on this pioneering work. It was not until the early 1930s, however, that another significant turning point was reached in research into the management of people at work. In the so-called Hawthorne experiment carried out at a Western Electric plant near Chicago[2] the effects of changing lighting and ventilating conditions were found to go contrary to management's expectations. It had been assumed that improving these environmental factors would have a favourable effect on production, and reducing the levels would have adverse results. In fact it was demonstrated that output increased regardless of whether these factors were increased or decreased. Although the experiment was criticized because it was not seen to be very scientific, it did give rise to a concentration of energy on analysing the effects of other factors, such as morale, recognition of effort and job satisfaction. It was suggested that people had feelings and needs and if management was to be successful in motivating them to perform, these needs had to be satisfied. This theory has persisted until the present day and so is a matter of some importance to training specialists.

The second world war brought about not only rapid development in technology but also a dramatic change in learning techniques in the work situation. In the interests of the nation's survival, ways had to be found of speeding up the training of people for the war effort, whether they were members of the armed forces, the civil defence organizations, the land army or the munitions factories. New approaches to training were developed, for example through the government's Training within Industry scheme, to accelerate the learning process so that people became skilled more quickly. Specialists in the use of these techniques began to emerge. Perhaps the training profession may be said to have arrived at that time, although curiously the immediate post-war period did not see many startling moves in its development in this country.

In America a fair amount of research into the behavioural sciences was going on in universities and business schools, and indeed in the business environment itself. This work was to have a considerable impact on the training scene there and, although generally much later, in the UK.

Several scientists, in studying what motivated people to work, concluded that they were stimulated to satisfy certain psychological needs. It was felt that if the acquisition of something which was desired satisfied a basic need, this would contribute to the person's motivation in his or her job. A K Maslow put forward his theory of a 'needs hierarchy'[3] which ranked a variety of identified needs in sequence of their desired satisfaction. A person did not worry too much about higher order needs like self-esteem and self-achievement until the lower order needs such as physiological (food, water, rest, shelter, etc) and safety factors had been substantially satisfied. Whilst the latter may not be too difficult to deal with, the satisfaction of higher order needs requires that the employer offers greater incentives, which may not be so easy to provide. Although little evidence has emerged since Maslow's work to confirm the hierarchy theory, his categories of needs are still used quite commonly today and are frequently treated in management training programmes on motivation.

From the 1950s onwards the work of Frederick Herzberg came into prominence. Assisted by Bernard Mausner and Barbara Snyderman, he developed the 'motivation-hygiene' theory[4] from work carried out among engineers and accountants in a number of establishments in the Pittsburgh area. The team sought to ascertain what people wanted from their jobs and in consequence what the pointers were for motivating them. It was found that in general the things that gave people happy feelings about their employment were factors related directly to the task, or 'motivators', whereas those which caused unhappiness or discomfort were factors which *surrounded* the job, such as money, security and environmental conditions, or 'hygiene' factors. If hygiene factors fell below an acceptable level, people became dissatisfied with their jobs. But improving these factors would not necessarily increase morale and motivation, as the Hawthorne studies had shown. The motivators, as several psychologists have also pointed out, led to positive attitudes to the job because they satisfied the individual's higher order needs for self-achievement or self-fulfilment. If we seek to motivate people through greater job satisfaction, therefore, we may have to concentrate on the motivators, such as achievement, recognition, advancement, responsibility and indeed the work itself. However, the hygiene factors cannot be ignored but have to be held at an acceptable level if they are not to have a de-motivating effect.

The idea that self-fulfilment could be achieved by individuals in organizations was questioned by Chris Argyris.[5] He argued that the independence which was an inherent characteristic of all of us was incompatible with an impersonal organization which expected people to toe the line. This mismatch stood a good chance of resulting in frustration and conflict. One wonders to what extent it has contributed to damaging industrial disputes in recent years.

Douglas McGregor introduced his Theory X and Theory Y concept[6] in the late 1950s and added his contribution to the discourse on the effects on motivation of punishment and rewards. A Theory X manager saw himself as responsible for organizing resources in the pursuit of economic goals. The average worker found work inherently distasteful, was unambitious, not amenable to taking responsibility and resistant to change. He required persuasion, coercion, control, punishment and, where appropriate, rewards. The Theory Y manager, whilst also seeing his role as an organizer of resources to meet economic goals, recognized that people were not by nature unresponsive to organizational needs, though they may have become resistant to them through long experience of working in organizations. He had to create opportunities and conditions which helped them to conclude that it was in their own best interests to work towards the objectives of the concern. Here was the basis of participative management. Whilst Theory X may work in certain situations, such as when employees were struggling to reach adequate subsistence levels, it was unlikely to be successful once their lower order needs were satisfied.

Another relevant area of study in the 1960s which sought to explain why people were satisfied or dissatisfied in their work was that which centred around the leadership or management style adopted by the boss. If the latter's style was such that he created an atmosphere in which his subordinates felt at ease, they were more likely to be satisfied with the work situation. Rensis Likert[7] used the word 'supportive' to describe the boss's approach to employee relationships when the climate produced contributed to the subordinate's sense of personal worth and importance to the organization.

Many managers and supervisory staff in organizations are quite oblivious of the leadership style that they use and the effect that it may have on their employees. Since understanding how one interacts with others is a vital factor in forging satisfactory relationships with subordinates, trainers would do well to explore these issues in their managerial and supervisory training programmes.

There has been no shortage of theories about what produces job satisfaction or dissatisfaction. How one seeks to motivate people depends on which theory or theories one accepts, and this places the training specialist firmly in the management role of making judgements. The evidence of many studies cannot be ignored, but it may be that what is acceptable and appropriate for one group of people is not necessarily transferable to another. John Hunt[8] of the London Business School has not only studied the work of others in this field, but carried out his own research into the subject during the 1970s. He has exhorted us to exercise caution and keep an open mind on the question of understanding job satisfaction. We shall be exploring the work of the key figures in the study of motivation in more detail in Chapter 5.

Throughout the last 25 years we have seen a marked upsurge in training activities in the UK employment scene. Employers have come to realize that human resources are important, indeed vital, for the attainment of their business goals. For a long time they have shown an almost fanatical concern for their machinery and equipment. If it let them down their maintenance staff worked long hours to put things right to ensure minimum disruption to production. Many managements went a stage further when they realized that some breakdowns could be avoided by planned maintenance, which aimed at keeping the machines and equipment in first-class condition at all times. Why should not the human resources attract the same care and attention as these fixed assets? Optimum performance from people can only be obtained when they are properly selected and adequately equipped by training to carry out their part of the job. Moreover, employees at all levels, from the top management down, have a right to expect professional training directly related to the established needs of the organization. It should no longer be reserved for apprentices and craftsmen.

Several factors have helped to lead employers to this conclusion, not least of which has been the policy of successive UK governments to give incentives and exert pressures to improve performance in the creation of wealth. The most significant legal measure directly affecting vocational training was the Industrial Training Act 1964,[9] which set the pattern for a national industrial manpower and training policy. Industrial Training Boards[10] were set up to improve training performance generally, by advice and practical help and by re-distributing the cost of training more fairly throughout industry (see p. 225). This was to the financial benefit of those employers who did their fair share of training to acceptable standards and to the disadvantage of those who did not. Government backing was given to the concept of training in transferable skills with the objective, as yet unproven, of creating greater mobility of skilled people between industries. The 1964 Act was amended by the Employment and Training Act 1973 (see p. 225) which introduced changes in structure, financing, etc. The Manpower Services Commission (see p. 226) was born and became responsible for the co-ordination and execution of public employment and training policies, including the provision of sponsored Skillcentres and adult re-training programmes.

The structure of the Manpower Services Commission, the national training body which reports on the whole of its activities to the Secretary of the State for Employment (and to Secretaries of State for Scotland and for Wales in respect of its plans and activities there) is reproduced in fig. 1 from its Corporate Plan for 1987-1991.[11] In October 1987, it relinquished to the Department of Employment responsibility for the Job Centre network and closely related programmes such as Restart, the Enterprise Allowance Scheme, the Professional and Executive Register and services for helping disabled people into open or sheltered employment. Legislation was also promised to enable the Secretary of State to appoint up to six additional employer members to the Commision and to increase employer representation on Industrial Training Boards.[10] Further information on the training activities of the Commission, renamed the Training Commission in 1988, are given in Chapter 10.

Another major influence on employers' attitudes to training has been the marked effect of inflation on an organization's operations.

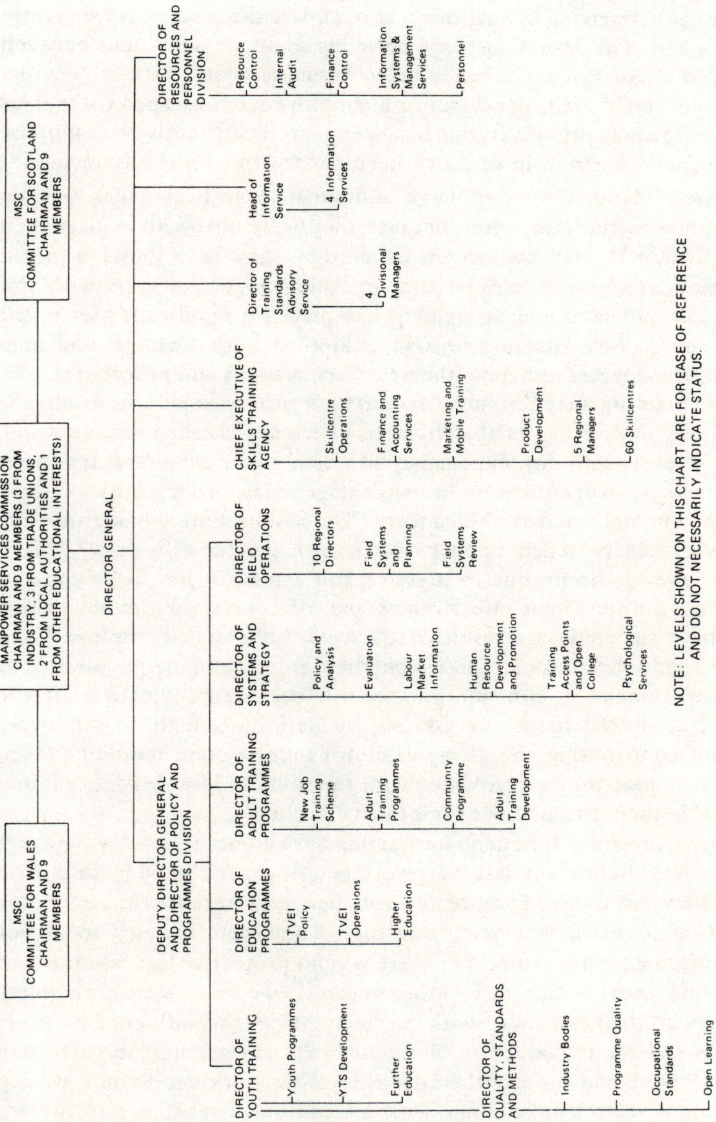

Figure 1. *Structure of Manpower Services Commission (Training Commission)*

The cost of employing people has risen alarmingly over the last few years, and is not confined to wages and salaries alone. To these have to be added the employer's contributions to national insurance and pensions, to say nothing of the proportion of other overheads an employee attracts, including the cost of supervision, which is frequently overlooked. The actual cost of employing someone now totals between one and a half times and twice his or her basic salary. No one, whether employer, employed, pensioner or unemployed, has escaped the vicious effect of rising costs. Everyone has been forced constantly to reappraise his financial position in order to keep pace with continually increasing expenses. Many businesses, large and small, have been taken over or have gone to the wall, often because they were unable to manage their cash flow,[12,44] even though on paper they may have shown a profit. Inflation accounting became the 'in' thing to try to cope with this situation and in this area training has played a significant part in the more progressive organizations in equipping both financial and non-financial managers to handle the necessary systems and procedures.

When an organization, manufacturing or otherwise, is not 'producing the goods' or meeting its objectives, its efficiency is called into question. To cut costs and for expediency it often takes summary action by reducing its workforce on a percentage basis, that is by a fixed proportion right across the concern. The assumption is made that the survivors can be relied upon to work with greater efficiency. This is not, however, borne out in practice and attention has to be given to their capabilities, their effectiveness and, of course, their morale which will have suffered as a result of the cuts. Enlightened employers will realize that the purpose for which they are employing people is that they will make a contribution to the corporate objectives of the organization and to its success. So, by definition, if those employees are not contributing and giving value for money, steps should be taken to ensure that they are provided with the skills and knowledge required to enable them to carry out their tasks effectively.

Other pressures for adequate training have come from the employees themselves. Before the last war, work people tended to be more passive than they are today. They feared for their jobs because the alternative to being in work was being destitute. They were inclined to accept despotic management because there was no protective legislation aimed at giving them a fair deal. More recently we have seen a complete change in their attitude, with an increase in the influence of trade unions and the introduction of a wide range of legal measures affecting employment and industrial relations.[13] More work people in a variety of employment sectors, some with a tradition of resistance to the use of the strike weapon, are now prepared to apply whatever sanctions they may feel are going to be effective in order to achieve their purpose, often regardless of the consequences for the organization. Since the state cushions them against the prospect of poverty in the event of their jobs being terminated, they feel that they have little to lose by taking their employers to the brink of bankruptcy. At the same time, there appears to be an inconsistent commitment to what is euphemistically referred to as the 'right to work'.

Current employment legislation promotes the concept of fairness in industrial relations and so employees are encouraged to pursue policies which they see as fair or as contesting unfairness. The immediate post-war boom in the economy also created further education and career opportunities for many more people and therefore the expectations of work people rose. They became attuned to the idea that career progression was more important than just getting a job. They began to volunteer for training when they thought they might benefit from it. Graduates progressed to positions of managerial responsibility at a much earlier age. This, coupled with improvements in the provision of occupational pension schemes, helped to ease the problem of over-employment by creating a climate where older workers could be offered early retirement on acceptable terms.

Thus, an environment developed in which both employers and employees were seeing training as a means of improving performance of individuals or groups, with an expected pay-off in improved organizational performance. Such improvements can come about in a variety of ways. Clearly, effective training can bring about an increase in knowledge required in the job, knowledge of the structure and business aims of the organization, the departmental objectives, the employee's individual duties and targets, the systems and procedures, and so on. Specific skills can be taught enabling the employee to carry out the job tasks to the desired standard; for example, manual skills, the skills of using techniques related to his function, behavioural skills of managing relationships with bosses, subordinates and peers. There is no doubt also that attitudes, towards the work, the management or other employees, can often be improved by training. Since counter-productive attitudes frequently arise from misunderstandings due to the passing on of inadequate, distorted or ambiguous information, one solution can lie quite simply in an open training policy directed towards honest clarification of the facts. This approach can hardly be called manipulation, as some sceptics of attitude training would have us believe. Fortunately there are very few trainers who, in the interest of self-aggrandizement, will resort to manipulative techniques or indoctrination.

There are, of course, other benefits to be gained from good training, such as improvements in safety standards. The factory nurse of an electronics plant in which an operator training programme was introduced reported that one of the immediate effects was to reduce dramatically the number of visits she had from people on the production line who had sustained minor injuries such as burns and cuts. Injuries to eyes from flying wire ends and from solder being accidentally flicked into them from soldering irons were completely eliminated. Morale increased because the work people were not only more confident in their own abilities, producing more and consequently earning more, but they also felt that the management were genuinely interested in them and valued them. The quality of the finished product was improved and the reject rate reduced to a more acceptable level. Labour turnover and absenteeism also dropped significantly.

One of the effects of a well-trained and committed workforce can be the projection of the right kind of image of the organization to the outside world. This can be extremely important, not only from the point of view of influencing customers, but also attracting the right kind of employees to the organization. It is possible to get the feel of a company from the way visitors are received by the staff and by observing the manner in which the employees go about their business. A slovenly receptionist who reads a book, files her nails or gossips with a friend on the 'phone whilst a visitor waits to be 'dealt with', is unlikely to have had adequate training for the job. Failure of the employer to appreciate this may result in a loss of business or in prospective employees of the right calibre changing their minds about joining the organization.

The acceptance of training as a valid means of contributing to the achievement of objectives, with the consequent marked increase in training activity, gave rise predictably to the establishment of a new profession. Training managers, training officers, training executives, trainers, instructors and training administrators sprang up all over the country and some of them formed their own professional association in 1964, the Institution of Training Officers. This body, re-named the Institute of Training and Development in 1979,[14] pledges itself to the advancement of the science and practice of training and to the setting and maintaining of high standards of competence and performance for those training staff engaged in industry, commerce and the public services. A much older body, the Institute of Personnel Management,[15] founded in 1913, represents professional people throughout the personnel function and so includes training staff in its membership. Its aims are outlined in Chapter 2. An attempt to merge the two organizations in the late 1970s failed due mainly to lack of support for the idea from members.

The training function, then, is now firmly established in this country. Managements who have recognized its importance as an investment rather than an overhead cost accord it the professional status it requires to meet its objectives. The biggest problem it faces in this age of competition for resources is that in many key areas it is extremely difficult to measure the effects of training in absolute terms. Whilst in a production environment it is fairly straightforward to assess output, quality, scrap, etc, the measurement of the effectiveness of, for example, management training is much less practicable since so many other dynamic factors can mask the results. The managing director who informed the author in all seriousness that he assessed the effectiveness of management training by the bottom line of the profit and loss account was deluding himself. Most training specialists would be overjoyed to have such a ready measure of their performance, but the reality is that there is no such simple measure which is unaffected by other factors. This lack of positive means of evaluation leaves many managers in the position where they see training as a greater financial risk than other options for investment of the organization's stretched financial resources. This is disquieting because such decisions are taken at the very time that an investment in training could help an organization along the road to greater efficiency and effectiveness and in some cases survival. One of the highest priorities for training specialists today is to find a means of evaluating training activities which will convince their managements of the contribution that training can make to the success of the business.[16]

The importance of top management commitment cannot be overemphasized. Without their active support the training department can only fulfil its aims at a low organizational level. Unhappily there are still many company training departments whose responsibilities are limited to apprentice, craft and clerical training. Undoubtedly some of them are very competent and achieve considerable success in these areas, but training should be seen as a corporate activity which embraces all levels in the organization structure, so providing the basis for consistency and coherence in training policy at the corporate level. This calls for a very high level of expertise and professionalism in the training function. It should have credibility throughout the enterprise and should not be seen as a corner of the business in which management can put tired executives out to grass.

Chapter 2

Training Objectives, Policies and Strategies

The training department's purpose

The purpose of the training department in an organization, and indeed the personnel function generally, is frequently misunderstood. It is convenient for managers, supervisors and others to refer to that department anything which appears to have a connection with training, however tenuous that connection may be. This arises understandably from the idea that one does not keep a dog and bark oneself, and also from the feeling that time does not permit one to concern oneself with work in which others specialize. It is true that training is a profession in its own right but the responsibility for it cannot rest solely within that profession. It has already been stressed that realistic employers acknowledge that if they employ people to carry out functions in an organization which will contribute to its performance, they must provide them with the tools to do the job. This means not only that premises, facilities, supervision, etc have to be available, but also that the employees themselves should be able to learn the requirements of their jobs and have guidance and training to enable them to carry out their duties to the necessary standards. The responsibility for training his subordinates has to rest very firmly on the shoulders of the manager or supervisor. He is accountable to top management for the performance of his staff, knowing better than anyone what their jobs entail, and he should be able to assess to what extent the requirements are being met. This obligation, to which he should be fully committed, should be explicitly stated in his contract of employment. This is not to say that the boss is expected to carry out all the necessary training himself, although he will sometimes be the right person to do so, for example in the coaching role[17] which should be part of his normal day-to-day duties.

Clearly, he will have to call upon the expertise of the training function in clarifying the training needs, in determining the most suitable means of satisfying those needs and in deciding who should undertake the required training. Sometimes the training department will recommend that the manager or supervisor carry out the training himself with assistance if required.[18] In other instances, where special expertise or training skill is necessary, they will be more practically involved themselves or will sub-contract the work, in whole or in part, to external consultants. The policy adopted will depend on the nature of the need and the training required, as well as the structure of the training department and the resources available (see Chapter 9). Training is therefore to be seen as a service function, providing management with professional support in meeting the organization's objectives. It should at no time be seen as undermining or taking away from managers the responsibility that is rightfully theirs.

The acknowledged professional association for people engaged in the personnel function, the Institute of Personnel Management (IPM),[15] states within its definition of personnel management that it is 'that part of management which is concerned with people at work and with the relationships within an enterprise. It applies not only to industry and commerce but to all fields of employment.

'Personnel Management aims to achieve both efficiency and justice, neither of which can be pursued successfully without the other. It seeks to bring together and develop into an effective organization men and women who make up an enterprise, enabling each to make his own best contribution to its success, both as an individual and as a member of the working group. It seeks to provide fair terms and conditions of employment and satisfying work for those employed.'

Herein lie the aims and the *raison d'être* of the training activity, which is usually an integral part of the personnel function. It is therefore concerned with people, with relationships, job satisfaction and fairness; with efficiency and effectiveness; and with organizational success. The size of the activity will dictate the range of expectations that the management will have of the function (see Chapter 9). Indeed the management may well have determined the size of the department having regard to the responsibilities it wishes it to carry out. If we choose a large organization in order to establish the limits of a training department's brief, we may reasonably expect its responsibilities to be:

- ☐ working with management to produce corporate plans (including manpower plans) and business strategies
- ☐ producing training policies, plans and budgets
- ☐ providing a training input to management development
- ☐ selecting trainees (eg apprentices, student trainees, graduates)
- ☐ arranging appropriate induction programmes
- ☐ carrying out job analyses
- ☐ assisting managers to identify training needs
- ☐ arranging and partly carrying out training programmes, including course design
- ☐ organizing further education for employees
- ☐ measuring, evaluating and following up training
- ☐ developing training staff

- ☐ liaising with educational establishments, government training organizations, professional associations, etc
- ☐ providing a training advisory and information service
- ☐ controlling all training resources
- ☐ advancing the cause of training as a profession.

The skills that training specialists have to bring to bear on these aspects of their work are discussed in Chapter 9.

Corporate plans and strategies

It is suggested above that the training function's responsibilities begin with involvement in the formulation of corporate plans and business strategies. Often training specialists are excluded from this vital activity, largely because their work is perceived to be of relatively low influence in the running of the organization. It is true that by the very nature of the organizational structure, which is commonly pyramidal in shape, their practical training operations will to a large degree take place at the lower levels. Yet the business decisions taken in the corridors of power directly affect the training department and its total strategy.

In no way can it respond to the overall organizational needs if it does not know what these are. Furthermore, if it is not involved in the initial planning, it cannot provide the input which management requires in order to decide whether or not the corporate plans are workable in training terms. For instance, it is futile for an organization to plan for a level of growth which is simply not achievable from the manpower availability point of view or which requires training for its workforce of such a duration as to make it impossible to meet delivery targets. A very good illustration of this type of problem is provided by a research organization which undertook to carry out government contract work. It landed a large contract which among other things required between 20 and 30 additional skilled draughtsmen within a very short time span. Fully trained draughtsmen of the calibre needed were virtually unobtainable at the time. The only way out of the dilemma was for the company to set up a new off-the-job training school for training draughtsmen from scratch, with the inevitable result that there were delays in bringing them up to the standards required to enable them to make an adequate contribution to the project. It is a reasonable assumption that if the training department had been involved from the start and had been aware of the manpower implications of taking on such work, the training school may well have been introduced at an earlier stage and may have had a fighting chance of producing skilled staff when they were needed.

Rapid changes in technology can bring similar difficulties for training specialists who may not be aware of the decisions being taken at the top, for example to mechanize or computerize systems in the factory or in the office. Often the first indication the training staff have that such a move is afoot is when they are given the date of the installation of the equipment! Much of the training planning that is required for a change of this magnitude needs to be done well in advance of the delivery of the hardware. Equipment suppliers are usually geared to these needs and are prepared to provide the training as part of the contract.

In an era of rapid change, the importance of business planning is self-evident. It is not sufficient for an organization simply to make forecasts about its future activity. Forecasts are mainly based on historical data. Assumptions have to be made that certain factors which upset previous forecasts will recur to a greater or lesser degree and allowances must also be made, with appropriate weightings, for new factors which may influence the situation. Thus very few forecasts, if any, can accurately reflect reality. Even when the most sophisticated computerized techniques are used, it would be quite unrealistic to rely upon them. They merely project past activities into the future and do not always adequately cater for the fact that tomorrow's world is likely to be very different from today's.

The essence of business planning is in the preparation of the organization to meet the challenges of the future, whatever they may be.[19] This clearly rules out any one immutable business strategy. Things will not be that simple and convenient. There has to be a number of alternative strategies to deal effectively with uncertainty and risk. For an organization to be successful it has to be able to approach the future with flexibility, to set itself up in such a way that it is equipped to deal appropriately with change, to seize opportunities, to cope with unexpected pressures, and so on. If forecasts of themselves are so unreliable, it is vital to be prepared for any eventuality and to plan accordingly. Whilst the perversity of nature is such that not all the angles are likely to be covered, the alternative strategy approach stands a better chance of success than one in which the organization commits itself to one solitary plan, come what may.

It is because of the existence of alternative business strategies in an organization that the involvement of the training department in the planning process is so strongly advocated. It is not reasonable to expect training staff to be clairvoyant or to have to change their own strategies without warning. However flexible they may be in responding to change, the lead time in setting up a new training activity or modifying an existing one can be considerable. It is often assumed by non-training people that results can be obtained overnight and a good deal of impatience is shown if the goods are not delivered when expected. Expediency in dealing with such problems thus dictates that the training department is aware in advance of what alternative strategies are incorporated in the business plans so that it is forewarned of the possible modifications it could be called upon to make to its own strategy.

The business strategy should therefore define the main aim of the organization and alternative approaches that may be used to advance it. The most favoured approach is selected by the top management and objectives are agreed for each of the functions in the organization. Part of this process would be a resource plan which would determine, among other things, what manpower would be needed and what results would be required from them. A management by objectives[20] approach may be adopted by some concerns, the objectives for each unit and each manager throughout the organization being derived in such a way that they integrate with the overall business objectives. Every manager would agree objectives with his subordinates, and they with their subordinates, and so on throughout the organization.

Manpower planning

Thus the business strategy and particularly the manpower plan would furnish the basis for a training plan embracing the whole organization. The manpower plan[21] provides an analysis of the manpower currently available and the movements in the workforce which are likely during the period of the plan, eg from resignations, retirements, deaths, redundancies, transfers, new entries. From this data can be derived a training needs analysis which will identify the training that is needed to satisfy the requirements of the business plan. (See Chapter 3 on establishing training needs.) One aspect of the manpower plan which should demand the careful scrutiny of personnel and training staff is the age profile of the organization's workforce. Fig. 2(a) shows the age data for four job classifications in the computer bureau division of an imaginary company and fig. 2(b) reproduces this information in graphical form.

The information illustrates among other things the manpower challenges that the company will have to face in the future. Irrespective of what labour turnover can be expected among the lower and middle age groups, the next five to 15 years will bring a mass exodus of nearly one third of the workforce due solely to retirement. The analyst and operator strengths will be sadly depleted unless steps are taken to feed in new blood at the lower end of the age spectrum, and clearly the implications for the training department are that more training than would normally have been expected will have to be provided. Over half the programmers employed are under 30 and will probably have been anticipating promotion for some time, so the middle age range in the systems analyst section could probably be replenished from this source. However, this will create havoc in the programming section and will require substantial recruitment, probably from outside the company, since there will be few operators available for promotion and re-training. The operator section will be having its own problems of manning, requiring a considerable injection of skilled employees, who may not

The NOP Data Company Ltd Date 31/3/88

Computer Bureau Division – Age profile of employees

Job classification	*Age range*						
	18-20	21-30	31-40	41-50	51-60	61-65	*Total*
A. Management and administration	–	1	10	1	–	–	12
B. Systems analysts	5	4	15	9	19	5	57
C. Programmers	12	17	10	2	–	–	41
D. Operators	–	5	2	10	18	5	40
Total	17	27	37	22	37	10	150

Figure 2(a) *Age profile data for four occupational categories*

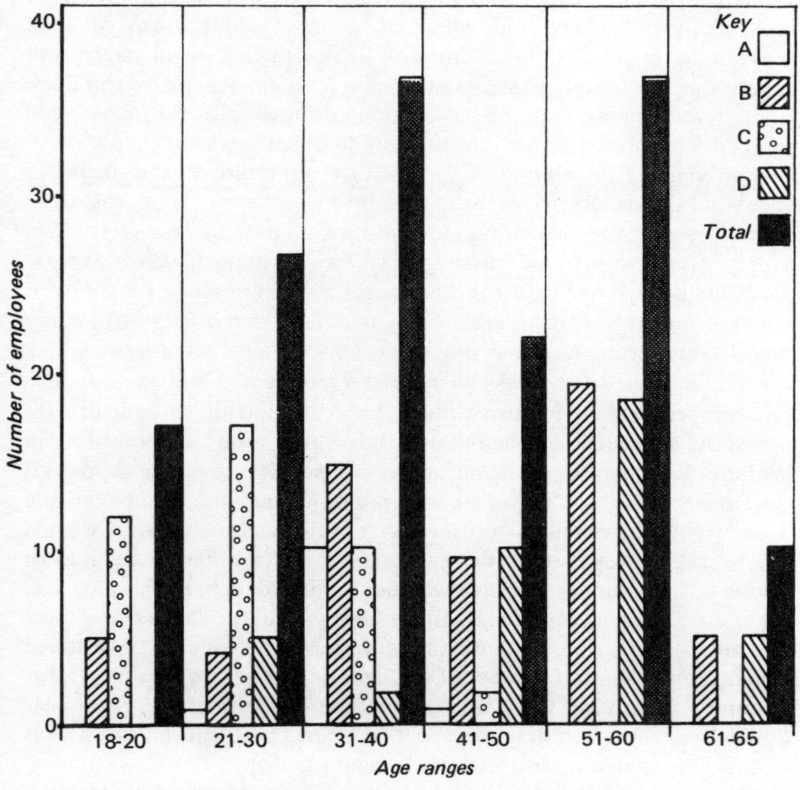

Figure 2(b) *Histogram of age profile data in (a)*

be readily available, or an intake of young people who will require training from scratch. If this is not properly planned there is a danger that the operator strength will be inadequate and the lead time in training new entrants will cause some embarrassment.

The indications are that there may be trouble in management areas, too. Most of these executives are in the 30 to 40 age range and it is reasonable to suppose that a significant proportion of them will be expecting to be promoted out of the bureau division in the foreseeable future. There is no-one to take their place unless there are promotions from the analyst or programmer ranks, or new managers are recruited from outside. In either event, some management training is indicated.

Management development

It will be obvious that the age profile only gives a very limited picture of the situation but nevertheless it sounds some very important warnings which have to be heeded. In order to obtain a more accurate picture, it is necessary to produce much more detailed information of the likely career progressions of individuals in order to be able to compute what movements are likely and what the training implications of such movements might be. One method of achieving this for managers and supervisors is through a management development scheme[22] and there is no reason apart from sheer volume of work why the same basic principles cannot be applied throughout an organization.

Management development[23] sets out to improve and maintain standards of managerial performance in an organization, at the same time providing the machinery for ensuring that there is a continuing supply of suitably trained managers to meet the organization's future needs. This objective calls for a comprehensive inventory of managerial talent, a means of identifying training needs to assist managers to equip themselves better to carry out their present jobs effectively and a succession plan which seeks to predict career paths and incorporates suitable preparation for promotion. The considerable amount of data necessary for such a scheme demands that it be computerized in medium to large sized organizations. In smaller concerns a manual system is workable. Whether mechanized or manual, it has to be capable of retrieving the details of prospective candidates for a vacancy when a job profile is keyed into the system. It therefore has to be able to handle a large number of variables. The personal data in the records also needs to be very detailed and, above all, up-to-date. The scheme must of course be flexible because, as with business forecasts mentioned earlier, only a limited number of predictions will become reality. If, for example, a manager who was earmarked for promotion next year suddenly decides to resign, there will be serious problems unless there is a contingency plan to deal with such an eventuality.

The monitoring of managerial performance is usually carried out by means of performance reviews.[24] The writer avoids the more commonly used term appraisal because it seems to imply a one-way autocratic approach. Performance review assumes that the interviewee takes an active part in the activity, in other words it is a democratic two-way system. Targets[16] which were *agreed*, not *set*, at the last interview are reviewed and where they are not met, reasons are sought. If these were outside the control of the employee, allowance has to be made for this and cognisance taken of the possible effects of such factors in the future. Where failure to meet targets satisfactorily points to shortcomings in knowledge or capability, training needs are identified and recorded in the training plan for suitable action. At the same meeting targets, including the satisfaction of the identified training needs, are agreed for the coming period. In this way, the employee will only agree to targets which he believes will be achievable and he will be able to talk through any difficulties that he may feel he is going to encounter. There is greater commitment to strive for achievement of the agreed objectives.

The training department's contribution to management development can be considerable but it depends to a large extent on how well managers carry out performance reviews. If they do not recognize what constitutes a training need when targets are not met, then the training machinery will not be set in motion, performance will not improve and the same problems may arise at the next review. It should therefore be stressed that an organization should not attempt to introduce a performance review system without taking early steps to ensure that all employees who will be involved are trained to carry out their responsibilities under the scheme effectively. This not only means being given assistance with interviewing[25] and discussion techniques but also with the recognition and identification of training needs.

In some management development programmes, potential managers are also included in the scheme. It is important for training specialists to recognize the special needs of these employees. Apart from the obvious requirements for them to become proficient in using management techniques, methods and systems, they require a major re-orientation in their thinking from operating as specialists to a total business approach as part of the management team (see Chapter 3).

Frequently employees complain that their managements are not concerned about their future; that the policy is to fill senior vacancies from outside; that vacancies are seldom if ever advertised internally; that they have been passed over for promotion, and so forth. Yet when management tries to introduce a management development scheme which, if properly operated, would remove these difficulties, there is often resistance to it. As has been said, the personal records of everyone in the scheme have to be comprehensive and up-to-date. Personnel departments have problems keeping their records up to the minute, since changes which they have not initiated themselves are seldom notified to them. It is therefore necessary to approach the members of the scheme for an update in their personal data and it is not unusual for them to refuse or at least give the return of the information a very low priority. This indicates a complete lack of understanding of the purpose of the exercise and once again points to an important training need, that of explaining the management's objectives and the implications, before introducing such a scheme.

Individual objectives

It has to be recognized that individuals as well as organizations have objectives, based on their experience, knowledge, attitudes, beliefs, home background, outside interests, etc. (See Chapter 5 on motivation.) These objectives, whilst quite logical and realistic in relation to the individual, may be in conflict with those of the business. Reconciling these goals may create problems for management, but trainers can give valuable support in exploring such difficulties in training programmes, making employees aware of how they arise and what will be the effect on the organization, and consequently on the individuals, if they are not resolved. Entrenched attitudes which are in opposition to the organization's goals can be very damaging but do not necessarily appear so to those who hold them. Better understanding may often be achieved through the medium of well-designed training.

Unified philosophy

It is thus necessary for the training objectives, policies, plans and strategy to reflect the philosophy expressed in the business plans. In the absence of training's involvement at top level, this is difficult if not impossible. It is not unknown for trainers unwittingly to adopt training approaches which are not always in harmony with the management ethos. This is clearly counter-productive and indeed can be exceedingly harmful, not only to the organization, whose employees may be misdirected, but also to the image of the training department which may be seen as incompetent. Training policy must echo management policy, and for this reason training managers need to convince those concerned with the corporate planning process that the function must be involved in that process if it is to meet management's expectations. It is true to say that many organizations still equate training with simply improving the performance of individuals out of context with the corporate goals. There is thus a risk that they will not get the priorities right and that a substantial amount of training may lack relevance.

Training policy

Every organization should have a declared training policy which is understood and supported by employees at all levels. It is not enough for the statement simply to say that it is the policy of the organization to ensure that everyone is developed to the limit of his or her ability, in the interests of corporate excellence.[26] Everyone should be clear as to how this will be carried out. An example is shown in fig. 3.

It has been said that the training policy should be supported by all employees. This is important since training can be abortive if there is no commitment on the part of those being trained. Part of this commitment comes from an understanding of what the training policy is all about, hence the need to explain it carefully to everyone. Training should not be seen by employees as a penalty but as an opportunity for them to further their knowledge and expertise both in their own and the organization's interests. The climate needs to be created in which they are eager to seize such opportunities and in their enthusiasm may well be able to identify some of their own needs. The importance of self-development should not be underestimated.[27]

Training strategy

The major purpose of training in an organization is to achieve performance from its employees at all levels. How the training department accomplishes this depends upon many factors including management and supervisory style, organizational climate, quality of the working environment, nature of the work and local community influences. These factors will differ from one establishment to another and thus the strategies called for will vary from one location to another. Clearly the morale of the workforce and what motivates them will have a direct bearing on the strategy adopted by the training department (see Chapter 5). It is therefore important that training staff can read the signals from both management and employees in order to assess what can be done and what cannot be done within the constraints that may be present. In some situations, for example, any attempt to introduce behavioural training overtly would court disaster. Thus in such instances if behavioural training is deemed necessary, it is vital to incorporate it in other, more acceptable, training in such a way that it does not become dominant.

Part of a training department's strategy is its total training doctrine. Some managements will wish to influence this, but others will say that it's a matter for the training function itself, and that as long as they deliver the goods, they are free to adopt what philosophy they wish. If given such a mandate, the training manager is able to determine a strategy which satisfies the organizational requirements in addition to the two criteria of meeting the psychological needs of the employees

The NOP Data Company Ltd Date

Statement of training policy

This statement sets out the company's training policy which has been agreed in the interests of ensuring that employees at all levels are given every assistance to optimize their performance in pursuit of corporate goals. These are set out in detail in the company's business policy document.

The main elements of this training policy are:

1. The training plan will be established by reference to the requirements of the company's business plan. Unit objectives will be agreed with the managers concerned and individual targets derived from these objectives and agreed with the employees. A performance review system will be adopted as described in the employee handbook.
2. Training needs will be identified through the performance review system or in special cases when there are changes in internal policies or systems or in external factors, such as government legislation.
3. The Training Department will comprise a Training Manager, a Training Officer, two Instructors, an Administrator and a Secretary/Records Clerk.
4. Where possible, training in satisfaction of identified needs will be carried out by management, supervision or members of the Training Department. Outside consultants will also be used where appropriate. Training methods will be determined by the Training Department.
5. All new employees will receive induction training on engagement. This will be designed to assist them to settle into the company and feel part of it at the earliest opportunity. It will include familiarization with the business as well as initial job training.
6. All employees under the age of 18 years will be given the opportunity of paid day release to attend suitable further education courses, if available, at the local technical college. Examination fees will be refunded when successful.
7. In approved cases, adult employees will be given assistance with time off to attend further education courses in furtherance of their knowledge of their jobs. Payment during absence on such courses or for acceptable correspondence courses, will be at the discretion of the management.
8. Four places on a sponsored 4-year sandwich course will be available to selected employees at . . . . . . University each year. (Further details from Training Department.)
9. Prescribed books for external courses will be paid for by the company provided they are returned to the Training Department library within six weeks of the end of the course. Otherwise the cost will be recharged.
10. All training costs will be borne by the Training Department budget. No such costs will be incurred without the written agreement of the Training Manager.
11. All training equipment including books will be on the Training Department's inventory and will not be removed without that department's permission.
12. The Conference Room will be the responsibility of the Training Department, to which all requests for its use will be made.

Figure 3. *Training policy statement*

whilst not conflicting with the management's philosophy. This is the happy situation in which every training man wishes to find himself.

The training department's doctrine will include its overall approach to learning. Training style may vary considerably from task to task and there is therefore a tactical element. Different situations call for different courses of action and hence the approach needs to be flexible. Nevertheless a common thread tends to run through a training department's philosophy, and this dictates its approach to both its overall strategy and its tactics. Firmly committed to a set of principles, it believes that by following them the training objectives will be fulfilled. This outlook, provided it is not too rigid, is important in that it gives the training function a purpose, a framework for the activity, which helps to build up a rapport and confidence with management and employees alike who soon learn to know what to expect from it. The training department which does not have a clear overall approach to its work is like a ship without a rudder, responding in an unco-ordinated way to the elements, in the shape of random training demands, but not to the helmsman who is trying to steer the vessel towards the desired destination.

It is the fashion nowadays for participative styles of training to be favoured, as there is a good deal of empirical evidence to suggest that this is more conducive to lasting learning than the more authoritative or formal approaches (see Chapter 6). Adopting such a style requires acceptance from employees who may be bewildered by something which is so far removed from the more traditional teaching styles to which they have been accustomed. The strategy therefore has to include consideration of ways and means of gaining such acceptance. For example, no training should be embarked upon without the most careful briefing. Trainees should never be left to find out for themselves what the purpose of the exercise is, what is going to be expected of them and what will be the trainer involvement.

The training strategy also has to recognize that the department's responsibilities are not discharged with the provision of training. The end result has to be monitored and measured against the criteria for success. If there is no strategy for achieving this and promoting acceptable transferability to the job, the process can be abortive or at least may only be partially successful.

It is an unhappy commentary on the performance in the past of a majority of training specialists that their activities have been carried on *outside* the organization rather than *within* it. Trainers have concentrated on teaching individual employees how to carry out the requirements of their jobs out of context with the current and changing needs of the organization of which they are part. The needs of an employee as perceived by him, by his manager or by the trainer can often bear no relation to what the organization itself requires of him in terms of achieving corporate success. The training department's strategy in this situation is parochial and thus of limited effect in meeting organizational goals. There is now growing support among professional trainers for adopting the approach of the organization development consultant (see p. 115) who concerns himself with total organizational strategy. Trainers become consultants to the management, working with them to establish organizational objectives, to monitor change and innovation and to formulate training strategies which are geared to the solution of real problems which affect organizational performance. In dealing with training opportunities on a total strategy basis, they may find themselves involved less in the design and running of training courses as in the past and more with those aspects which help to ensure that the training is getting to the root of the organization's needs.

In summary, a training department's strategy should therefore embody:

- ☐ an overall sense of direction
- ☐ an assessment of environmental influences, including leadership style in the organization
- ☐ a doctrine geared to training intervention at organizational level,[28] and thus to satisfying true organizational needs as well as those of the workforce
- ☐ methodology which aids the satisfaction of those needs
- ☐ planning and tactical flexibility
- ☐ an acceptance of the importance of measuring results and modifying strategies where necessary.

Training plans

The training plan is a practical document which brings together all the training needs derived from the business and manpower plans, the performance review system and any other recognized sources. It not only sets out what the needs are, how they were established and what standards are to be achieved, but also indicates the means by which they are to be satisfied, with the estimated time scales. The person or persons who will be responsible for the training are specified and budget allocations stated. A suitable form may be as shown in fig. 4. The budget figures are purely fictitious and should not be assumed to be typical.

Conclusions

One underlying principle which has been stressed throughout this chapter is that of the unification of training objectives, policies and strategies with the business plans of the organization. This is a key factor if training departments are to be truly effective in terms of carrying out their purpose of improving organizational performance.

The NOP Data Company Ltd								Training Plan 1988
Source	*Department*	*Trainees*	*Training targets*	*Training planned*	*Responsibility*	*Dates*	*Training completed*	*Budget (excl. trainee's salary)*
Self	Management	Financial Controller	General appreciation of Management by Objectives as a corporate management technique	Prescribed reading 'Management by Objectives' by John Humble	Self-development	Book to be borrowed from Training Dept Library for 1 month from 4.2.88	4.3.88	—
Performance review	Management	Trainee Manager	Introduction to (1) Management a/cs and (2) Cost a/cs. Must achieve 80% correct responses in Finance questionnaire FM1	On-the-job assignments in Finance Department	(1) Senior Management Accountant (2) Cost Accountant	(1) 10-12.2.88 (2) 7-9.3.88	(1) 12.2.88 (2) 9.3.88	75 65
Training policy	Management	Junior Secretary	Pitmans 100 wpm shorthand certificate	Continuation of day release to Cottenford Tech. College (1987/88)	Training Manager	Thursdays to 30.6.88	30.6.88	40
Performance review	Systems	4 Senior Analysts	Update on provisions of Employment Acts 1980 and 1982	External course by Harbury Consultants	Training Manager	2 analysts 19.2.88 2 analysts 18.3.88	19.2.88 18.3.88	200 200
Manpower plan	Programming	3 new programmers starting 1.3.88	Standard induction and initial programmer training to grade 2 standard	(1) Induction (2) On-the-job training in accordance with programme TP1	(1) Chief programmer and Personnel Dept. (2) Senior programmer	(1) 1.3.88 (2) 3-31.3.88	(1) 1.3.88 (2) 31.3.88	45 575

Figure 4. *Example of training plan*

Unhappily, this condition is not always met. Commonly training departments find themselves setting their own objectives, producing plans and developing strategies in blissful isolation and without any detailed knowledge of the corporate goals of the organization. The result is that the true objectives are not identified and such training as is carried out is done piecemeal and without any idea as to what should be the priorities.

This is not necessarily the fault of the training manager. He may apply himself assiduously to the task of trying to convince his management of the desirability of his closer involvement with the affairs of state, and his efforts may be met with a negative, even hostile, response. Gaining his management's support to the desired extent may be an uphill climb, but nevertheless this goal should be pursued with the utmost vigour (see Chapter 9).

A successful training function has to be built on teamwork (see Chapter 6). Not only should everyone be aware of its aims in organizational terms, but they should also recognize that they each have a part to play and should be fully committed to making training policies work. Creating this climate should be one of the training manager's primary objectives.

Chapter 3

The Training Process – Establishing Training Needs

One of the most important steps in the training process is the establishment of the training needs.[29] In using this term we are implying that there are weaknesses somewhere in the system which demand strengthening by means of training in some form or other. It is common to define a training need as the gap which exists between the true requirements of a given job and the present capabilities of the incumbent. However, we must not confine our definition solely to the individual, although in the last analysis the satisfaction of needs will have to be carried out through individuals. The organization is seen to have needs when it recognizes that it is not geared to meeting the objectives which it sets itself. In other words, when setting its targets it cannot make the assumption that the resources already available will be suitable or adequate. It therefore has to examine any shortcomings and make suitable provision in its plans for eliminating them. This involves among other things, establishing whether the organizational structure and capability are right to meet the challenges of the future and identifying the needs which arise in the various functions or occupations throughout the business. Finally, individual needs will become evident when employees carrying out those functions are found not to be fully equipped, in terms of knowledge, skills or attitudes, to meet the requirements of their jobs (see Chapter 5).

In order to be able to measure the gap which has to be closed by means of training, it is therefore necessary to follow a three-stage procedure. We need to ascertain, in some detail:

- ☐ the desired performance of the organization and its shortfalls in meeting its objectives due to training deficiencies
- ☐ the training needed in each occupation to enable that function to be carried out comprehensively and
- ☐ the expected contribution and present capability of each member of the workforce.

It has already been indicated in Chapter 2 that the overall training needs in an organization will be highlighted by the business plans which indicate what the concern's activities are expected to be over the period of the plan. Corporate plans may be for any period from a few months to five or even ten years. It is, however, most common for organizations to produce short-term plans for periods of one year and long-term plans for periods of four or five years.

Let us suppose that the 1988 short-term corporate plan of a manufacturing plant, which is part of a large group, includes the following objectives:

- ☐ to complete development of product B by 11 December 1987. This model to supercede product A. Pre-production models to be available by 19 February 1988. Commence production 7 March 1988. Output target 500 units/month for the first two months, thereafter 1000 units/month. Total output for 1988 9000 units; 1989 12,000 units
- ☐ to phase out product A by 2 May 1988. Forecast monthly requirements in 1988: January 840; February 730; March 380; April 420
- ☐ to introduce incentive bonus scheme on product B line with effect from 7 March 1988
- ☐ to install two model PX870 word processors in Sales Department by 29 January 1988
- ☐ to adopt the group financial reporting systems by 3 January 1989.

This information, although limited, provides the training department with some clues about future training needs, which may be summarized as follows:

1. It is assumed that production workers will not have been sitting around idle, and that their numbers will be in line with the needs of production in January and February 1988. This means that since the level of output is expected to rise considerably from March onwards, more production workers will be required, unless productivity can be dramatically improved! The numbers will be revealed in the manpower plan[21] and there will be two obvious training needs. First, the existing workforce will have to be re-trained on the new model and second, the new intake will require induction and job training. If the new model is very different from the old, the supervisors may also need familiarization with the revised requirements.
2. An incentive scheme should not be introduced without adequate communication with the workforce. If management wishes it to work, the people involved must accept it and fully understand it. Thus training is again indicated for the operatives, the supervisors and possibly the managers. Members of the wages/salaries department will also have to be familiarized with the scheme.
3. The installation of equipment which will change working practices in a department will inevitably give rise to the need for training

those affected. The employees in the sales department who will use the word processors will have to be instructed in their operation.

4. Changing the financial reporting system in an establishment by directive from head office can have far-reaching implications. Not only does the financial department itself have to be initiated in the revised procedures and possibly in a new philosophy, but the managers and supervisors who are parties to implementing the system will likewise require training in carrying out the new requirements. Failure to prepare both specialists and managers to operate modified reporting systems in this way can cause considerable confusion and make the transition from old to new much more difficult than it needs to be.

The findings at this stage are vague. They really only tell us that some training will have to be done. Although numbers of potential trainees will be available from the manpower plan, the magnitude of the task is not evident since we have not yet established how much new knowledge or skill has to be acquired by them. The first step, then, is to analyse the new requirements.

Job analysis[30] is the term used to describe a process which involves the analysis of a job into its component parts or tasks to provide the data required for a variety of purposes. These include recruitment, management development, developing organizational and wage structures, improving job methods and safety and, of course, establishing training needs. The general principles of job analysis are applicable to all situations, whether in the factory, the office, maintenance or servicing departments both in-plant and in the field, in fact anywhere where work is being done. It tends, however, to be associated in people's minds more with manual and craft jobs and possibly clerical work, than with management, supervision or other professional areas. This arises from the fact that manual jobs generally involve more easily definable processes or activities and consequently they would appear to be more suitable areas in which to use analytical methods. Management and professional work is less clear cut, and attempts to analyse such jobs are likely to meet with greater opposition from the people concerned, who feel that much of their work is empiric and not susceptible to detailed examination. Nevertheless, the analysis of such work can pay dividends in, among other things, improving the management of time[31] and thus helping to optimize managerial performance. It is a common criticism of managers that they spend unnecessarily long hours at work and need to learn to manage their time more effectively.

In the course of carrying out a job analysis, a job description or a job specification is prepared. The distinction between these terms is that a job specification states what a job should be whilst a job description sets out what it actually is, taking into account the specific knowledge and skills the job-holder brings to it. Clearly when someone is recruited to a job, he seldom matches the job specification precisely and often it is necessary to modify the duties and responsibilities to make use of the skills and knowledge that the newcomer can bring to the position. In some instances, the job descriptions of other people in the department may well be modified in order to accommodate the new arrival and to optimize departmental performance. Note that this does not mean that either of these documents tells us how *effectively* the job is performed by the job-holder. That is taken care of in the performance review (see pp. 47 and 189) or by some other means of assessment.

It will thus be seen that where we are examining a newly created job, we produce a specification based on what we think the job should look like. Where the position is already occupied by an employee, it is possible, with the benefit of the experience of the job-holder, to write a job description setting out precisely what it entails. In either case the document should normally cover:

- ☐ the scope and purpose of the job and its objectives
- ☐ the work performed in the job: the detailed functions/duties and whether operational, supervisory, or managerial etc
- ☐ the responsibility for (a) resources, quantified where possible under the six M's: manpower, machines, materials, methods, money and minutes (time), and stating clearly where accountable; (b) policy decisions, whether individually or through committees
- ☐ the organizational relationships, ie position in the hierarchy, cross-functional interfaces
- ☐ the training and experience needed
- ☐ the working conditions, eg (a) location; (b) nature of work activity (mobile, sedentary, etc); (c) hours of work (shift work, flexitime, etc); (d) whether member of a group; (e) health/safety risks
- ☐ the pay scale and conditions of service (including overtime)
- ☐ the opportunities for advancement within the organization.

To produce such a document we therefore need to know a good deal about the job and where it fits into the general scheme of things. If the post is deemed to be necessary to the future of the organization, it should not be too difficult to define its purpose. No job should exist without a clear statement of its scope and intent and the objectives the job-holder is expected to achieve. For example, the objectives of a personnel manager may be:

- ☐ to promote and maintain sound industrial relations practice throughout the organization
- ☐ to recruit employees at all levels below first line management in sufficient numbers and of acceptable standard to meet the needs

of the manpower plan

- ☐ to contribute to the formulation of company personnel policies and agreements and to ensure their effective implementation
- ☐ to establish the training needs of employees at all levels and to take the necessary steps to see that these needs are satisfied
- ☐ to provide a welfare service to employees at all levels and to implement health and safety policies.

Tabulating the work performed in the job may be more difficult. We can readily establish whether it is a managerial, supervisory, specialist or operational job but ascertaining the detailed functions to be performed requires analysis and may have to be approached in different ways depending on the job. One thing is certain. The process entails the collection and examination of a good deal of data, some of which will be considered appropriate for inclusion in the job analysis and some of which will be rejected. Where the job is already being carried out, one way in which such data can be accumulated is by discussing it with the job-holder. He should be in possession of as much information as anyone and often he will be able to offer facts, gleaned from experience, which no one else knows about. Of course, approaching the employee for such a purpose requires care. He needs to be put at his ease and reassured as to the reasons for the exercise. He must not see it as putting him under any threat, for example of being moved, or worse, of losing his job altogether. Once such worries are dispelled, he will normally be very happy to talk about his job.

It is not enough merely to ask the job-holder what he does. If we have training needs in mind we shall want to know how he does his job and why he does it in a particular way. We may discover that he has got into the habit of employing inefficient work methods. This may point to the need for a closer examination of the whole job by the work study department, who will establish by scientific means the most suitable methods to be used in carrying out the job.[1]

TWI job breakdown

A job involving a number of operations, processes or tasks may have to be broken down into manageable parts. There are several ways in which this may be done. Perhaps the most simple of these is the Training Within Industry (TWI) breakdown for job instruction. Although the TWI courses run by the Manpower Services Commission were phased out in May 1984, the method of breakdown used has stood the test of time and is still found to be helpful in the absence of anything more sophisticated. The trainer is recommended to work through the job once to identify stages or units which he believes contain no more than the average learner is able to master at a time. He then goes through the job a second time and looks for essential factors in doing it properly. These are called key points and are factors:

- ☐ that may make the job easier to give special guidance on carrying it out
- ☐ that may have safety implications, or
- ☐ that may affect the quality of the finished work.

A typical TWI breakdown covering the replacement of a mains plug on an electrical appliance is shown in fig. 5.

Stage	*Instruction*	*Key points*
Remove old plug	Remove cover fixing screw. Loosen cord grip retaining screws. Loosen terminals on connecting pins. Release wires from plug. Remove fuse.	
Check wires	If fractured or insulation chafed: ☐ cut off damaged wire. ☐ strip outer sheath by 5 cm. Tape end of outer sheath if braided.	Using stripper or cutters, avoid damage to wires.
Position wires in new plug	Clamp end of outer sheath under cord grip by tightening retaining screws. Run wires to appropriate pins. Cut wires to suitable lengths. Strip 1 cm of insulation off each wire.	Avoid damage to cable through over tightening. Brown wire to *LIVE* Blue wire to *NEUTRAL* Green/yellow wire to *EARTH*. Do not fracture wires with stripper or cutters.
Fix wires to terminals	Wind wire ends clockwise around threaded pin. Screw down terminal.	Twist wire ends clockwise if stranded. Wind around pin as closely as possible. Firmly but not enough to fracture wires. Check no stray ends.
Make secure	Insert fuse in fuseholder. Assemble cover and secure with central screw.	Check value of fuse suitable for appliance. Check cable held firmly by cord grip. Firmly – no looseness and not too tight.
Test appliance	Insert plug in mains supply socket. Switch on appliance and socket switch.	If appliance does not function, switch off, remove plug from socket, check fuse and review assembly stages.

Figure 5. *TWI breakdown for replacing a mains plug*

Task analysis

Task analysis[32] is another method of breaking down a job. This is defined in the MSC's *Glossary of Training Terms*[33] as 'a systematic analysis of the behaviour required to carry out a *task* with a view to identifying areas of difficulty and the appropriate training techniques and learning aids necessary for successful instruction'. The tasks in a job are listed and each one is then analysed in order to evaluate its importance and the degree of difficulty that may be experienced. The means of dealing with the task in training terms are then identified. By way of a simple example, fig. 6 shows part of a task analysis of the job of a sales assistant in a retail shop.

FENELLA FASHIONS LTD			page 3
Task Analysis			Job: Junior Sales Assistant
Task	*Level of importance*	*Degree of difficulty*	*Training method required*
18. Dealing with dissatisfied customers	Top priority requirement – customer's complaint must be dealt with satisfactorily in the interests of Company reputation and further business	Requires skill and ability to take heat out of situation, to show particular concern, to keep level head, to analyse the problem and to give positive help	Off-the-job role playing, reinforced by suitable film
23. Cashing-up. Checking day's takings against total rung up on till	High level importance but subject to check by supervisor if cash does not balance with till-roll	Relatively easy. Largely a question of the ability to count notes and coins accurately and with the minimum of delay	Instruction and practice in adding up notes and coins in mixed denominations, preferably off-the-job

Figure 6. *Part of task analysis of sales assistant's job*

Faults analysis

Where the incidence of errors or faults in a job can be fairly high, the faults analysis method can be useful. The reasons for and consequences of the faults or errors are assessed and the necessary training action planned. An example of the use of this technique is as follows:

> A service engineer has an adequate technical knowledge to understand the basic operation of all the products he is likely to encounter, but he has had no practical experience of trouble-shooting on Unit X. This unit has a fault pattern which is fairly consistent, eg 80 per cent of faults are failure of component Y resulting in certain symptoms and the other 20 per cent are also fairly predictable. The need is quite obvious here. He does not have to be acquainted with the detailed operation of the unit, but does require a run-down on the most frequently recurring faults. Just how much information has to be imparted depends upon his existing knowledge and expertise.

Another example of the use of the faults analysis approach is with the job of a conference organizer.

> It is relatively easy to produce a checklist of the basic activities and duties of such a person, but the acid test of his or her success comes when things go wrong and have to be dealt with promptly to avoid a disaster. A list of such eventualities can be made. For example, the failure of a speaker to arrive at the appointed time, the breakdown of a visual aid during a presentation, the outbreak of fire in the building, hiccups in the catering services ordered, and so on. Being forewarned of the most common critical incidents in this person's job, it is possible to provide suitable training to enable them to be dealt with effectively should they arise.

Skills analysis

Perhaps the most common method of analysing the skills required in work of a non-supervisory nature in industry or commerce is that known simply as skills analysis. The main requirements of this method are that it should be systematic and that it should provide enough information to enable a suitable training programme to be designed. It may be used for simple or complex jobs. An example of a very simple job is shown in fig. 7.

This breakdown does not give detailed information on how to use the shredding machine. This would have to be provided in the training programme developed from the skills analysis (see Chapter 4).

In more complicated jobs it may be necessary to incorporate an ergonomic study of the job. Ergonomics, as defined by Professor W T Singleton in his *Introduction to Ergonomics*,[34] is 'the technology of work design', and is 'based on the human biological sciences: anatomy, physiology and psychology. In general terms, anatomy is concerned with the structure of the body (the size and the way it is constructed); physiology is concerned with the function of the body (the biological processes that maintain it); and psychology is concerned with behaviour (the adaptive responses of the organism to its environment).' Thus in analysing a job which involves more complex skills, we may have to concern ourselves with:

- ☐ matching the working conditions to the physical build of the employee (height of chair with respect to bench or desk, for example)

Item	*Skill*	*Knowledge*
Preparation of machine for operation	Installing and connecting up.	Basic understanding of working principles. Correct position for efficient operation.
Use of machine	Feeding paper into machine. Ability to clear when jammed.	Capacity of machine, size and thickness of paper which may be handled. Removal of pins and clips. Need to switch off when clearing machine on jamming.
Maintenance and inspection	Regular lubrication. Daily inspection of machine and mains lead for wear. Replacement of polythene bag.	Lubrication procedure as set out in handbook. Consequences of not carrying out lubrication and inspection regularly. Knowledge of where to obtain replacement bag and how bag is fixed to machine. How to deal with filled bag.
Safety	Operating machine without risk to self, others or machine.	Electrical and safety factors and emergency procedures – see handbook. Physical safety factors.

Figure 7. *Simple skills analysis for using a paper shredder in an office*

☐ the precise movement patterns of the limbs used in carrying out work manoeuvres
☐ the physiological and psychological effects of environmental conditions such as heat, light, dirt, noise, vibration
☐ the employee's motivation and attitude towards the job.

In general, such a detailed scientific analysis of a job requires a specialist who may be found in the internal work study department or among the ranks of independent consultants.

Since it is not possible to do justice to the subject of ergonomics in a few paragraphs, a description of its various aspects will not be attempted here. Training staff who wish to explore the topic in detail are recommended to read Singleton's book mentioned above.

Returning to the employee's job description, we have examined the objectives of the job and analysed the work performed in it by breaking it down into its various duties and functions. A further part of the job analysis is the establishment of responsibilities for resources and policies. The manager or supervisor who is on the next rung up in the hierarchy will usually be most concerned with settling his subordinate's responsibilities. Being accountable for the total operation of his department, he will allocate responsibilities by delegation[35] and the extent of that delegation will depend on a number of factors, including the training which he has given his staff to fit them for duties at a higher level. Unhappily, this is not the average manager's strong point. He often avoids delegation because of his fear of the subordinate being unable to cope, failing to carry out the job satisfactorily and thus bringing the manager himself into disrepute. Another fear is that if the subordinate knows too much the manager feels that his own job may be under threat. The first situation is less likely to arise if the employee is a suitable person to take on more responsibility, is given the necessary training and help to prepare him for it and is monitored periodically without his feeling that he is being closely supervised. The second fear, whilst being shortsighted, is understandable, but it is fair to say that no organization worthy of the name is going to sack its managers if they show the competence that is expected of them in developing their subordinates to the full.

Assuming, then, that the manager is carrying out his own responsibilities adequately, he will be able to establish those of his subordinates with little difficulty. He will know what the organizational structure of his department is and thus how many other employees report to each of his immediate subordinates. Similarly, the responsibility for the other resources such as materials and equipment will be clearly defined. What may not be so evident is the policy-making machinery. Whilst this should be quite clear in the interests of avoiding misunderstandings, it very often emerges as an *ad hoc* activity, with disastrous results. In the absence of any clearly understood policies, people will make their own. This may work quite well for a long time if the quality of the personnel is high, but sooner or later something will go wrong. The most likely problem will be that *ad hoc* policy decisions will be inconsistent and this can often cause reactions which are worse than those from decisions which are downright bad. Training managers would be wise to stress the importance of the responsibilities for policy decisions being clearly defined in job descriptions, and the training needs in this area should be carefully explored. Some employees have a group responsibility for certain aspects of policy decision-making through the medium of committees or working parties. Many attend such meetings without knowing precisely what their obligations are. Shared responsibilities become diluted responsibilities and there is in general a lower level of commitment to shouldering one's share of the burden. Most people who are in this situation would benefit from some training in obtaining optimum results from committees.

The organizational relationships of the individual will be reasonably easy to establish. He will have contacts with other departments in the organization, some on a regular basis, others infrequently. The interface between those departments and his own has to be managed in the best interests of furthering his objectives. Frequently personal factors affect this. He may get on very well with some and find others difficult to handle. If this is so, the cause of difficulty has to be analysed and suitable steps taken to deal with it.

Listing the important working conditions in the job description should not present too many problems. Most of them could be the source of training needs. Physical working arrangements, eg where the job is a sedentary one, may create difficulties of an ergonomic nature. Shift-working may prove unsuitable for some employees because it is out of phase with their normal metabolism. Flexitime may cause problems in terms of getting the work done at times convenient to the business. If the employee works as a relatively isolated individual, he may experience problems of integrating his work with that of other parts of the organization. If he is part of a working group, there could be interpersonal difficulties. There are, of course, health and safety risks in all jobs to a greater or lesser degree. It is important that every employee knows what the hazards are in his particular situation and what he can do to avoid them. All such problems can come to light by exploring the areas covered by the job description and can, of course, highlight a number of training needs. This list is by no means exhaustive.

It was mentioned in Chapter 2 that performance review, whether used as part of a management development scheme or not, is an effective means of establishing training needs, provided those carrying out the review are competent to recognize those needs when subordinates do not meet their targets.[24, 25] If we assume that this condition is fulfilled, the following example will illustrate how training needs might be identified at such a meeting. The dialogue is between a training manager, Peter, and one of his subordinate trainers, Clive, in a large group of companies.

Peter: Morning, Clive. It's nice to see you looking so bright and cheerful on a Monday morning! How are things going?

Clive: Oh, pretty well, I think. I have found the work most absorbing over the past few months. Hectic, but certainly rewarding in terms of job satisfaction. I only wish there were more hours in the day. I think I'm beginning to feel the pressure a bit.

Peter: Yes, there's so much to do, I think we're all feeling a bit pushed. Anyway, the purpose of this meeting is really to look at our performance over the past year and to make plans for the coming one. Are you happy with the way things have gone?

Clive: I've had my unpleasant moments, but on the whole I think things have worked out reasonably well. You've seen the figures and no doubt had quite a bit of feedback from elsewhere. What do you feel?

Peter: Well, certainly you have carried out all the jobs that we targetted for last year and I must congratulate you on your stamina and determination. On the whole, the feedback I have had has been very favourable but there are one or two areas which I think we ought to have a look at. Have you any idea which they might be?

Clive: I've no doubt one of them is the supervisor course I did in June . . .

Peter: What problems did you have with that?

Clive: It was odd. As you know, I've done quite a few of these now, and as far as I can tell they have all gone down pretty well. But with this one . . . well, I just did not seem to be able to get onto the same wavelength as this group. We always expect things to be a little difficult at first when they are feeling their way and weighing things up, but these chaps never seemed to be at ease and at times I felt they were openly hostile.

Peter: How did they show this hostility, then?

Clive: In a number of ways. They criticized the exercises quite frequently, and at times they ganged up on me with the clear intention of opposing anything I said. I can't think what I did wrong.

Peter: Do you really believe you did anything wrong? Was this not just a case of the group mix? We know that no two groups are alike and we have to take the rough with the smooth. We can't win 'em all, Clive.

Clive: But I have never experienced anything quite as serious as this before, Peter. I was at a loss to know what to do.

Peter: What did you try to do?

Clive: Well, I must say I tended to take the easy way out by avoiding anything too controversial. Which of course was not over-helpful from a learning point of view. I really felt outnumbered and told them so, and they said 'Rubbish!'.

Peter: Did these problems arise as much during recreation periods as during training sessions?

Clive: Come to think of it, no. They behaved quite differently off the job and I didn't feel so isolated. In fact, I played darts with them quite a bit.

Peter: It sounds as though there was no personal animosity, then?

Clive: No, I don't think so. They were perfectly friendly in the bar.

Peter: Then, it seems to me you were up against a reaction to authority, and didn't know how to handle it.

Clive: That's exactly it. I remember now that they spent quite a bit of time both in syndicates and full-group sessions knocking the management. It became almost an obsession with one group . . .

Peter: . . . and they saw you as representing the management.

Clive: Yes, evidently, but how do I cope with this sort of thing in the future?

Peter: You may not have to. This may be a one-off. But if you feel nervous about the possibility of it recurring, I suggest we look for an advanced course on interpersonal relations and managing groups. Preferably one in which the consultants specialize in dealing with real problems brought by the participants. I'm not sure who would be the best people at the moment, but I'll make some enquiries and perhaps you'll do the same. We'll meet again at the same time next Monday and get it sorted out.

Clive: Thanks!

Peter: Now about the other problem . . . .

In this example, a problem has been talked through and a training solution agreed upon. It may not necessarily be the right solution, because the assumptions made may not be correct. Nevertheless, there is a rationale for the identification of the problem and for its solution. Training needs can therefore arise in this way. It is more common, however, for needs identified in performance reviews to be more clear-cut. For example, if a target is easily quantifiable it is much easier to decide whether or not it has been met. If a salesman's target requires him to sell a given number of products in a given time, it will be obvious whether he has met it or not. It is important, however, to establish what factors may have prevented him from reaching his target. Some may be completely outside his control, for example, changes in the law affecting credit agreements or failure of the factory to deliver the goods on time, although he may have a limited influence on the latter. Where his failure arises from lack of knowledge or skill, or from having the wrong attitude towards the company or his job, the need for training[18] will show itself fairly readily. The value of performance review in establishing training needs lies in the fact that boss and subordinate arrive at conclusions jointly. This tends to remove the objection that *ad hoc* and arbitrary decisions are taken to send people for training. The needs emerge naturally from a regular process which is accepted as part of the day-to-day operation of the department.

The use of pre-testing is usually associated with selecting people for employment. The aim is to obtain guidance in ascertaining what kind of work a person is suitable for or whether or not he is suited to work of a particular kind. Aptitude tests cover clerical work, shorthand/typing, mechanical comprehension, manual dexterity, languages, vision and artistic skills, technical attainment (eg engineering, maths or science) and there are also tests of personality characteristics. These tests, among others, may be used in selecting people for training. If it is possible to discover in advance whether or not an employee has the capacity for learning to do work of a particular kind, time and resources may be saved in selecting out those who are unsuitable. In the past, work in this area has been concentrated mainly on manual operations. At the time of writing, however, there is evidence of a growing interest in the design of such tests for cognitive skills. Several agencies[36] produce catalogues of test materials available and some of them apply strict user qualification conditions. In other words, they insist on users of their test materials having undergone approved instructions in their use.

Psychological testing[37] has met with mixed reactions from training specialists over a number of years. There are some users, of course, whose experience has confirmed their belief that such tests are a valuable aid to measuring characteristics which cannot be measured by other means. There are many more sceptics, however, who feel that psychological tests have to be treated with some reserve and cannot be relied upon to give them the answers they are seeking. They may be prepared to use them to confirm their findings by other methods, but when the tests conflict with those findings they prefer to back their own judgements.

There are signs, however, that interest in occupation-related psychometric testing, in particular for employee recruitment and performance review, is on the increase. One firm of consultants has developed a set of Occupational Personality Questionnaires (OPQ)[38] which, it is claimed, 'marks the first major British initiative in personality research for some years' and promises significant improvements on existing techniques.

Some special aspects

In this chapter so far we have considered the identification of training needs using the business and manpower plans, performance reviews and certain forms of job analysis. In practice we may also find that we have to use our judgement and knowledge of the business to pinpoint training needs which are peculiar to particular jobs in the organization but which are not highlighted by the above means. We shall therefore be looking at some of these aspects in the following pages.

Managers

Since most of the blame for things going wrong in business is popularly laid at management's door, it may be thought that managers are more in need of training than anyone else. It is often argued by the cynics that managers are not competent to carry out the heavy responsibilities entrusted to them. No doubt there is justification for such criticism in a small proportion of cases, but the vast majority of managers that the writer has worked with over the past 30 or more years have not been seriously lacking in knowledge or experience. They have been dedicated, energetic, hard-working people whose main deficiency, if any, has been the lack of ability to use their attributes to optimum effect. A good deal of the training required should therefore be centred around harnessing their knowledge and experience in the interests of achieving the improved performance of which they are capable. Methods of achieving this are discussed in Chapter 6.

It is not at all difficult to identify areas where managers would benefit from an update in the knowledge required in their particular jobs using the means already described. Often these requirements become clear to the manager himself when he finds that his decision-making capacity is hampered by a lack of information about, for example, internal factors like how other departments in the business operate or external factors such as the national economy and government legislation. Training managers will also be aware of the inefficiencies and frustrations that arise from managers working as isolated individuals rather than as teams pursuing corporate goals (see pp. 110-16).

The needs for training in interpersonal skills[39] are not always easy to deal with. Few managers will readily concede that they have problems in handling people. Rather than admit that they lack the requisite skills, many will blame the society in which we live for difficulties experienced with people and resign themselves to being powerless to do anything about them. If this were true, why are some managements so much more successful in handling their workforces than others? This phenomenon presents the training manager with a challenge. He needs to be able to find a way to test the value of training in interpersonal skills within his organization. Where there may be opposition to tackling this head-on, there will be many opportunities to introduce behavioural approaches into other training programmes. Once managers have seen the value of dealing with their interpersonal problems in a certain way, they will be more receptive to the idea that training needs that they have dismissed in the past as being non-existent are worth exploring in greater depth.

Training staff need to adopt a proactive as well as a reactive role in identifying training needs. It has been said previously that the responsibility for training in any department is that of the manager or supervisor. That is fine as long as he recognizes the need when it exists, but many instances arise where something changes and the manager may not know about it. Examples of this are:

- ☐ government legislation, affecting the business or employment, which the manager does not monitor adequately
- ☐ changes in working practices in other departments which may have repercussions in the manager's department
- ☐ changes in rules, regulations and recommendations of professional institutions
- ☐ internal policy changes which have not been properly communicated to those who need to know
- ☐ changes in further education arrangements at technical colleges, etc
- ☐ changes in Industrial Training Board requirements.

In such instances, managers rely on the training staff to keep them informed of what is happening and what the training implications for their departments may be. There are also countless situations where, because of the extensive contacts that the training department has throughout an organization, it becomes aware of needs of a general character which may not become apparent to individual managers. It is true to say that, however varied managers' jobs may be, there is a core of common training needs. That is, there are fundamental skills which every manager, regardless of function, should possess. These include interviewing[40] (in the broadest sense, not just selection interviewing), running meetings,[61] delegation,[35] coaching,[17] counselling,[41] instructional[18] and presentation skills.[42] When a need of this kind is identified

NOP Data Company Ltd Form NTS

Training Survey Date:

Subject Business Presentation Skills for Managers

Details
In discussions with Mr X and Mr Y we have learned that they would appreciate some training in addressing a group and making business presentations to management. We feel that a course covering these skills would be beneficial to a number of other managers in NOP. We have in mind a 3-day programme which would examine in detail the theory of effective speaking and would also provide individual coaching in making presentations to a group. Closed circuit TV and video recording would be used on the third day. If you are interested, will you please return the completed form to the Training Department by 31 March.

Questionnaire
We have training requirements in this area and would support an internal training programme.

1. Department/Division . . . .
2. Approximate number of managers who would be nominated . . . .
3. Over what period? . . . .
4. How many of these nominees could be released at a time? . . . .
5. Are there any specific requirements that you would want incorporated in the programme?

. . . .

. . . .

. . . .

Signed . . . .

Job title . . . .

Figure 8. *Suggested training survey form*

by the training staff, a survey should be conducted in the organization to ascertain the demand before any internal training activity is set up. Where the demand does not justify such an internal course, external facilities may have to be used to satisfy the limited needs.[43] Fig. 8 shows a design for a survey form suitable for use in medium to large organizations.

It is very common for specialists to be promoted within organizations into managerial jobs without any preparation for their new roles. The assumption is often made that, if they have proved themselves competent in the specialist role and have generally gained acceptance from the management and their work colleagues, they are suitably equipped to carry out the new responsibilities satisfactorily without training. Most organizations will have witnessed the calamities that this policy has brought about and yet the practice still persists. Even at the highest level the theory can be held that management is a sink or swim situation; if you do not succeed in swimming on your own you are unfit to be a manager. This is, in the writer's opinion, a fallacy. There are many competent specialists who would make competent managers if given the tools to do the job. Apparently, it is seldom recognized that moving from a specialist job, which has rightly or wrongly been carried out in a parochial fashion, to a management one, entails a dramatic re-alignment of one's working objectives, one's attitudes and, frequently, one's allegiances. There has to be a re-orientation from carrying out one's limited role in a specialist function to approaching the new job within a total business framework. Every move in effect has to integrate with the business policy and the business objectives. Indeed, one is party, to a greater or lesser degree, to the formulation of that policy and those objectives. It follows, then, that a newly-appointed manager needs to know far more about the business and about its philosophy than was required in the specialist role that he has just relinquished. It is sometimes argued that those who aspire to high positions in organizations owe it to themselves and to those who promote them to learn what they need to know about business by self-development. Certainly this is a reasonable argument where a general knowledge of business management is concerned, but it is not as practicable in dealing with the idiosyncrasies of particular organizations. Training managers are therefore urged to recognize the need to provide adequate training in business orientation, specially tailored to the organization's needs, for those who assume managerial responsibilities. Such responsibilities involve a thorough knowledge of the business plans, strategy, policies, systems, and so on. Promoting someone into management also opens up a need to train him in those day-to-day skills which he is expected to have as a manager, such as the common needs skills already mentioned.

Supervisors

The role of the supervisor in an organization is a unique one. It is commonly said to be the most difficult of jobs, not because the duties are particularly arduous, necessarily, but because there tends to be a conflict of loyalties. Supervisors find themselves at one and the same time representing the interests of both the management and their workpeople, and this can lead to difficulties in carrying out their jobs effectively. It must be said, however, that some of the dilemmas that arise are not so much due to any organizational conflict as to the fact that the supervisors themselves are not always suitably trained to carry out their responsibilities. Here again, as with managers, we can have a situation where someone is promoted into a supervisory job without adequate preparation. He has been working as a craftsman, operator, clerk, for example, in a department in which the supervisor's job becomes vacant. Because of his knowledge and experience of the *work* carried out by the department, it is assumed that he is the man for the job. There should, of course, be a substantial re-orientation around the new duties, but frequently the supervisor continues to involve himself in the technical or operational aspects of the department's work because that is what he knows most about and is most interested in and the supervisory duties which he should be carrying out are given scant attention. He cannot be wholly blamed for this because no one has told him precisely what is required in the job. He knows that he is expected to produce output, but when problems which are only indirectly related to output arise, he does not recognize them as coming within his remit. For example, he will refer all problems remotely concerned with personnel and training matters to the specialist department, when many of them should be dealt with by him personally. He will accept new employees from the personnel department without having interviewed them to assess their suitability for the work or to satisfy himself that they will integrate with his existing workforce. And yet he will still acknowledge responsibility for their performance.

Some years ago a medium sized manufacturing company called in some efficiency consultants with the object of improving organizational performance. They interviewed the supervisors and discovered that the amount of time they actually spent on supervision was minimal. They therefore told the supervisors what their jobs should really entail, and said that as from Monday morning they would no longer have to involve themselves directly in the practical work of the department or the keeping of records. In other words, their duties would be solely supervisory. Two of them said they would rather go back onto the shop floor!

The message for the training department is clear. Every individual who is promoted to a position of supervisory responsibility generates training needs, and every effort should be made to equip such employees with the skills to carry out their new responsibilities adequately.[80] A good deal of care is needed in drafting job specifications and the utmost attention should be given to ensuring that supervisors understand precisely what their jobs entail.

It is easy to produce supervisors for training programmes which are unsuitable because the training needs have not been properly established. One should not fall into the trap of assuming that because they have responsibility for subordinates, their needs are similar to those of managers. A knowledge of the financial structure and reporting systems in the organization is important to managers, for instance, but does not have the same relevance for supervisors. The financial knowledge that they require is probably confined to costing systems to which they have a direct input. However much it may be deemed a good thing to introduce them to balance sheets and profit and loss accounts, it will not have the same importance for them and they are unlikely to be receptive, unless they are seeking promotion to managerial status.

Specialists

Most organizations, whether in industry, commerce or the public sector, employ a substantial number of specialists, that is, people who devote their energies to particular functions or professions. They will be employed in finance and accountancy, engineering, science, drawing office, marketing, sales, production, personnel, training, materials management, administration, architecture, surveying, planning, work study, maintenance, servicing . . . and so on. Each group has a sphere of influence, each has its own jargon and each approaches its work in its own special way.

Frequently one group will not communicate with another simply because it does not understand the language used. An accountant may avoid going near an engineer for fear of being blinded with science. Ironically, the engineer may avoid contacting the accountant for the very same reason – financial jargon means nothing to him. There would therefore appear to be a substantial need to help specialists understand each other's language in the interests of their working together for the common good. Strangely, these needs seldom emerge from the systematic approaches described earlier in this chapter, partly because people do not see training as a means of overcoming the lack of communication between departments or individuals. Here, then, is an area in which the training manager can be proactive. Since everyone else claims to be unable to communicate with accountants, it is rewarding to start here.[44] Accountants and non-accountants alike will welcome the introduction of training programmes in finance for non-accountants. It helps the non-accounting specialists to ask accountants the right questions, and to be able to understand the answers! It also helps to impress upon those specialists that the fault for lack of communication rests just as much on them as on the accountants. From there one can move on to engineering for non-engineers, marketing for non-marketing specialists, and so on.

There is a common misconception that engineers and scientists do not make good managers. This stems from the fact that they are seen to be very much wrapped up in things, as distinct from people. They are deeply involved in and committed to their technical activities and may not therefore see what is going on around them. This is no reason to assume that they will not make good managers if they choose to move into the management ranks. The important thing is to recognize that this is so and thus to ensure that the machinery is available to enable them to cross that bridge and to be suitably trained for the new position.

Many of the training needs that arise for specialists are to update them in their particular field. This is a serious problem for technical people because of rapid technological change. It is, however, just as necessary for people in other areas to keep abreast of developments in their own fields. The difficulty that training staffs have is how this can best be done. They have to rely very heavily on the ability of the specialists' bosses to identify areas of development which are pertinent. One way in which assistance can be given is to ensure that access is obtained to publications which report important new developments. Larger organizations have their own libraries which simplify the problem to some extent.

Field service or installation and commissioning personnel pose particular problems in assessing performance and consequently in establishing training needs. They have considerable freedom in discharging their duties on remote sites and it is uneconomical and impracticable to provide supervision on the job. Much of their work therefore has to be taken on trust, because in the absence of any feedback from the customer there is no way of knowing whether they have carried out the requirements of the job satisfactorily or not. This points to a need to ensure that the highest selection standards are used for this type of employee in the first place. Some organizations deal with the training needs problem by arranging regular., not necessarily frequent, training sessions at which the participants are encouraged to discuss their experiences in the field in some detail. Special difficulties are brought out into the open and, where appropriate, training solutions sought. Feedback from customers can also be of value in some instances. An atmosphere of openness and trust between managers and their field staff has to be created in order to make it possible for help to be given when needed.

Office workers

For some years the Industrial Training Boards have recommended training programmes for clerical workers which are just as detailed as those proposed and adopted for other workers.[45] In spite of this, less attention seems to be given to the needs of office workers compared with, say craftsmen or operators. The explanation probably lies in the fact that clerical work is not seen as requiring any skills that cannot be easily picked up as you go along. This attitude is unfortunate, because it can lead to gross inefficiencies in offices which would not be tolerated on the factory floor. There is sometimes resentment among blue-collar workers that whilst they are subject to tight restrictions on their activities and are required to meet demanding targets with the utmost efficiency, the white-collar workers appear to be free to work at a leisurely pace, to be wasteful in their use of office materials and not to be closely monitored. Whether this is true or not in particular situations, there is little doubt that in general office workers deserve more training than they get. Training specialists know only too well that properly planned and well directed training can have valuable pay-offs in any area of business and the offices are no exception. In periods of economic recession, departments which are seen to contribute to overheads as distinct from wealth-creating activities are the first to suffer cutbacks when businesses run into difficulties. It is therefore important that those who remain to carry the burden with reduced resources should be helped to do so as efficiently as possible.

One difficult area in offices is secretarial work. No two so-called secretarial jobs are alike, because each reflects the attitude to the job of the executive for whom the secretary works. The result is that she can be anything from a competent personal assistant who virtually runs the executive's job for him to an underqualified typist who is only sitting there to boost his prestige. There is often a high turnover in secretarial staff due to the fact that competent women are not given the responsibilities that they are capable of carrying out. When having to replace employees who leave for this reason, personnel departments would do well to insist on an undertaking from the executive that if someone with true secretarial skills is appointed, her capabilities will be suitably applied in the job.

The basic secretarial skills, such as shorthand, typing, office routine, arranging appointments, are usually learned at secretarial college or by day release or evening study at a further education establishment. The skills needed to carry out a particular job, as has been said, centre around the relationship that exists between the secretary and the executive for whom she works. There is therefore merit in carrying out off-the-job training in which both parties are involved. This helps to remove some of the misunderstandings which frequently arise in interpreting the requirements of the job. It also provides the opportunity for promoting the idea in the minds of the executives that a good secretary properly employed is an invaluable asset. The jobs of both executive and secretary would have to be analysed before such training could take place.

Craftsmen

Analysing the job of a craftsman, whilst it may be quite complicated if more than one skill is involved, is not difficult. It is largely a question of the observation of what activities are actually carried out by a skilled employee. It is not surprising then that when the Industial Training Boards came into being after the Industrial Training Act 1964[9] (subsequently modified by the Employment and Training Acts 1973 and 1981) was passed, this was the area in which they concentrated their initial efforts.

Considerable help and guidance has been given by Training Boards in the analysis of training needs for craft apprentices, in providing basic training programmes and also additional modules to enable craftsmen to extend their range of skills. Comprehensive information may be obtained from the appropriate Board.[10]

Operators

Like those of craftsmen, the analysis of the jobs of operators is fairly straightforward, and the job analysis methods covered earlier in this chapter are appropriate. In the interests of enabling operators to reach experienced worker standard without too much delay (see Chapter 5), a scientific approach to the analysis is desirable. In other words, after observing a skilled operator carrying out the job, it is helpful to have the working methods analysed by the appropriate work study specialist to ensure that the most efficient methods for the particular activity are being used.[1] As mentioned elsewhere, it is not unheard of for even the best operators to lapse into undesirable work practices and take short cuts which are not acceptable either from the point of view of efficiency or safety.

Graduates

When organizations employ graduates, it is with the expectation that they are acquiring employees with trained minds who will fairly quickly be able to take on responsible work in the business. Two major mistakes are made repeatedly. First, it is sometimes thought that graduates require as much detailed training as other young people and second, there are those who feel that graduates are capable of taking responsibility within a very short time which other people have taken many years of their lives to equip themselves for. In the first case, it is important to realize that their minds are geared to assimilating information quickly and it is asking for trouble to expect them to operate a machine on a repetitive process for a period of months when they have learned all they need to know about the process in a week. It is generally true to say that for the types of jobs that they will aspire to, they only need to have an *appreciation* of the various processes that go to make up the end product. There is no requirement for them actually to acquire the skills needed to carry out those processes. In the second case, whilst they come to work imbued with the confidence that they can very quickly assume responsibility, it is quite unrealistic to expect this without making certain that they are suitably equipped for it. It is therefore imperative that when we analyse the job that we ultimately want a graduate to do, we take special care to see that he is given the opportunity to acquire all the knowledge and skill needed to carry out that job effectively. He will, of course, be capable of acquiring a good deal of such information himself, but that does not exempt the employer from providing a comprehensive programme[46] and adequate facilities to satisfy the graduate's needs. It makes economic sense to capitalize on a substantial investment.

The question of age and its possible influence on the establishment of training needs has not so far been mentioned. It would be very convenient to be able to say that its effect is negligible and can therefore be ignored. In practice, however, it is not possible to treat all employees alike in such a wide age range as 15 to 65 (or even higher) years. There is a temptation to believe that what is good for a mature adult in his 30s is suitable for everyone, but this is not the case. At either end of the working life there are particular needs which require special consideration. The young person entering the world of work for the first time faces a major adjustment to a totally new environment. He has spent much of his life in the company of young people and has been almost wholly dependent on his parents and the staff of the educational establishment that he has been attending. He not only has to adjust to the idea that he is moving into a period of relatively independent adulthood but also that the situation that he finds himself in is quite different from anything he has encountered before. Most of his working colleagues are likely to be mature adults, the work he is given to do will be new to him, the business environment itself will be strange and the new rules, regulations and routines may be a little difficult to come to terms with. The training specialist has to be sensitive to these difficulties, the magnitude of which will vary with the individual, and must ensure that they are adequately catered for when establishing the training needs of young people. This not only calls for understanding on the part of the training staff themselves but also on the part of the managers and supervisors for whom the young employees will be working. It is in the latter relationships that things sometimes go wrong, due to prejudices about the younger generation and a lack of appreciation of what problems they are having to face when they first go out to work. Trainers can make useful contributions to the handling of such difficulties by suitable inputs on this subject in management and supervisory training programmes.

The needs of adults at the other end of the age scale are different, though no less important. They centre around reassurances about their capabilities and a realization on the part of managers, supervisors and trainers alike that learning in late adult life takes time and requires special understanding. The problems of adult re-training are discussed in Chapter 6.

The writer makes no apology for repeating what was said at the beginning of this chapter, that the analysis of the training needs is one of the most important stages in the training process. It is unfortunate that so much training is carried out without regard for the basic principle that a clearly defined need should be established before deciding what training should be done. It is embarrassing for training departments to be told by course participants that they did not know why they were sent on the course because they could not see how it would help them in their jobs. Public courses have tended to encourage managers to adopt the line of least resistance. When they see details of a course which looks as though it might be interesting, they either nominate themselves or a subordinate without attempting to find out precisely what it covers. They find out too late that it is quite unsuitable, their needs are not satisfied, the company suffers and the training department loses credibility for allowing it to happen. The importance of analysing the true needs cannot therefore be overstressed.

Chapter 4

The Training Process – Planning the Overall Programme

In studying the process of training in an organization, we have so far established how its objectives are arrived at and the means by which we are able to identify specific training needs. We have seen how these needs have been brought together into an overall training plan which gives brief details of how we shall set about satisfying them, who will be responsible and what the time scale for implementation of the appropriate training activities will be. Before we can in fact enter the time scale in the training plan, however, we need to give the matter very careful consideration, as the timing and the setting of priorities can be critical.

Where the organization is small and the training needs consequently limited, the problem probably does not arise, except in so far that any training carried out at the wrong time can cause problems. In the larger business, however, the requirements can be many and varied, giving rise to the need for judicious planning. It is obvious that not all the necessary training activities can be carried out at once. This would be impracticable in terms of training resource allocation, disruption of the work of the departments involved and, if on a large enough scale, would have a significant effect on the cash flow of the business. In other words, the financial commitment would be concentrated in one limited period instead of being spread reasonably evenly over the financial year. Much of a training department's expenditure is subject to short-term credit. One's creditors, particularly those providing external services such as hotels and conference centres, will not want to be kept waiting for their money and may well withdraw their services, or at least their credit facilities, if they are not paid on time. This places a constraint on the training manager when planning his overall training programme. His accountant will be much more amenable if he arranges the expensive training activities, such as external residential courses, so that the load on the exchequer is evenly spread over the year, than if he presents such bills for payment in a random fashion regardless of the magnitude of the sums involved.

On-the-job training has to be carried out when it is needed and when it is practicable for everyone concerned. It should never be simply squeezed in when a trainer, instructor or supervisor can find a minute. It is sufficiently important to justify adequate time being allocated to it and for the instructor to give it his undivided attention. It does not help the trainee to find that his instructor is preoccupied with matters not directly concerned with his training. Apprentices in particular suffer from this problem. They require a fair amount of individual attention from their instructor or supervisor in the early stages of every phase of their training but are often forced to come to terms with a situation where the instruction is constantly being stopped down by the day-to-day needs of the business. Indeed, they are frequently required to satisfy the pressing needs of production before they are fully competent to make the contribution expected of them. This is clearly undesirable and should be avoided wherever possible. What is apparently gained by having the apprentice 'producing' can too often be offset by a lack of work pace due to insufficient stamina training (see Chapter 6, p. 100) and an increase in the number of rejects at the end of the day. Somehow this difficulty has to be overcome. There has to be an understanding between the training staff and management that to equip people to carry out their tasks adequately their instruction must be taken seriously. It has to take place at the right time and appropriate periods of uninterrupted time must be set aside. The right time is when it will integrate with, and not disrupt, the normal activities of the department and will also suit the trainee. This last condition would not be satisfied for instance if the training were commenced a few minutes before a natural break or immediately after a situation where the trainee had been put under abnormal stress. The conditions must be such that he is going to be receptive to the training and will learn as quickly as possible from it.

Off-the-job training has to be arranged with similar considerations in mind. As mentioned in Chapter 5, in which the two training approaches are compared and contrasted, one of the disadvantages of off-the-job training is the fact that it occurs outside the work situation and thus may appear to lack relevance. The timing is therefore very important, because it must be seen to integrate logically with what has been going on or what is expected to happen in the real world of work. Where the trainees are managers or supervisors, one of the key factors will be when they can reasonably be released from their jobs to undergo training away from the work situation. Because managers are probably able more readily to delegate their work to subordinates, this is less of a problem for them than for supervisors whose continuous presence on the job seems to be expected. Top management will nearly always argue that they themselves are not able to get away during the working week and they may have to be persuaded to attend training sessions at weekends. Sales representatives and field service engineers may have difficulty in allocating time to training activities which will involve them in travelling to a remote centre. Employees who normally work on the night shift may be unable to attend off-the-job training courses unless these can be arranged at night. These are only a few of the areas where difficulties arise from the specific nature of the job.

Every training situation appears to have its own problems in terms of timing and these factors cannot be ignored when the overall training programme is being planned. A system has to be devised which will take all the relevant factors into account and, where they conflict, achieve the best compromise. This really requires being able to see information on all trainees at a glance so that their training periods may be fixed as part of the overall plan and not piecemeal. Where large numbers of training assignments are involved they will have to be grouped. Some will not have to be included at all if they are not seen to be dependent in any way on the others. For example, where the training involves prescribed reading (see the training plan, p. 35) this will not affect other training activities or resources and so can be ignored for this purpose.

The main criteria to be considered, then, when deciding at what time training should take place are:

1. When will it be most appropriate from the trainee's point of view? When will it integrate best with his work, with the remainder of his training and with his part-time studies? When will he be most receptive?
2. If the trainee is already a contributing member of a team, when will his training cause the least disruption to the work of that team? Will other members be absent at the same time?
3. When will the instructor, trainer, supervisor, who will be carrying out the training be available? What other commitments will he have? Can he give the task his undivided attention?
4. When will the required training facilities (premises, equipment, paperwork, etc) be available?
5. Where significant costs are involved, when is the most suitable time to incur them from a cash flow point of view?

Depending on the type of training involved, the factors mentioned will have varying levels of significance. When considering apprentices, for example, whose on-the-job training will go hand in hand with carrying out part of the job and will have an immediate impact on performance, continuity of effort may be important. Thus, when one apprentice leaves a department another comes into it. The periods during which several apprentices undertake a particular training activity will thus be staggered and not concurrent. The cost of the operation will vary little from month to month so the effect on cash flow will be fairly constant.

Contrast this with the situation where a number of managers from different departments are to attend a one-week residential course to sharpen up their decision-making and problem-solving skills. They are being prepared to meet the needs of the future and may not have the opportunity to put their learning to immediate effect. There is not the same urgency to embark on this training and priority will tend to be given to dealing with the day-to-day problems in their jobs. Furthermore, this type of training activity may be very costly, measured in thousands of pounds rather than hundreds and thus could have a marked effect on cash flow if it has to be paid for in a month in which the business is already short of cash. Under normal economic conditions this is seen to be of little importance. In an inflationary era in which the management of cash flow can determine whether or not a business survives, it cannot be ignored.[12,44]

It is common practice in training departments to record the various training activities planned on wall charts in the form of calendars covering a whole year. The bar chart principle is adopted, the simplest form being as shown in fig. 9. In practice a coding system using adhesive coloured strips, dots etc will be used to identify various items of information according to what may be required from the chart. This chart shows at a glance how the time allocations for the various trainees are related to each other and it is relatively easy to ascertain whether any overlaps are of importance or not. For example, two people from the marketing department are going to be tied up for the same three days in the second week of January and this may be undesirable. On the other hand, the overlap of one day in the fourth week between the employees from the purchasing and personnel departments may have no significance at all, since their jobs are not directly connected.

What the chart does not show is how the periods were arrived at in the first place, and it is suggested that some formal system be adopted to ensure that the questions listed on p. 63 are taken into account. To avoid the necessity of repeating information about the trainees already recorded on the master chart, a transparent acetate sheet is recommended on which is drawn with a spirit-based pen a grid which corresponds with that on the calendar. This can then be placed over the calendar, with the grids on both in register, enabling further bars to be drawn by means of a water-based pen (see fig. 10). This information may easily be removed by using a damp cloth if necessary.

For every trainee a line is allocated for each of the first four questions. Bars are drawn, in different colours if desired, to indicate all the possible periods in answer to the appropriate questions. For example, the most suitable times for Barton to attend the one-week internal course in the early part of the year are 11-15 and 25-29 January. However from his workgroup's point of view the most convenient times are 13-15, 18-22, 25 January and 1-2 February. The instructor's availability is 11-15, 18-20 and 26-29 January and the internal facilities may only be used on 11-15, 19-20, 25-28 January and 3-5 February. From this information the chart shows clearly that the most favourable week for Barton to attend is 11-15 January. Although on the first two days of that week his workgroup may find his absence inconvenient, this is the best compromise that we can make.

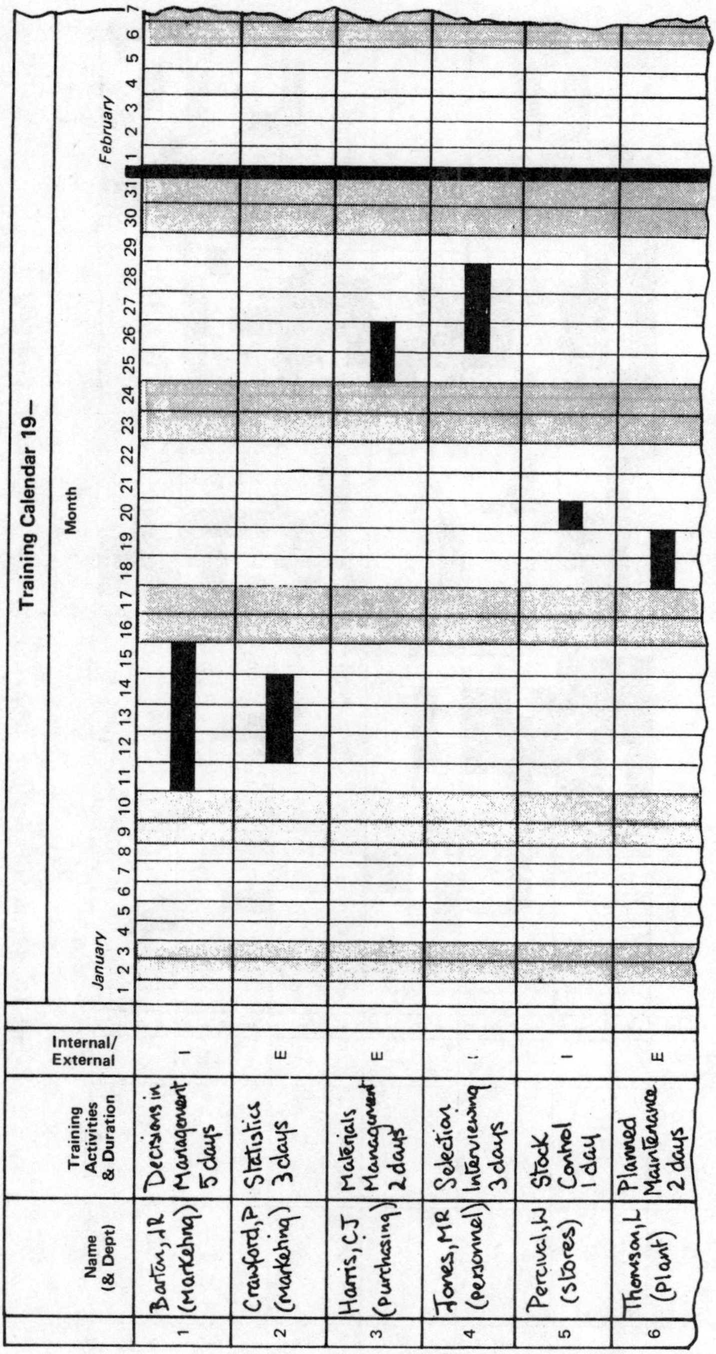

Figure 9. *Bar chart recording training activities*

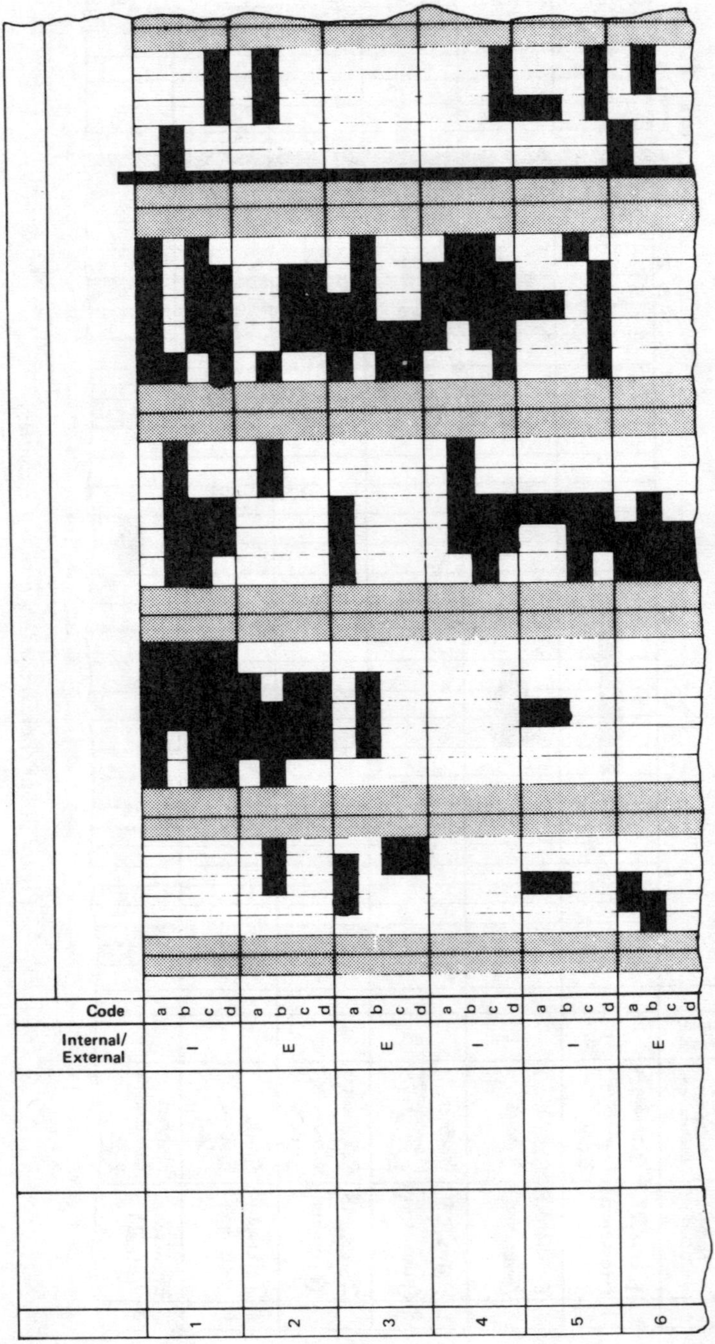

Figure 10. *Acetate overlay for computing most suitable times for training*

The only other time that he is available is 25-29 January but this would not only be a greater inconvenience to the workgroup but he would find himself without an instructor on the first day!

If the same instructor(s) and facilities are used for the other internal courses it is important not to commit the same periods for those courses. For example, having decided that 11-15 January is the likely period for Barton's course, this period can only be shown again on the chart for trainees being considered for that course. It cannot be shown in Percival's or Thomson's case, because the services will not be available. If it is found, when all the other trainees' information is recorded, that Barton's course cannot be run, then clearly the dates which have become available can be inserted on the charts for other internal training commitments.

Figs. 9 and 10 have illustrated off-the-job training activities which may involve internal facilities used by staff from the training department or external facilities staffed by independent consultants. The system is so flexible, however, that it may equally well be applied to on-the-job training. In this case, the training facilities will be in the trainee's department and the instructor will most probably be his supervisor or a work colleague.

When the most suitable period for each activity has been established, it can then be transferred to the main chart shown in fig. 9. At this stage, question 5 has to be considered. The chart(s) will now show the distribution of training activities throughout the year, and it is necessary to assess their impact on the cash flow. If there are any peaks above the average level in a particular month this should be discussed with the accountant. It may be found advisable to return to the information in fig. 10 in order to try to make suitable adjustments.

This method may be thought cumbersome by those who use more arbitrary approaches to training programme planning. It is, however, an attempt to take all the relevant factors into account when organizing training activities, at the same time providing a ready means of relating those factors in the best interests of the trainee and the organization. Much of the information required may be collected and recorded by a relatively junior member of the staff, leaving the training executive with the main task of interpreting the facts and taking action on them.

Some larger organizations, particularly those employing significant numbers of technician and craft trainees, operate an off-the-job training centre, often remote from the main work establishments. Such centres provide first year training and are usually approved by the appropriate Industrial Training Board[10] if they meet the required standards (see Chapter 10). Other centres, generally confined to the very large organizations, specialize in management and supervisory training.

Small organizations which are unable to provide the resources or the numbers of trainees required to justify the setting up of such activities internally, are often able to combine with other businesses to form a group training scheme. They share responsibility for running the scheme and are often able to obtain a grant from one of the Training Boards (see Chapter 10).

Planning in all these training establishments requires a systematic approach to activities which may on the face of it seem fairly straightforward and will therefore offer the temptation of tackling them in a random or casual way. As most training specialists will readily agree, graphic representation is helpful when a substantial quantity of data is involved (see Chapter 9 on visual aids). Less systematic methods can lead to important factors being overlooked and difficulties being experienced in handling a large number of variables.

One of the problems that training staff have to face is that of establishing the right climate for effective training to take place. This is only partly associated with the commitment of top management (see Chapter 9), although that clearly determines the organizational attitude towards training. Many of the barriers arise lower down in the hierarchy, among the departmental managers or supervisors, the employees themselves and their colleagues. Managers and supervisors may resist or ignore training for a variety of reasons, and these are discussed in Chapter 10. Bearing in mind, however, that they have the overall responsibility for the development of their subordinates, their attitudes are crucial to the creation of a climate enabling training of the right kind, quantity and standard to take place. There has to be a constant awareness of the value and indeed the indispensability of training in the battle for effectiveness. This requirement in itself demands that managers and supervisors are trained to recognize the needs of their employees and to take the necessary action. It also means that there must be greater involvement in the process on the part of the boss. Quite apart from his willingness to play a practical role in the training activity, passing on some of his own expertise and actively encouraging teamwork, he must show a lively interest in the outcome of his employees' training. The oft-repeated story of the employee returning to work after a training course to be greeted by the boss bearing a full in-tray and saying, 'Thank heavens you're back. These things have been piling up and they're urgent . . .', is unhappily only too true. The effect of such a reception is for the employee to feel that his training was seen as of no importance and so might as well be forgotten. It was good while it lasted . . . . Managers and supervisors owe it to their employees, themselves and the organization to de-brief their subordinates after training. They need to ascertain what the trainee felt about it, what he learned from it and above all to what extent it satisfied the needs which they had jointly established. Furthermore, it is important to decide what the next move should be. If the training failed to meet the target, something has to be done about it soon. It is no good waiting until the next performance review which may be many months away.

The employee's attitude to his training will clearly be affected by how involved the boss shows himself to be. A clear statement of the organization's training policy and an efficient induction programme when he joins will also impress upon the employee that training is given the importance that it deserves. If he starts off with such a picture he will most likely take training seriously and will be willingly and actively geared to making it work. It is a significant step forward to achieve a climate in which employees are committed with enthusiasm to improving their performance by any means available to them.

The use of outside consultants

Circumstances can arise where outside consultants[81] are employed to carry out training for the organization. This can be either on an internal or an external basis and can come about in any of the following circumstances:

- ☐ where the specialized expertise that the consultants have to offer is not obtainable internally
- ☐ where the internal trainer resources are stretched to the point where the training department has to limit its activities, even though the finances may be available
- ☐ where the consultants are hired to carry out an overall efficiency programme of which training forms a part
- ☐ where the management seeks confirmation of conclusions it has reached internally before they take action which may prove expensive or which may have other far-reaching implications.

Needless to say, the hiring of outside consultants should be approached with caution. Whilst there are many who provide a first-rate professional service there is a minority whose expertise may be questioned. Bearing in mind that it may be uneconomic to engage the services of consultants whose advice is not accepted and implemented, it is important to ensure that a reputable firm is used. No organization can really afford the damaging effects that can result from using unprofessional 'experts'. Quite apart from the organizational disruption that may be suffered, the effect on morale can be harmful for a very long time. One precaution which can be taken is to ensure that the organization is not left high and dry when the consultants withdraw. If, for example, they are introducing a new technique, it is desirable that their continuing presence is not required to implement it throughout the organization. In addition to an explanation of the technique, the programme should include adequate training to enable the staff to give effect to it as required. Incurring the cost of a resident consultant to carry out the implementation stage of the project is unnecessary, although it is advisable that the contract should allow for access to a consultant for advice.

When using outside staff to augment the organization's training resources, adequate briefing is essential. The initial discussions will have just covered enough ground to enable the decision to be made to engage the consultants in the first place. More detailed consideration has to be given to the substance of the programme, what particular points the management requires stressed and the methods that will be used. As suggested in Chapter 2, the training department will have a strategy which, among other things, favours a particular style of training, and the introduction of a philosophy or methodology which conflicts with that style may have undesirable effects. This is particularly true where highly participative methods have been accepted throughout the organization and a trainer attempts to introduce a more didactic style (see Chapter 6). In the writer's experience a minority of participants will acquiesce, whilst the reactions of the majority will range from a passive lack of interest to open rejection. It is therefore important that external consultants fully understand the training ethos in the organization, and match their inputs to it. They need also to know what the management philosophy is, so that they are aware of what they may be able to say or not to say in order to advance the interests of the organization. In other words, a consultant needs to be primed with a good deal of information about the organization and how it works to help him to understand it and to develop a rapport with the employees on the programme.

One major advantage of using outside consultants for training assignments is that it frequently enables employees to compare their organization with others. The more competent consultants have usually had a wide variety of experience of working in different industries or professions and the information that they are able to impart is invaluable to employees whose knowledge and experience may be restricted to their own organization. These insights into how other people handle similar problems can be extremely helpful in suggesting alternative approaches to decision-making and problem-solving. They are also useful sometimes in boosting confidence when participants learn that the world outside is not so very different from their own. Confirmation that one's views and theories have support from others is good for the ego.

The value of sound administration

It is often held that effective training is purely a function of the quality of the instructor or trainer. In fact, there are many who will delude themselves into believing that if they have a first-class trainer or consultant, success is assured. The more enlightened training specialist will be well aware that this is very far from the case. If training is to be worthwhile and is to meet its objectives, the quality of the tutor is indeed a key factor. However, if he is not supported by efficient administration, he is just as prone to failure as his less professional colleagues. Indeed, the writer firmly contends that it is a characteristic of a truly professional training man that he recognizes that good training can only be achieved by teamwork and the administrator is a vital member of the team.

Training administration tends to be taken for granted because it is seen as an ordinary or mundane activity. Much of it is concerned with paperwork, with providing creature comforts, with ensuring that training facilities and aids are there and with trouble shooting. Because these are the sorts of things that people almost subconsciously expect, they are unaware that someone who is working away quietly in the background has in fact had to provide them. That is, until something goes wrong. Failure to provide a service which is relied upon, however minor it may be, will give rise to disruption of the training programme and charges of inefficiency and poor organization. However good the trainer's own performance, the trainees are distracted from it. This disrupts their learning and has repercussions out of all proportion to the magnitude of the problem, particularly if the standard of the training is high. When the training is good, there is nothing else to knock but the administration!

A simple case in point is where the training programme provides for coffee or tea to be supplied at a prescribed time. When the participants become aware that the time has passed and the service has not materialized, it becomes a talking point which can divert their attention completely from the matter in hand. Even after the service has been provided, the event appears to have been indelibly imprinted on the trainees' minds, as evidenced by their trotting out references to it at later stages in the programme.

The apprentice mentioned earlier in this chapter whose training is repeatedly interrupted by the day-to-day needs of the business is another example. The effects of such disruptions on some trainees could be very damaging indeed and could in extreme cases lead to their terminating their contracts of employment. Of course, there is always a strong argument that the immediate needs of the business have to come first, but managements cannot abdicate their responsibilities for providing their employees with the training they need to carry out their tasks satisfactorily. As previously pointed out, ways have to be found to set aside adequate time for such training to be given.

There are, of course, many other ways in which poor administration can create havoc. Inadequate joining instructions can give rise to difficulties where participants are not properly informed about what is expected of them before a training programme. It is not unheard of for them to get lost when trying to find a training venue as a result of poor directions. They need to be told in advance what facilities will be provided and what they are expected to bring with them. The aims and objectives of the training should be clearly stated and trainees should also know in advance who will be responsible for the programme and what methods will be adopted. The sample documents shown in fig. 11 together with a map showing the location of the venue would be sent under cover of a personal letter welcoming the employees to the programme and offering any help if there are any points on which they are not clear. Thus many of the anxieties and reservations which they may have had about the experience will have been removed. Participants like to feel that the activity is organized, that everything is under control, so that all they have to concern themselves with is learning. That is how it should be.

When the training is in-house, the preparation is usually more straightforward than when it is off the premises. The facilities needed are usually easily accessible and even if something is forgotten it is

Supervisory Skills Page 2

Aims
This programme is designed around the concept that supervision is one of the processes by which the objectives of the organization are achieved. It sets out to give supervisors an understanding of, and practice in, the more important skills involved.

Objectives
More specifically, the programme will help supervisors to:

- ☐ appreciate that supervision involves making the best use of resources available to find effective answers to complex problems
- ☐ improve their understanding of themselves and their roles in the organization
- ☐ learn how to use their existing knowledge and experience as a basis for further development
- ☐ formulate plans for using the skills practised in the programme in their future work.

Methods
Various aspects of supervision will be explored informally in small groups by means of exercises written by the tutors and reflecting the realities of supervision in our organization.

Participants will be asked to seek solutions to the various problems posed by the free exchange of their knowledge and experience, and will report their findings to the full group at the end of each exercise. After full group discussion, handouts will be provided which should not be taken as authoritative. They will merely suggest one possible solution to the problem. Help will be given to pursue alternative approaches so that judgements may be made as to which solution is likely to be the most workable.

We shall therefore be adopting 'learning by doing' rather than lecturing or direct teaching methods.

Duration
5 days.

Figure 11(a). *Joining instructions – aims and methods*

Administrative Information

Page 3

1. *Duration of programme*
From Monday 22 February 1988 – 09.00
to Friday 26 February 1988 – 16.00 (approx)

2. *Venue*
The Crossed Fingers Hotel,
Lime Green, Casselton, Sussex
Tel: Casselton 45678

The hotel is situated at the southernmost corner of Lime Green where it joins the High Street. Routes are shown on the enclosed map.

3. *Training rooms*
All sessions other than syndicate discussions will take place in the Garrett Room on the third floor. Syndicate rooms will be notified on Monday morning.

4. *Tutors*
Keith Packman – Training Department – Monday to Wednesday inclusive
John Masterton – Oxbridge Management Training – Wednesday to Friday inclusive.

5. *Accommodation and services*
The programme will be fully residential to encourage optimum participation and to avoid external pressures. The company will pay the following charges direct:

☐ bed and breakfast, morning coffee, lunch, afternoon tea, evening meal for the duration of the course.

Participants incurring other charges, eg for drinks, telephone calls, newspapers, should settle their accounts for these before leaving on Friday.

Bedrooms are centrally heated and have bathrooms en suite. Radio and colour TV are also installed, and tea-making facilities provided.

Early morning calls and newspapers should be arranged with the porter.

Breakfast will be served at 8 am, lunch at 1 pm and dinner at 7.30 pm in the main restaurant, ground floor.

The Cromwell Bar serves real ale. A snooker room is situated in the basement. Arrangements may be made through the hotel reception to use the Lime Green Golf Club at privilege rates.

Branches of the big four banks are within walking distance of the hotel. Barclaycard, Access, Eurocard and American Express may be used to pay hotel bills if desired.

6. *Programme continuity*
In fairness to other participants and to ensure maximum benefit from the programme, it is essential that it be seen by members as a package requiring full-time attendance for the 5 days.

It is also important that the course which is tightly scheduled is not interrupted by telephone calls or messages for members. All messages unless especially urgent will be passed on at suitable breaks in the programme and outgoing calls should also be made at these times.

Telephone calls may be made from the call-boxes in the foyer or from one's bedroom. In the latter case a service charge will be added by the hotel.

7. *Programme material*
All programme material, stationery, etc will be supplied in the Garrett Room.

8. *Reports*
Members are assured that no reports on individual performance will be made. Whilst continuous evaluation of progress will take place on a group basis, individual anonymity will be preserved.

9. *Car parking*
Adequate car parking space is available in the hotel forecourt.

10. *Dress*
Members will be free to wear casual clothing throughout the programme if they should wish to do so.

Figure 11(b). *Joining instructions – administrative information*

relatively easy to rectify the omission. What has to be realized when providing training activities externally, however, is that everything that is in any way likely to be needed has to be packed. If the venue used is remote the chances of obtaining anything that has been forgotten within a reasonable time are slim. So as not to leave anything to chance, therefore, an inventory such as the one shown in fig. 12 should be used for each programme. Furthermore, when operating at an external venue, the services available are not under the administrator's direct control. A relationship has to be established with the hotel or conference centre staff which will ensure that they respond adequately to the needs of the programme. This simply cannot be taken for granted and therefore the briefing given to the staff of the establishment has to be detailed and close liaison and monitoring are essential.

Not all the mistakes or failures in administration have to be made public. Often a hiccup in the organization of a training programme can be readily put right without the participants having an inkling that anything has gone wrong. So if the correction can be made without the error having any adverse effect on the programme, why publicize it? Trainers would do well in such circumstances not to incur the displeasure of their administrators by asking the participants, however jocularly, 'What's gone wrong with the admin today?'. The most effective administration is unobtrusive, and this means that the administrator is unlikely to be able to enjoy the limelight. Indeed, mistakes that come to light are more likely to attract publicity than all the sterling work done behind the scenes to ensure that the programme runs smoothly.

It goes without saying that the training administrator should be of a high calibre. It is important that the trainer should not have to concern himself with organizational problems. He is fully occupied with problems associated with the training itself and he therefore needs a

Training Equipment and Materials Inventory

Programme:
Dates:
Venue:

Equipment	*Tick*	*Programme Materials*	*Tick*	*Stationery etc*	*Tick*	*Stationery etc*	*Tick*
Overhead projector	☐	Transparencies for OHP	☐	Pens for flip charts	☐	Mapping pins	☐
Spare lamps, fuses for OHP	☐	Films	☐	Pens for OHP	☐	Envelopes	☐
Screen	☐	Slides	☐	Pencils	☐	Masking tape	☐
16mm film projector	☐	Video tapes	☐	Sharpeners	☐	Sellotape	☐
Spare lamps, fuses for FP	☐	Sound tapes	☐	Erasers	☐	Bulldog clips	☐
Extension speaker	☐	Flip charts	☐	Rulers	☐	Paper punch	☐
Extension leads	☐	Flip chart clips	☐	Ruled paper	☐	Stapler/staples	☐
Multiway socket leads	☐	Admin notes (spare copies)	☐	Plain paper	☐	Staple extractor	☐
35mm slide projector	☐	Handouts	☐	Graph paper	☐	Penknife	☐
Spare lamps, fuses for SP	☐	Programme files	☐	Paper clips	☐	Tape measure	☐
CCTV (see handbook for breakdown)	☐	Place boards	☐	Reinforcing washers	☐	Cloth for OHP	☐
Tape recorder	☐	Lapel badges	☐	Drawing pins	☐	Blackboard rubber	☐
Flip-chart stands	☐	Participant lists	☐	Glue stick	☐	Chalk	☐
		Trainer's notes	☐	Rubber bands	☐	Matches	☐
				String	☐	Venue information	☐
						First aid box	☐
						Toiletries	☐
		Tools		*Reference Books*			
		Pliers	☐	Dictionary	☐		
		Screwdriver	☐	. . . .	☐		
		Scissors	☐	. . . .	☐		
		Cleaning kits	☐	. . . .	☐		

Figure 12. *Training programme inventory*

back-up which can be relied upon. It is taking risks to entrust the task to an inexperienced junior. An otherwise effective training activity can be so easily undermined by a lack of administrative skill. Paying a competent administrator a rate truly commensurate with the job is a worthwhile investment. The necessary skills are discussed in Chapter 9.

Summary

In this chapter we have considered what has to be done to ensure that all the training activities in an organization are integrated so that they take place at the right time in terms of the needs of the trainee and the organization and the availability of resources. A systematic approach to programme planning is therefore recommended.

It is almost inevitable, in an organization which takes training seriously, that at some time or other the stretched resources of the training department will have to be supplemented by external means. Care is advised in the use of consultants, who should be selected because of their proven expertise in the desired areas and with particular regard to the manner in which they conduct their assignments. The use of external training facilities which are not under one's direct control calls for an administrative back-up of a high standard.

Chapter 5

The Training Process – Learning and Behaviour

The change agent

The training specialist in an organization is often referred to as a 'change agent',[47] although there has been some confusion as to what is really meant by this term. Until a few years ago it implied reacting to changes which take place outside his direct control. For example, much of the training which he initiates tends to stem from variations in working requirements arising internally or imposed from outside the organization. These modifications might sometimes be of a major nature, such as would arise from changes in the top management, resulting in substantial re-framing of organizational policies. They can more frequently come about at employee level where an individual or small group requirement to augment knowledge or skill in the job has been identified.

Organizational changes can give rise to a diversity of training needs. A change in management philosophy will have far-reaching effects throughout the organization. For example, a switch from an entrepreneurial to a bureaucratic management style, or *vice versa*, will have a dramatic impact throughout the business and may well give rise to confusion at all levels until retraining in line with the new philosophy has been carried out. Managers and supervisors may themselves have to change their leadership style to fit the new ethos.

Changes taking place at the policy-making rather than the individual or small group level may involve new corporate strategies, which manifest themselves in such areas as: financial control and investment policies; product innovation and diversification; change of product mix; computerization; new equipment, tools, systems, procedures, methods; manpower planning.

At the employee level, changes arise for example from staff turnover resulting in the need for the induction of new people. Existing employees, particularly in fast developing technical areas, also require continual updating in their specialisms in order to keep abreast of the competition. A knowledge of the latest developments in the law affecting employment and in the standards set by professional institutions will be important for many managers and supervisors. Interpersonal relationships and collective relationships with trade unions will always be in a state of flux and will give rise to recurrent needs for training in interactive skills.

In times of organizational growth there are continuing training requirements which have to be satisfied in order that the concern may meet the challenges of progress. Even when the business is in a contracting situation, training needs arise from the re-organization of activities around a smaller workforce. The training department therefore has to be a progressive unit which is geared to keep pace with changes in the organizational structure, the external influences, technology, pressures for efficiency and cost effectiveness and so on.[16] In addition, there are changes taking place in the employees themselves, in their educational and professional levels, knowledge, skills, attitudes, expectations and group allegiances. This demands constant monitoring of the dynamic situation and the needs of the organization, keeping up-to-date with relevant training research, matching training methods to the needs, evaluating the results and using those results to assess the performance of the training function in the interests of maintaining its efficiency and effectiveness.

What has been said suggests a reactive role for the trainer. That is, he is responding to needs which become evident to him or some other member(s) of the concern from traditional methods of analysis, management policy, performance review, intuition, etc. The current concept of the change agent in training is that of the trainer's direct intervention in the organization to bring about change himself. Instead of simply reacting to situations which appear to have training implications as they come to his notice, he adopts a proactive role, consciously setting out to seek opportunities for change and exploiting them by whatever means are appropriate. Commonly the change which he initiates in this way would not come about without his intervention.

Clearly the proactive approach requires that the trainer operates at the source of corporate decision-making, since this is the area in which he can make the greatest impact. With his knowledge of the business and the capabilities of the workforce, he may wish to influence the management in the options it takes when embarking on certain courses of action (see p. 24). A manpower policy may take on a whole new aspect, for instance, if the training specialist is involved right from the start. Since such involvement in decisions at the corporate level enables lower level training needs to be more readily assessed, the resultant training is likely to be more relevant and training effort more effective. It follows then that, in carrying out a change agent role, the trainer can wield considerable power in an organization. To what extent he is able to do so depends on his credibility at the top.

Knowledge, skills and attitudes

Whilst the purpose of training in the business context has changed very little over the post-war years, the approach, the methods and the techniques used have progressed considerably. Specialists have become more aware of what their role should be, what tends to motivate people to work in various kinds of employment and what are the most acceptable and profitable ways of achieving the desired performance from individuals and groups. Employers too have grown to recognize the value of investing in training with these ends in view.

It has been accepted for some years that all training can be categorized under the headings of knowledge, skills and attitudes. These were briefly mentioned in the first chapter but require closer attention. At one time little distinction was made between these three training areas. Skills were seen to be acquired when knowledge of the method, process or system was passed on, either by word of mouth or in writing. Learners were expected to become proficient in a job after being told what to do. The unfortunates who were unable to absorb the information and apply it fairly quickly were considered idle or untrainable and were discharged. The approach to attitudes in training was negative. Employees were often seen to have the *wrong* attitude when they failed to meet the employer's demands, but it did not occur to anyone that inculcating the *right* attitude, that is one which was accepted as constructive, could have a reinforcing effect on learning. The work of behavioural scientists, coupled with pressures from the workforce calling for the application of fairness and common sense, have helped to bring about a change in approach in recent years. Trainers are now well aware that people cannot be treated as machines and the extent to which the employer's goals can be achieved by simply telling them what to do is limited.

The distinction between knowledge and skills has also come about as much by reason of worker pressures as because of managerial enlightenment. In the early part of this century it was not considered necessary to give employees any more information about the organization and its business than was directly related to the skill for which the person was employed. Indeed it was normal for owners and managers carefully to guard all information about the running of the establishment. Since people did not regard it as their right to know what was going on in the corridors of power, they were content to leave such weighty matters to the management. The bosses were able to run their businesses as dictatorships and nobody questioned them. In this restrictive environment, the work people lived in blissful ignorance of the aims of the organization and the significance of their place in it. Gradually throughout the 1900s employees in industry particularly have realized that as contributing members of the wealth-creating team they are entitled to be treated as participators in more than name. Progressively greater demands have been made for information about the business and its goals, its policies and procedures. The growth of trade unions[48] has resulted in greater importance being given not only to the provision of better terms and conditions of service, but also to the dissemination of information about them and about opportunities available in the business. The law has also added weight to the need for information to be passed on to union negotiators for the purpose of collective bargaining.[49]

Managements have become aware of the fact that employees who are kept in the picture about what is going on are more likely to accept and give commitment to management decisions. Uncertainty can have a more damaging effect on a workforce than bad news. Employees, although seldom amenable to the idea of being made redundant, will generally be more able to come to terms with the decision if they know the real reasons why the management has had to take it and if they have been kept informed as the situation has developed. When they know that something unpleasant is brewing but are uncertain as to what it is or how it will affect them, they will become concerned and anxious. Their morale, and consequently their efficiency, will suffer and they will react unfavourably and without sympathy for the management's problems when the ultimate decision is made. These decisions can often be taken without thought for the possible effects. The employer may well want to re-engage redundant employees at some time in the future when the organization is growing again. He may meet with a rebuff from them if they feel they have not had a fair deal from him.

Coupled with these requirements for employees to know more about the organization is the need for them to be continually updated in specific areas of their jobs. Many employees are sufficiently dedicated to their work to undertake private study to keep abreast of the latest developments in their field. Indeed, most trainers will argue that self-development is the most effective means of training because of the unsolicited commitment involved.[27] Nevertheless, employers have a responsibility for ensuring that their employees are equipped to cope with change in their particular specialisms. Thus there is a continuing need for 'knowledge' training. Not only is it necessary to cover the knowledge required to enable an employee to carry out a specific job, but a good deal more information about the business has to be imparted if he or she is to feel a contributing member of the team.

The simple wheel shown in fig. 13 illustrates the importance of seeing the training of an employee as a total concept and not a question of showing him how to carry out his particular task in isolation. At the hub of his working existence is the job. This has to give support to the organization and the environment through the knowledge, skills and attitudes which he brings to it. Failure to provide the necessary training in any of these areas weakens the structure and is therefore to the

Figure 13. *The total training concept*

detriment of the organization. Here the analogy with a true wheel ends, as clearly the length and strength of the 'spokes' will vary with the nature of the job. Knowledge of the firm's business which may be required, for example, will increase the higher the employee's position in the hierarchy. It would be fatuous to suggest that an operator on the shop floor or a junior clerk in an office should be as knowledgeable about the enterprise as a director or senior manager. It is nevertheless reasonable that people at the lower levels in an organization should at least know what the firm is in business for, what it makes or does and what their place in the scheme of things may be.

There is often a need for specific training in skills and attitudes relating to the organization and the environment. If an employee has to have contact with others in the business, and in particular work in cross-functional teams, he needs to be able to communicate, to be able to understand instructions from above and the views of other specialists. He may have to interpret and use figures and information provided by, for example, the accounts department. If he is in a supervisory position he would have to be able to implement disciplinary and grievance procedures[50] and other organizational policies, rules and regulations.

Negative attitudes towards the organization can often have far-reaching effects. The growth of trade unions is testimony to the fact that work people felt that they needed to combine in order to get a fair deal from their employers. Whilst ruthless autocratic managements are fast disappearing, a good deal of suspicion still persists and one feels that this is largely due to lack of communication about the management's intentions, be they long- or short-term. The establishment of trust between management and workforce, which may be reinforced by means of training as well as by normal day-to-day communication, can go a long way towards creating a cohesive team which can meet the challenges of the future. Loyalty cannot be bought but has to be earned by ensuring not only that justice is done but that it is seen to be done. People will usually respond if it is demonstrated by word and deed that management respect their feelings and are open and honest with them.

The employee's relationship with the environment in which he lives is often completely ignored. The way he behaves in the community outside the workplace can have marked repercussions on the organization's image. When he relaxes in the company of his personal friends he may feel freer to voice his criticisms of his employers and work colleagues than when at work. This can have damaging results, not only in terms of possible loss of business if overheard by customers, present and potential, but also in deterring suitable candidates from applying for jobs with the concern. It is therefore in the long-term interests of management to create, by all the means available including training, a climate that is conducive to their employees being ambassadors for the organization outside the workplace.

On- and off-the-job training

The decision as to whether training should be carried out on or off the job cannot be made arbitrarily. A judgement has to be made as to which method is more likely to meet the required objectives. On-the-job training generally takes place in the normal work situation, the task very often contributing directly to the output of the department. Off-the-job training is conducted away from the work situation and therefore is more often than not simulated and/or hypothetical. In some production establishments, an off-the-job training area is set aside within the plant for the purpose of training operatives and other production employees. Other requirements are accommodated by the use of training rooms on site, or using conference centres or hotels off-site.

The most significant advantages and disadvantages of the two methods are shown in fig. 14. The main argument for taking training away from the workplace is that it provides an opportunity in low-risk surroundings to study important problems in greater depth than would be possible in the midst of work pressures and interruptions. This makes it particularly appropriate for management training,[39] where it is necessary for managers to study complex problems and make considered judgements. Too often the decision to carry out training on-the-job is taken on purely financial grounds and becomes a 'sitting next to Nelly' activity, which can only be as effective as Nelly's instructional skill allows.

The teaching/learning debate

Much has been said in training and education circles about whether the role of a trainer is as a teacher or as a facilitator of learning.[51] Throughout our school careers we were conditioned into regarding the teacher

On-the-Job	Off-the-Job
Advantages ☐ no special facilities needed ☐ no additional staff needed ☐ real life situation, not simulated ☐ productive in terms of department's work ☐ trainee can establish work relationships from the start ☐ learning can be controlled ☐ no 'off-the-job' cost involved ☐ no transferability of training required	☐ away from work and home pressures ☐ more time available ☐ trainees' specific difficulties are easier to explore ☐ relaxed atmosphere more conducive to learning ☐ easier to obtain full attention of trainees (distractions reduced to minimum) ☐ able to test hypotheses and ideas in low risk environment (exchange of knowledge and experience) ☐ improves morale and motivation for self-development
Disadvantages ☐ cost lost in departmental budget ☐ risk to machines, equipment, etc and increase in scrap due to lack of experience ☐ part-time instructor may lack skill in training ☐ lack of time due to pressures of production ☐ difficulty of accommodating trainee idiosyncrasies ☐ psychological pressures on trainee due to exposure before experienced workers	☐ cost of external facilities ☐ artificial sheltered environment ☐ difficulty of simulating work problems ☐ resistance of trainees being away from home ☐ difficulty of transferring learning to work situation ☐ generally more time-consuming ☐ often involves travelling costs and inconvenience

Figure 14. *On- and off-the-job training: pros and cons*

as an expert and one who could tell us whether our answers to problems were right or wrong. When we went out into the world of business, we naturally believed that there would always be someone there who could give us the right answers, and we could eventually learn to provide them ourselves. We were surprised to find that many business problems, and particularly management problems, do not have 'book' solutions or 'right' answers. There were only solutions which had been tested by practice and experience. From the welter of options available one had to use one's judgement to decide which was likely to be the most workable solution in the particular circumstances of the case. It was not realistic to expect that precisely the same conditions would ever occur again. In other words, no two problems were ever exactly alike so they could not be solved by means of a magic prescription.

It might be assumed then that the choice between teaching and learning methods of training should not be difficult to make. In situations where a concrete and indisputable answer to a problem is possible, it may seem reasonable to adopt a teaching style, whilst learning by other means may be necessary when dealing with problems requiring a choice of workable options. However, since learning is central to all training and a prerequisite for success, if a trainer does not create a learning climate his efforts are likely to be abortive. Unfortunately, teaching is not synonymous with learning: telling someone something, however convincingly, by no means guarantees that the message will be received and understood. Thus, if a teaching style is adopted, it must be accompanied by other reinforcing conditions in order to be successful. The trainer should at no time adopt the attitude that trainees *ought* to be receptive to what he is trying to put over. The conditions must be established which come as near as possible to ensuring that they are receptive.

Learning theory

Most dictionaries define learning as 'knowledge got by study'. This implies that there has to be a conscious discipline and willingness on the part of the learner to acquire knowledge. Bernard Bass goes further and in considering learning in the industrial training context, suggests that it is 'a relatively permanent change in behaviour that occurs as a result of practice or experience'.[52] If we accept this definition we cannot consider learning as anything but dynamic. It takes place when there is a practical demonstration, or an activity, or an experience giving rise to some perceivable change in behaviour, however small. This theory therefore reinforces the idea that the learning process must be an active one if the end result is to be achieved.

For trainers to be able to create the right conditions for learning to take place they need to have an understanding of what is going on in the learning process. One way of looking at this is suggested in the simplified model shown in fig. 15.

When a learner is introduced to an external stimulus, there are two major factors which will influence his reaction or response. One is his

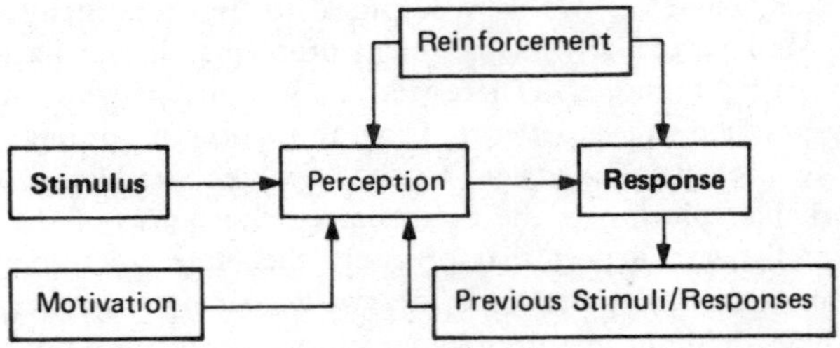

Figure 15. *A simplified learning theory model*

motivation, or willingness to be influenced, and the other is his perception of the nature and importance of the stimulus. This perception, or impression, is based on his past experience of handling and responding to earlier stimuli. Other external factors, known as reinforcers, may be used by the trainer to support or increase the level of the response, and the learner will again have a perception of these related to his previous experience. It is true to say that a good deal of learning can occur subconsciously, so that the learner may be unaware of it, although his actions will indicate to others that learning has in fact taken place. This makes anecdotal feedback about training activities somewhat unreliable, since a learner may not readily concede that his behaviour has in any way been changed.

It is no accident that 'perception' appears at the centre of the learning theory model. It is a key aspect of learning theory. If the information he is trying to learn can readily be organized in the learner's mind within a framework of previous experiences, he will have relatively little difficulty in assimilating it. Where the material is complicated or not easily related, however, a bridge has to be built between the new and previous knowledge, for example by the use of appropriate symbols or terminology. We are all much happier when dealing with familiar things and often switch off completely when people start talking to us in their own specialized language. Some years ago the author was asked to mount and run courses on finance for non-financial managers; at first he was reluctant not because he did not feel competent to answer most of the questions which tended to come up, but because he often did not recognize the questions! In this case, the language needed to be right to provide the bridge for the trainer to be able to interpret the needs of the participants.

Learning can take place by a variety of means. One of the most common is experimentation, or trial and error. Provided there are no serious risks involved, for example, to physical or mental health, safety, reputation or work output, it is possible to learn successfully by actually trying out solutions to problems and observing whether or not they work. Whilst this method of learning may be effective in terms of retention of knowledge so gained, it tends to be a time-consuming and therefore inefficient process. It can also lead to over-confidence if results are generally favourable or to frustration if they are not.

Experience provides the vehicle for a major part of learning. We may learn by observation of others around us and often model our own behaviour on theirs. They may change our behaviour by simply feeding in appropriate information based on their own experience of a comparable situation. We may also consciously analyse the previous success or otherwise of the total process shown in fig. 15. If such experiences give rise to some sort of reward or positive feelings, we are encouraged to repeat the same formula, in particular where we recognize similar ingredients in the new situation. Any kind of punishment or negative result deters us from using the same prescription again.

Earlier in this book the importance of employee self-development was mentioned. Clearly this calls not only for commitment and self-discipline but also for the ability to learn. Learning to learn[53] is in itself a skill and the training department should not make the error of assuming that everyone possesses it. Any form of education relies on the ability of the learner to acquire information by reading, listening to lectures, taking part in discussion groups, watching television, etc, but it is often overlooked that he may be lacking in the very skills needed to do those things adequately. His reading ability may fall short of what is required, he may not have mastered the difficult skill of listening, his knowledge of the English language itself may not match up to the requirements, and so on. Many training managers may be disturbed by the educational standards of school leavers, in particular in literacy and numeracy. They will argue that it is not their job to educate, but to train. New employees should have an acceptable level of basic education before they start work. But what if they have not reached such standards? Something has to be done about it; it is a fruitless exercise to try to build on inadequate foundations. It may be necessary to train employees in, for instance, English, mathematics, reading and writing skills. This can be done in the training room, by the use of coaching, programmed learning, reputable correspondence courses or other open learning methods, or by attendance at a further education establishment.

One of the difficulties encountered by training staff in introducing formal training into an establishment is the reluctance of the manager to allow adequate time for the training programme. Output is the god which everyone is expected to worship and taking time out to train is preventing the output target figures from being met. Trainers are well aware of the fact that untrained employees cannot meet the targets anyway and training properly carried out will enable them to reach experienced worker standard (EWS) much more quickly than if they are left to their own devices and 'learn from experience'. The learning curve shown in fig. 16 makes the assumptions that all learners are alike in their acquisition of knowledge and skill and the task to be learned or information to be acquired is fairly straightforward.

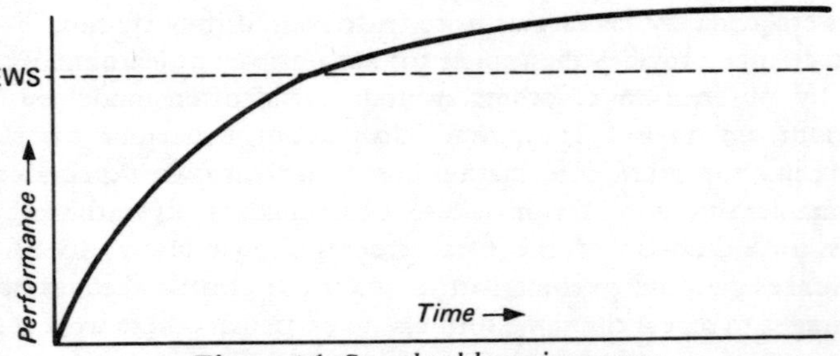

Figure 16. *Standard learning curve*

This is clearly an oversimplification. Even when the task is seen to be simple by the trainer or instructor, it can have varying degrees of complexity and ease of assimilation in the minds of the learners. In other words, their perceptions of the task, the environment and the trainer will vary, with consequent effects on their rate of learning. It may well be, therefore, that the initial slope of the curve will differ considerably within a given sample of learners. Those who have difficulty in relating the task to their past experience and knowledge, who are not suitably motivated or are affected by other psychological constraints, will get off to a slower start as shown by the solid curve in fig. 17.

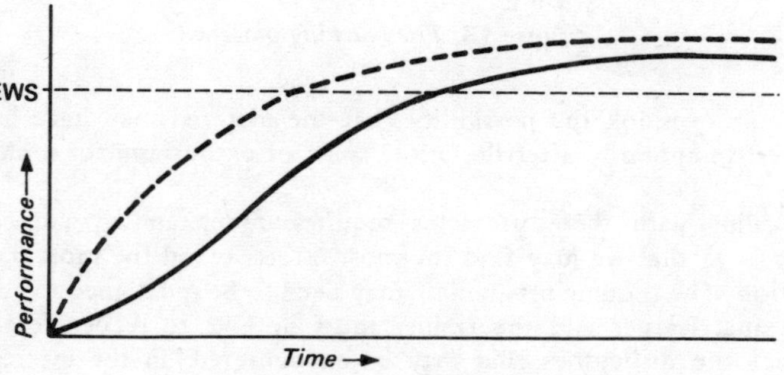

Figure 17. *Differing rates of learning*

The slope of the curve following this initial period of acclimatization will assume a steady or a steep increase depending on the learner's capacity for learning. The fact that his learning rate may be very high during this stage (see dotted curve) means that he reaches experienced worker standard quicker than other learners. It does not in any way indicate that he will achieve a higher level of expertise and ability in the end. We all know that 'late developers' often reach levels of performance above those of the people who make rapid strides at the start and then lose impetus as things get more difficult.

Another phenomenon which must be understood is that of the 'learning plateau'. It has frequently been observed that some learners reach a point in their training when they appear to be at a standstill, that is, little if any learning is taking place (see fig. 18).

It is dangerous to assume in this situation that the learner has reached the limit of his capability and we should always seek the reasons for the plateau before accepting that this might be so. It may be simply that the training has been organized in definable steps and the learner is taking time to absorb the subject matter of the last step before proceeding to the next. He may be pausing to unlearn some of his previously acquired knowledge before accepting the new. We should

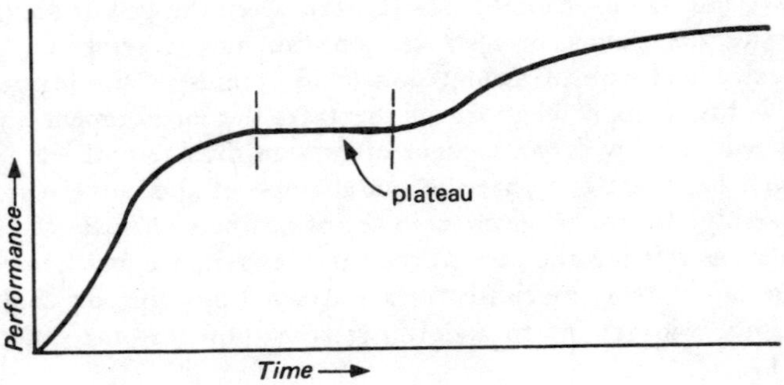

Figure 18. *The learning plateau*

also not overlook the possibility that the material may have lost its interest temporarily after the initial spurt of enthusiasm for something new.

Dealing with these problems requires understanding and careful analysis so that we may find the most effective and the most painless solution. The training programme may need to be redesigned to suit the individual learner and the trainer must be able to recognize and so predict the difficulties that may be encountered. In the interests of reducing unproductive periods to a minimum we should try to eliminate plateaux from the training process. Having identified a plateau, however, it will be necessary to provide reinforcers, incentives or a bridge to help the learner on to the next productive stage.

The careful planning of training in easily learned steps goes a long way towards easing the stresses arising from attempts to teach too much too quickly. It should always be borne in mind that when learners are acquiring new knowledge or skills, which may appear revolutionary to them, they are under stress and need to be given time to cope with the change. Pre-arranged pauses between the steps enable the learner to absorb the last portion of information and the trainer to collect his thoughts, and if necessary re-arrange them, for the next one. Some of these pauses should be specified rest intervals, giving the learner the opportunity to wind down and recharge his batteries, particularly where the overall period of training is lengthy or where the material is complex. More frequent pauses may be effective in the earlier stages when the learner is adjusting to the new circumstances. We may reasonably expect that learning will be more lasting when stages are short. The practice of cramming may be effective for getting one through some written examinations but is not generally conducive to acquiring lasting knowledge.

Providing the learner with feedback is essential if learning is to be effective. In addition to the benefit of reassurance in confirming that his learning is along the right lines and relevant to the job he is going to do, it enables him to correct errors before they become indelibly imprinted on his mind. If he knows that he is going to be checked and his progress monitored in this way at every stage, he is more likely to be motivated to apply himself to the task. He may, of course, require guidance from time to time. This should not be given to the extent that he becomes too trainer-dependent.

The importance of motivation

It was mentioned earlier in this chapter that one of the major factors influencing a learner's response to a training stimulus is his motivation. If we are to make any impression on his work performance we must understand what motivates him to work in his current job or for that matter in any job. We are tempted to assume that all employees are motivated to work for the same reasons. However, as we shall see, this is very far from the truth.

Motivation has been defined in a number of ways. In the training context, the simplest concept is the willingness of the learner to put effort into his training and into the ultimate performance of the job.[54] This usually implies involvement and commitment, that is, an active interest in the job and the appropriate training for it and a readiness to accept that training and decisions made affecting it. Clearly this is of vital importance to trainers. If employees are not willing learners, there is no way in which the training objectives and those of the organization will be met. An understanding of what induces employees to work is therefore imperative. The work of the behavioural scientists gives us some help in this direction although they cannot tell us how to deal with any particular case, but can only offer basic guidelines of where to look for a solution to the problem.

The idea which is fundamental to many theories of motivation is that people are spurred on by psychological and physical needs, some of which are inherited and some acquired by learning. Their attitudes and consequent actions are directed towards meeting goals which they set themselves in order to satisfy certain needs.[55] For example, if an employee feels a need for the exercise of power in his job, he will set himself goals, consciously or otherwise, which will be directed towards that end. Failure to achieve such goals can give rise to frustration which may be manifest in all kinds of, sometimes apparently unaccountable, behaviour. Knowing what goal the employee is failing to achieve can help us to understand the behaviour resulting from it.

A significant milestone in motivation research was achieved by the Hawthorne studies in the late 1920s and early 1930s. A group of researchers from Harvard University headed by Elton Mayo, carried out experiments among groups of workers in the Western Electric plant near Chicago.[2] Whilst it had been popularly believed that environmental conditions had a material effect on employee motivation, it was demonstrated at Western Electric that the supervisor/worker relationship was of much greater significance. Management had believed that by improving working conditions such as ventilating and lighting levels in the factory they could expect improved performance from the workforce and that reductions in those levels would have the reverse effect. In fact, a controlled experiment showed that production increased even when the levels were reduced. A study of the effect of the supervisor's presence was also made. It was recorded that the working group set its own levels of production regardless of incentives, but that performance was demonstrably better when the supervisor was present and showing a direct interest than when he was away from the job. The presence or absence of research observers had similar effects, which gave rise to suggestions that the experiments were invalid. Nevertheless, they did divert the attention of the behavioural scientists away from environmental factors and towards such considerations as group cohesion, morale and job satisfaction.

In 1943 Abraham H Maslow[3] put forward a theory of human motivation in which he identified five sets of basic needs:

- ☐ physiological (survival needs eg water, food, sleep, shelter, sex)
- ☐ safety, security, stability
- ☐ belongingness (love and affection)
- ☐ status and self-esteem
- ☐ self-actualization (sense of achievement)

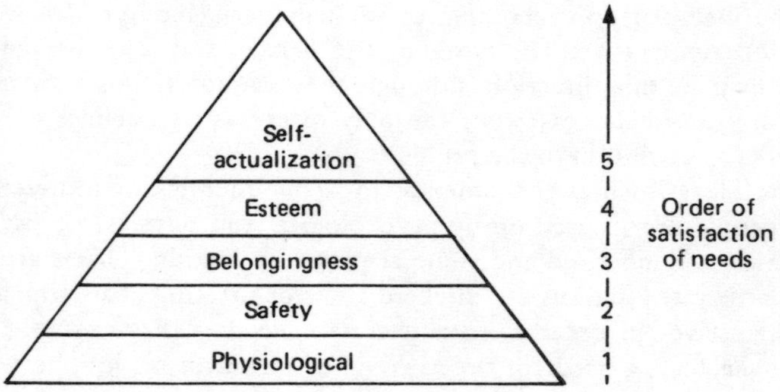

Figure 19. *Maslow's 'needs hierarchy'*

It will be seen from fig. 19 that Maslow arranged these needs in what he referred to as a hierarchy. This means that they are in a specific sequence through which one tends to move as each level of need is satisfied. Thus, for example, when physiological and safety needs are substantially satisfied, the next higher order need in the hierarchy (belongingness) emerges and demands attention. As one moves up the pyramid, so the incentives to be furnished by the employer tend to become increasingly difficult to provide. Clearly the opportunities available to give employees status and a sense of achievement in their work are fewer than those to satisfy normal survival needs. The dissatisfactions that people experience are therefore likely to increase as they move up the hierarchy.

The level to which they progress in the hierarchy will vary from one individual to another. Some people will have nothing but a passing interest in status, for example, but will have a very strong need to be wanted. Others will not be satisfied until they have reached the top of the pyramid, being motivated strongly by the prospect of achievement and reaching the peak of their capabilities. The problem is that it is not at all easy to establish what really motivates any particular individual and yet this information is important to the training specialist who seeks to achieve optimum results in his training activities. This calls for a close relationship with the learner in which every opportunity is taken to get to know him, to discover his interests, his attitudes and his beliefs. His receptivity to training will generally be improved if he is relaxed and not under threat in any way, and one means of achieving this is to encourage him to talk about his outside pursuits and those things about which he is enthusiastic. Exploring these interests can very often provide the gateway to discovering how he feels about his work and his career.

The 'motivation-hygiene' theory of Frederick Herzberg[4] was developed in the 1950s, as a result of research carried out in eight heavy engineering establishments and one major utility in Pittsburgh, Pennsylvania. A cross-section of 203 managers, engineers, accountants, production workers and clerks was interviewed. The team analysed the positive and negative feelings of the employees in relation to their jobs. They concluded that positive or good feelings resulted from task-related factors which they classified as motivators, whereas negative feelings arose from factors associated with the environment or context of the job, which they called hygiene or maintenance factors:

Motivators (or satisfiers)	*Hygiene/maintenance factors (or dissatisfiers)*
sense of achievement	company policy and administration
recognition (for achievement)	supervision
the work itself	salary
responsibility	interpersonal relations
opportunity for advancement	working conditions

Hygiene in the medical sense implies prevention, not cure. It helps to remove health risks from our environment. In the motivational context, attitudes towards the job may be unfavourable if there are harmful circumstances or factors surrounding it. Removal of these factors does not necessarily bring about improved satisfaction with the job but it may well help to remove obstacles to creating the right conditions for job satisfaction to be exploited by other means. If we want our work people to be satisfied with their jobs, therefore, we not only have to establish which motivating factors have to be provided but also which demotivating factors have to be reduced to an acceptable level.

Although the 'motivation-hygiene' theory has enjoyed fairly wide acceptance over a number of years, not all behavioural scientists are prepared to go along with its assumptions. Both Herzberg's and Maslow's theories assume, for example, that it is realistically possible for an employer to create the conditions for employees to fulfil themselves at work. Chris Argyris contends, however, that most organizations are impersonal bodies which demand servility and dependence within a fairly rigid framework.[5] Healthy, mature people generally expect to have a certain degree of independence and control over their own lives, but this is not compatible with the nature of the organization. Some concerns have recognized the constraints that the organizational ethos places on them in this regard and have taken steps to modify the climate, not just the physical conditions, in which people work in order to improve the match between individual and organizational goals. This demands a re-appraisal of management thinking, in particular in respect of interpersonal relations, giving rise to a variety of training needs for managers and supervisory staff generally.[39]

The studies of Douglas M McGregor during the late 1950s were centred on this matching of human effort to the needs of the organization.[6] The conventional view of management, which he called Theory X, was that it was concerned with organizing resources, men, machines, materials and money, towards economic ends. To achieve the objectives, employees had to be managed. But the average worker was self-centred, averse to work, lacking in ambition, resistant to change and generally unconcerned about the needs of the organization. He therefore needed persuasion, coercion, threats, close supervision and control in order to perform acceptably. In the days of full employment, this hard-line approach became increasingly difficult to operate and was frequently resisted by the workers who combined in an attempt to force management's hand. In some instances, the pendulum swung too far the other way, and some employers adopted a permissive style which had equally disastrous results. Giving people considerably more latitude resulted in their taking advantage of the management, and performance and output suffered.

The results of using a controlling or directive approach to management have shown that people are no longer readily motivated by such means. Most employment in the post-war society has provided the basic requirements of living and people are now inclined to be stimulated more by the prospect of self-fulfilment than by physiological factors. McGregor therefore postulated another theory which he felt more nearly met the requirements of the time (late 1950s). His Theory Y suggested that whilst management's objectives had not fundamentally changed, it had to modify its approach in sympathy with the considerably changed motivational needs of the workers. Employees were no longer seen to be inherently apathetic towards the organization or unconcerned about its needs, but were thought to have acquired those traits because of their experiences of working in organizations. The way in which they had been treated by the management and the restrictive administrative machine may well have stifled any enthusiasm they may have had for the source of their livelihoods. They were in reality equipped with the basic ingredients necessary for them to be able to take a responsible role in the organization and it was incumbent upon management to recognize this and to provide the opportunities, support, incentives, etc for them to develop their capabilities towards that end.

There is no easy way of effecting the transition from Theory X to Theory Y management. Attitude changing both at management and shop floor level is a long-term operation; it will not happen at the drop of a hat. Management, having been used to autocratic control, giving orders and having the satisfaction of seeing them carried out without question, will find it hard to adjust to a style which encourages active rather than passive co-operation from employees. The employees themselves may well be bewildered, and even suspicious, when they find themselves being treated as adults rather than juveniles.

McGregor's Theory Y has stood the test of the past 25 years or more. During the 1960s and 1970s other behavioural scientists have added weight to the importance of a management and leadership style which takes account of the needs of the employee as well as those of the organization.[5][6] His sense of personal worth and importance to the enterprise can be exploited by creating a supportive climate (Rensis Likert 1961).[7] Many employers have made the change, in total or in part, and in general it may be said that is has been of benefit to both sides. It has certainly not solved all industrial problems, but it is true to say that a willing co-operative workforce, backed by a sympathetic and helpful management, is much more likely to produce the goods than one which is apathetic and constantly looking over its shoulder. The sharp rise in unemployment in more recent years tempted some managers to try to revert to a Theory X approach, feeling that they were in a stronger position to do so when employees lived in fear of losing their jobs. The employees resisted with all the power at their command.

We have seen that motivational research has centred on factors which provide employees with satisfaction or dissatisfaction at work. In the late 1970s, John Hunt of the London Business School[8] suggested an updated list of such factors, using some of the earlier theories, but modifying them in the light of his own research findings.

Satisfiers	*Dissatisfiers*
Challenge	The formal structure – control, rewards, rules
Recognition	Bosses
Freedom	Salary and wages
Control over one's own work, power, status	Working conditions
A complete job	The people we work with
Knowing what the goals are	Boring work
Individual growth	No contact with users of our products or services
Working with compatible people	Poor communication within the hierarchy
Developing 'satisfying' relationships with those people	Limited opportunities for promotion
Belonging to a worthwhile organization	Loss of control over one's life (ie power)
Being rewarded at a level commensurate with expectations	Failing
Succeeding	

In providing this list, Hunt suggested that we kept our minds open about understanding employee satisfaction. Separating sets of factors in this way was not realistic because they were so interdependent as to be inseparable. Dissatisfactions might produce conflict which in turn generated a response with a positive outcome.

In the second edition of *Managing People at Work*, Hunt provides a summary of his research findings over a period of more than 15 years, during which time he obtained personal data from over 10,000 people. This data, which included their rankings of certain work goals, was used to build up profiles in histogram form which demonstrated, among other things, significant changes in people's goal orientations as they went through different phases of their lives. Not only did the goal orientations vary between individuals as a result of their different backgrounds, characteristics, etc but they also varied in any given individual as he progressed through the successive stages of his development from childhood to old age. It was concluded that these factors had to be taken into consideration when managers sought to understand their people's behaviour at work. Managers had to understand what their employees might be experiencing before they could begin to appreciate why they behaved in a particular way. If a match could be achieved between the employee's job design and his profile at any particular time, this would be a first step towards motivating him in the direction of optimum performance in the job.

The writer's experience in industry is confirmed by this research. Clearly we should not ignore the fact that people do not come in convenient packages, responding to situations with consistency throughout their working lives or in similar ways to their colleagues. They are individuals and have to be handled on a one-off basis, with due regard to *all* the circumstances. Moreover, success in dealing with one problem will not guarantee success in handling another, even if the same employee is involved. Nevertheless, experience of resolving or failing to resolve difficulties with employees adds to our store of knowledge and helps to provide guidelines for the future.

The study of motivation has two major purposes for the training specialist. First, since the receptivity of his learners depends on their willingness and co-operation, he has to be aware of the effects of the various factors on their motivation and so create the right learning climate. Second, if the organization's managers and supervisors are to obtain the best results from their workforce, they themselves have to receive training in which they learn how to identify and handle the employees' idiosyncrasies. It is important that those who are appointed to manage others are given the appropriate tools with which to do so.

Summary

In this chapter we have considered:

- ☐ the trainer's initiative for and response to change
- ☐ training as a total concept
- ☐ on- and off-the-job training
- ☐ aspects of trainee behaviour and how it affects learning.

The trainer's skills should embrace both proactive and reactive approaches to training. Traditionally it has been the pattern to respond to needs as they arise and by looking at the individual in the job as an entity rather than as part of a total dynamic system. There is however a strong argument for the trainer initiating change as opposed to waiting for it to occur through other agencies. If this happens at the highest level, training is able to operate most effectively and make optimum impact on the fulfilment of corporate goals.

Training needs to be seen as a total concept. An organization depends for its effectiveness on performance from all its members. Lack of attention to detail in terms of the knowledge, skills and attitudes required of them can therefore have a stultifying effect on the ultimate success of the enterprise. Training on a piecemeal basis should be resisted wherever possible.

When selecting the method of training for the solution of a particular problem, a fundamental decision to be taken is whether the training should be done on-the-job or off-the-job. The choice should not be made simply in the light of what is more convenient, but having due regard to the factors listed in fig. 14. The circumstances of each case should be weighed carefully before such decisions are made.

Effective training demands the creation of conditions in which true learning with understanding can take place. A learner's response to a stimulus will be influenced by his motivation and by his perception of its nature and importance. The research of behavioural scientists into what makes a person put effort into his work provides a number of clues as to what factors are important when an employer seeks to obtain the best from his employees. These factors need to be considered if the right conditions for learning are to be achieved. It is important to realize, however, that the behaviourists do not provide us with one simple solution which can be applied to every case. Different people respond to situations in particular ways for very different reasons.

Chapter 6

The Training Process – Methods and Techniques of Training

Against the backcloth of behavioural theories discussed in the last chapter we can now consider what methods are available to us as training managers. We can conveniently divide these methods into two major categories, didactic and participative. The former may be defined as direct teaching (with authoritarian overtones) whilst the latter implies two-way communication between two or more persons, with or without a leader. It has already been suggested that direct teaching methods are valid vehicles for learning provided suitable safeguards are introduced in the form of feedback. Some will be tempted to say that when this happens they become participative techniques. This is not so, because a true participative style requires a total commitment on the part of the trainer to creating a learning situation in a group. He is not seen as an expert armed with authoritative answers and solutions to problems, but as an equal member of the group, a resource on which the group can draw when necessary.

The following list of training methods and techniques is by no means exhaustive. Most methods fall into these categories, however, and the training specialist needs to be aware of them. He must be the judge as to which is the most appropriate to use in the specific circumstances.

Didactic methods

One-to-one instruction

The direct teaching approach[18] to the training of apprentices, operators and other individual learners is still used extensively. Whilst an authoritarian style of one-way communication may still survive in some of the smaller establishments where there is no professional training function, it is now widely recognized that successful instruction depends upon an active rather than a passive learner. Directive instruction tends to create dependency, and this is in conflict with the aim to bring a learner up to experienced worker standard at the earliest possible time. This objective requires the use of a systematic method, backed up by a comprehensive two-way information flow, adequate reinforcement of learning and a practical demonstration of that learning under skilled supervision.

The work on instructor performance carried out in the mid-1970s by the Industrial Training Research Unit supported the view that having a systematic approach to instruction did not of itself produce an effective instructor.[57] The style of instruction that he adopted could have a significant effect on learning. Whilst one style may be beneficial another may be a hindrance to meeting the desired objectives.

The research was carried out with a sample of 43 instructors and every statement and action recorded whilst they were supervising their trainees. From this data it was possible to identify different styles of instruction. For example, the instructor who was an automaton simply operating the system could be distinguished from the one who was flexible and took into account the specific needs of his trainee whilst still working within an overall master plan. The period of each instruction included basic training and specific operational training.

Information on the past performance and success rate of each instructor was obtained from an independent record source, and a comparison was then made with the identified styles. The results gave a strong indication that there are preferred styles of instruction which have a better chance than others of achieving success. These preferred styles were in general centred on the two-way rather than the one-way process of communication. Whilst they conformed to an overall plan which ensured that nothing important was ignored or overlooked, they were characterized by instructor behaviour which showed an awareness that no two trainees and no two tasks were alike but all demanded individual attention and consideration. Each trainee required the right amount (for him) of basic information to enable him to learn by doing in a challenging and supportive climate.

All the effects of adopting a good instructional style would appear to be positive. They include a better understanding of the job requirements coupled with the ability to carry them out satisfactorily, the generation of enthusiasm for the job and what may be seen as desirable attitudes towards the organization and other employees at all levels.

It is not the purpose of this chapter to give a blow by blow account of every conceivable move in the instruction process[10] but it is felt that the following factors are worthy of mention:

1. The question should be asked initially as to whether one-to-one formal instruction is the best way of imparting the required knowledge or skill. There may be a more suitable method, depending on the objective.
2. The job must be analysed in detail and the learner's present knowledge ascertained. The gap constitutes the learner's training need.
3. An instruction plan must be made, and appropriate targets

identified. The most important questions to be asked at this stage are: 'What must the learner be able to do when I have finished the instruction?' and, 'What standards should he be able to achieve?' Bearing in mind that there is a limit to the quantity of information a learner can absorb and retain at any time, the instruction should be planned in easily assimilable sections or units, separated by clearly defined breaks. Important points which may make the job easier or affect the quality of the finished work, or which may prevent injury to the person or damage to equipment, etc should be defined so that they may be impressed on the learner as key parts of the instruction. Where visual aids are deemed to be necessary to reinforce learning they must be appropriate to the information one wishes to impart. They should never be used just for effect, nor to excess.

4. The instructor who organizes himself in such a way as to reduce problems to a minimum clearly stands a better chance of success than one who takes no precautions at all and is content to play everything by ear. There is always the danger of familiarity breeding contempt and important issues consequently being overlooked. It is axiomatic that conditions should be created in which the learner is relaxed and receptive. This requires that the environment is reasonably comfortable and that disruptions to the training process are avoided. Interruptions either visual or verbal not only disturb the learner but can equally give rise to the instructor losing his train of thought. For the same reasons, care should be taken to ensure that everything needed for the instruction, eg tools, equipment, diagrams, manuals, are to hand before the process is started.

   Accepting that no two learners are alike in personal characteristics or learning capacity, the right relationship has to be established with them, taking into account their particular psychological needs. An extrovert instructor whose manner is overbearing can be very intimidating to a nervous trainee and can thus restrict the learning process. In order to obtain commitment from the trainee, an interest in learning has to be created. This is not always easy particularly where the task is mundane, but that is no excuse for not trying to find some way of making the job satisfying.

5. When carrying out the instruction it is advisable to give the trainee a preview of the task to be performed. This helps him to re-organize his thoughts around the new task before he has to cope with the detail. He needs to know the purpose, the approximate time and the scope of the instruction. An indication of how the job which he is required to perform fits into the general scheme of things is usually useful in creating interest.

   It is important for the instructor to get things right first time, because he is depending on his message getting across so that he does not make problems for the future. This necessitates instructing clearly, patiently, naturally and comprehensively at a reasonable pace, using skilfully whatever tools or aids are required to reinforce learning. Needless to say, any distracting mannerisms have to be controlled.

6. Generally the sooner the trainee can get involved in the instruction process the better, provided the activity is safe and does not risk unnecessary cost. For example, if he is learning how to use a micrometer gauge, his progress will be improved if he is able to handle the instrument at an early stage.

   Some instructors, having shown the trainee the job, go away and leave him to practise on his own. This is the very time they should be present, since a trainee left to his own devices will try to take undesirable short cuts and when in trouble may be afraid to call for help. It is important that his early attempts are closely monitored and that his understanding of the activity is thoroughly checked. He should be quite clear at the outset what is required of him and should know what to do if he experiences any difficulty.

7. Operator jobs in a production plant usually demand high speed working to acceptable standards of quality in order to meet output targets. There is a tendency for some instructors to allow trainees to take their time and not concern themselves with speed until they have mastered the skill. This is undesirable in that it introduces two ways of working into the training programme. A crisis in the form of a learning plateau (see p. 88) may arise when the transfer has to be made from a low to a high speed mode. The trainee should be encouraged to accept the idea of working at speed from the start, and ergonomic factors and work methods should be established for each process. In other words, the ultimate workplace conditions, including the recommended physical movements and methods involved in the process, should be closely simulated in the training situation. Clearly it is unrealistic for a trainee to be expected to carry out a production process initially at anything like experienced worker performance levels. What can be done, however, is to introduce the trainee to small units of the process at a time, requiring the achievement of a target speed for each unit before proceeding to the next. When all units in the process have been satisfactorily completed at target speed, it is then necessary to bring them together and to achieve that speed for the total cycle. Extending the number of cycles, or the run, whilst maintaining and improving on the target speed, is known as stamina training and this is the stage at which a trainee may become disheartened if sufficient help and encouragement are not forthcoming. Adequate explanation has

to be given for every stage of the training process, and the need to achieve a target speed should not be interpreted by the trainee as slave-driving. It is important that speed is maintained whilst the trainee is actually working but that ample relaxation time is also built into the programme. As the trainee gains confidence and competence, so the relaxation time can be progressively reduced.

8. The record of progress should be freely available to the trainee throughout the instructional process. It is helpful for him to know just how much additional effort is needed to achieve target performance. Frequently it can be quite small and knowing this can remove a good deal of anxiety.

   When teaching skills to, among others, craft and technician apprentices, it is strongly recommended, and indeed is a condition of ITB approval for such training, that the trainee keeps a log book. It records the major elements in the training programme and should be signed by the instructor at the end of each stage of off-the-job instruction and by the supervisor during on-the-job training. This record can make a useful contribution to the reinforcement of learning. It also helps to some extent to assess the trainee's progress and provides him with a handy reference book for the future.

9. Finally, the trainee's progress is monitored at suitable intervals until it is confirmed that target performance is being maintained. There is a joint responsibility at this stage between the supervisor and the instructor. Until the supervisor is happy with the trainee's contribution the instructor should not consider his job complete. The trainee will have built up a working relationship with the instructor during this training and will expect his help and advice to be available until sufficient confidence has been gained to carry out the job required with competence.

Where the initial training is undertaken in an off-the-job area, as recommended for example by the Industrial Training Boards, the time that the transfer from training room to workplace is made will vary considerably with the degree of complexity of the job and the rate of progress of the trainee. One important consideration, particularly when re-training adults, who may be over-anxious, is that the move should not be made too soon simply in the interests of getting the work out. Trying to solve one problem in this way may merely result in creating others, such as low morale with consequent low performance, high scrap rate, increased accidents, absenteeism and possibly even higher labour turnover. The work and morale of the longer serving skilled workers can also be affected by their pre-occupation with the problems of the newcomers, with adverse effects on their own productivity.

Lecture

The lecture[58] is a time-honoured means of communicating with a group. Usually defined as an informative discourse delivered to an audience, it clearly implies a one-way talk to a number of people given by someone who is knowledgeable about his subject. It normally covers a specific, discrete topic rather than a range of subjects, and for it to be successful it demands a high level of skill from the lecturer.

Often a lecture is used when it is necessary to convey messages to a large audience, since other methods of a more participative nature would prove too cumbersome to operate. This creates problems, because the prospect of significant learning taking place with a large group is greatly diminished by the lack of interaction, not only between the lecturer and members of the audience but also between the members themselves. Unless the lecturer is expert at arousing individual attention and creating audience involvement, there is a severe risk of members becoming inattentive and distracted. Some lecturers use humour to create interest, and, if they are naturally humorous people who choose the time and the subject carefully, this can be very successful. The speaker who is not a natural humorist, however, can be a disaster if his jokes are irrelevant and misfire. The danger of relying on humour is that the audience may remember the quips but not the subject matter, and one must always remember the objectives of the exercise and ask oneself whether or not these are being achieved.

It is frequently assumed that someone who is master of his profession is worthy of the attention of his audience. This is very far from the case. The nation's greatest authority on a particular subject can also be the nation's biggest bore in the lecture room. If the object of the lecture is learning, then it is essential that the speaker is not only knowledgeable in his subject but is also skilled in creating a learning climate in which he can get his message across. This requires an understanding of the needs of the audience. Sometimes they are not volunteers and therefore have no vested interest in the topic, finding it unstimulating. They may have their minds full of other problems. Somehow one has to be able to break into their thoughts and re-direct them. Creating the right conditions for learning to be effective requires attention to a number of factors. The most important of these are summarized below.

1. The environment, including whatever services have to be provided (eg catering), must be suitable. As with any other type of training the trainees must be comfortable and reasonably relaxed. Anything short of this will create a distraction and inhibit learning.
2. The needs of the audience in terms of subject matter must be ascertained in advance. There are real problems here, since they may not be a homogeneous group, that is, their level of knowledge of the subject may vary considerably. Setting the level of the

lecture to ensure that the more informed are not bored is likely to leave those with limited knowledge of the topic well behind. Starting from a much lower datum point in order to cater for the less informed may well frustrate those who have heard it all before. This problem is typical of many which managers and specialists have to decide upon, and calls for the exercise of skilled judgement. The lecturer who succeeds in getting it right is hailed as an interesting and absorbing speaker; the one who fails to do so attracts less favourable epithets. One obvious solution to this difficulty is to split the audience into groups, each comprised of people with common interests. This is seldom practicable, if only for the reason that one usually does not know who will be coming until they are there. The writer would suggest that a reasonable approach might be to try to set the talk at such a level that the less knowledgeable are stretched but are not entirely out of their depth. This may be tedious for the better informed members in the early stages, but they should be asked to bear with the speaker until he has filled in some of the more fundamental information for the benefit of the newcomers to the subject. Reassurance can be given that the talk will move on to more advanced aspects as soon as is practicable. This avoids the trap of allowing the more knowledgeable to feel that the whole lecture is going to be at a low level. It cannot be over-emphasized that there are dividends to be reaped from letting the audience know right from the start exactly what they can expect.

3. The subject must be thoroughly researched and the lecture carefully planned to meet the perceived need, care being taken to structure it logically in steps separated by natural breaks. Both speaker and audience need time to collect their thoughts between stages. Although there are no hard and fast rules about the duration of such stages, in general it is unlikely that the audience's span of attention will exceed about 20 minutes. It is often advantageous to use the intervals to invite questions or to circulate written information. The vital factor is that no activity is so long that the speaker loses the audience's attention. How the breaks are used is of less importance.
4. Visual aids and handouts should be used with discretion. It should never be assumed that the use of training aids is essential for a lecture to be successful. Many a lecture has been ruined by visual aids which have been badly produced or equipment which has been inexpertly operated. These devices should be used to reinforce, not to do the lecturer's job for him (see Chapter 9). Handouts are a valuable means of consolidating and supplementing information provided in a lecture, but they must be well designed and reproduced and must be used at the right time to be effective. Giving them out at the commencement of or during

a talk is inviting the audience to absorb itself in reading them and to ignore the speaker. Whenever handouts are distributed, whether during breaks in the programme or at the end, time must be allowed for them to be read without interruption. The audience should also be told at the beginning how visual aids and handouts will be used, whether or not they need to take notes, the approximate duration of the talk and when questions will be taken.

5. The skills expected of a lecturer differ very little from those required of any public speaker. Creating and maintaining the interest of the audience demands that the speaker considers the following points among others.

   He should adopt a natural, relaxed style. Some people believe that when addressing a group one is expected to behave as a totally different person. Since few are good actors, they fail dismally. Individuality is an essential feature of effective speaking. The lecturer should not try to emulate someone else, but project his own personality. He should therefore behave quite naturally but, as in one-to-one instruction, should avoid mannerisms which are in any way distracting. He should not appear slovenly or take up a stance which impedes his delivery. Needless to say he should also be wary of saying or doing anything which may cause offence to any member of the audience. The way he uses his voice can make or mar a lecture. Its level should be right for the distance it has to travel and the natural acoustics of the room. Variation in tone and pace also helps to maintain interest and so he should try to refrain from speaking in a monotone.

   The lecturer should use straightforward language which may be interpreted by everyone in the audience without too much difficulty. Jargon should be used with care and only when it is known that the audience will understand it. Sentences should be short and to the point and padding should be avoided.

   Every member of the group should be made to feel that the lecture is a dialogue between the speaker and himself even though words may not in fact be exchanged. This requires eye-to-eye contact with as many people as possible, and a determined effort not to direct one's comments to the ceiling, walls or floor or to one's notes. It also means that the speaker has to be able to read the non-verbal signals of the audience and respond to them as if they were spoken. However, a temptation that he should avoid is to address all his statements to one person who gives him a warm feeling by hanging on his every word and nodding sagely!

   The way in which lecture notes are used requires careful consideration. Detailed notes which are read out verbatim often create a dependency which results in a stilted performance. If the speaker expects his audience to respond to him, they deserve more than a mere reading of the lesson. They will expect him to have done his homework and to have planned and rehearsed his talk so as not to have to depend on comprehensive notes. Subject headings on small cards should usually be sufficient to provide the necessary triggers except where the lecture treats a highly technical or involved subject, in which case more detailed information may be necessary.

When expounding a controversial argument, other points of view should not be ignored. Dogmatism may lose an otherwise receptive audience. That is not to say that a speaker cannot be positive or even forceful but he should be wary of sweeping aside views which do not coincide with his own.

The lecturer should be honest with his audience. If he finds that a member of the group knows more about the subject than he does, he should not try to cover up but should make use of the available expertise. This can be done by involving the member and encouraging him to share his knowledge with everyone. Furthermore, if asked a question to which he does not know the answer, it is far better that the speaker should admit it and should promise to find the answer for the questioner at some later time. Most people will accept that the man who knows all the answers has not yet been born, and they will respect a lecturer who is prepared to admit that there are gaps in his knowledge. Trying to bluff one's way through such a situation does nothing for one's reputation.

Control over nervousness is important. Even the most accomplished speakers will say that they are apprehensive when they first go on. Once having got under way and having established a rapport with their audiences, however, they can relax and even enjoy the experience. A common mistake made by the inexperienced lecturer is to allow himself to be carried along at a fast pace by nervous energy at the start, not giving himself time to think about what has to be said. If he takes his time right at the beginning the audience is able to get used to his delivery. At the same time he has the necessary breathing space in which to marshal his thoughts. The pacing of each stage of the talk helps in this regard. A lecture should not be a long continuous tirade but a well balanced talk suitably broken up with pauses between statements. A pause of several seconds seems much shorter to an audience than to the speaker and he should rehearse his lecture with the aid of a tape recorder, experimenting with pauses of different duration. The effect is likely to be a reduction in the speed of delivery with marked improvement in the quality of performance.

6. The lecture should always end on a positive note. People like to go away feeling that they have been stimulated and have been given food for thought. The end should never be an anti-climax.

Sometimes, a brief review of the main points of the talk is in order and useful in putting everything in perspective. Often a call to future action is required and needs to be put over with conviction. Where such action is being initiated, members of the audience must know precisely what is expected of them.

7. It is usually helpful for the audience to be thanked for their attention and participation and where appropriate an offer of future help may be made.

In spite of criticisms by the advocates of participative learning, the lecture still has its place in certain training situations. Indeed it may be the only practicable way to handle a large audience. Since by its nature it tends to be relatively passive and unstimulating, however, it needs to have a built-in participative element in order to stand a reasonable prospect of satisfying its objectives. It is not only necessary that feedback is obtained from the audience but also that it is acted upon and not ignored. The skilful use of audience involvement can turn an unstimulating recitation or mere entertainment into a dynamic learning experience for everyone, including the lecturer.

Participative methods

The following training methods rely to a major extent for their success as learning media on the active involvement of the trainees. The degree of this participation varies from one method to another but the overall philosophy implies that learning by doing[52] or by getting personally involved, even if only in discussion, is the most successful route to acquiring knowledge and skill, or towards changing attitudes. The cross-fertilization of beliefs, attitudes, knowledge, experience, etc between people who have matured in widely differing environments is seen to be invaluable for the broadening of their outlook on life in general and on their work in particular. Furthermore, by inviting total participation of the trainees, a climate is created in which they feel that they are being treated as responsible adults and that their views and their knowledge and experience are valued. The trust and confidence thus engendered go a long way towards obtaining optimum contributions from members of the group, and the most effective learning from the activity.

Conference

No apologies are given for including the conference in the list of training methods. Although few conference delegates will consciously think that they are attending a training session, if they do not learn something from it, what is its purpose? They expect to go away wiser than they were before they came, but they may have little idea in advance in what way they will benefit.

The conference[59] is usually a highly structured device for conveying a message or messages on a large scale, often to an audience of several hundred people. It attracts delegates with common interests, usually from a wide cross-section of society, who seek the opportunity to hear and comment on the views of recognized authorities in the areas covered. The literal translation of the word conference implies consultation. In other words, delegates should not only hear an authoritative discourse from the speakers but should reasonably expect to be able to obtain answers to questions concerning the topic or topics covered. It is in this respect that conferences often fail to meet their objectives, either for the reason that the objectives were not properly formulated or communicated to delegates in the first place or because the chairman conducts the discussion badly.

The chairman is a key figure in the conference. He wields considerable power and is expected to have complete control both of the speakers themselves and of the audience. He should know in advance what he can expect from his speakers and should plan adequate question time after each talk. Having to curtail question time due to bad planning can result in a number of dissatisfied delegates, and can turn an otherwise good conference for most into a disappointment for many. One of the weaknesses in the system is that it provides an excellent opportunity for the *prima donnas* to take the floor and play to the gallery. They tend not to have anything constructive to say but nevertheless take up an inordinate amount of time, to the detriment of those who may have valuable contributions to make to the debate. Handling this situation demands skill on the part of the chairman and a firmness which cannot be wrongly interpreted as dictatorial. There will, of course, be a good deal of reticence on the part of many delegates to stand up in front of such a large audience to make their points or to put questions. The benefit of the aggregated views and experience of the assembly can thus be lost in the conference situation.

Another major task of the conference chairman is to sum up at the end. Relevance and brevity are the keynotes here. The audience have listened to speakers for a number of hours and are now ready to go home. Prolonging the conference for very long whilst adding nothing to what has already been said does nothing to help send them away with warm feelings about the meeting. What is said depends on the style of the chairman but the temptation to indulge in the expression of personal viewpoints at this stage is to be avoided. Summing up should involve briefly summarizing the major points arising from the conference, and thanking the speakers and others involved for their contributions. It is often appropriate to re-state the objectives of the conference, expressing the hope that they have been achieved. Sometimes valuable feedback is obtained by audience reaction to this.

Many see the conference more as an opportunity for meeting people, particularly the speakers, than for learning much about the subjects discussed. Training specialists are not alone in this. There is certainly a pay-off for them in making contact, at coffee or lunch time, with recognized authorities in fields of direct interest to them and indeed with fellow specialists. The more aware they are of what is going on in their profession the better in terms of keeping up-to-date and coping with change.

Seminar

The more common seminar is a conference on a smaller scale but incorporating a greater degree of participation from the members. The word is derived from the Latin for 'seed-plot' and thus suggests that it is a well prepared situation for sowing, nurturing and developing ideas.

The seminar[60] is usually centred around a single theme which is examined in some depth. The speakers are acknowledged specialists who make brief presentations outlining the topic or topics to be discussed and lead the members towards certain tasks which they want them to explore. The size of the seminar should be such that it can be readily divided up into small syndicate groups. The syndicate size is determined by its effectiveness as a discussion group. Too small a group limits the expertise and views that can be drawn on and so produces frustration and a sense of inadequacy. Too large a group tends to result in domination by a few and the inhibition of members who feel overshadowed by those who are more forthcoming. This suggests, say, a minimum number of four and a maximum of five or six. Syndicates of over six, unless very carefully selected, can suffer from the same problem as the large conference in which valuable contributions are forfeited.

The number of syndicates used depends upon the reporting-back procedure. It is assumed that after each input from a speaker the seminar breaks into separate syndicate groups to examine the task. They are given a time limit to reach their conclusions by democratic processes and they each appoint a spokesman, who is not necessarily chairman of the group, to report back to the full group session. Clearly, if a large number of spokesmen have to report back on the same topic, the full group session becomes a lengthy process with a good deal of repetition. The writer would place a limit of four on the number of groups in these circumstances. Of course, if a number of tasks is allocated concurrently, the limit of four groups can be applied to each different task.

The amount of time devoted to the various activities in a seminar needs to be arrived at very carefully and can be quite critical. It is not an uncommon reaction from members that they feel that they obtain greater benefit from the syndicate discussions than from the full group sessions to which they report back. This is not surprising, since they have explored the problems in some depth in the small groups, where they are more closely involved as individuals, and then find the full group sessions as so much repetition of the same themes. This suggests that more time should be allocated to the syndicate discussions 'where the real work gets done' than to the full group meetings.

Handouts summarizing the main points made by the speakers are useful at the end of seminar sessions to provide reference material for members. To encourage them to make use of the information in the future, handouts should be brief and to the point.

Winding up a seminar may differ very little from closing a conference. The trainer may have to summarize, if appropriate, but again he must be on his guard against spending too much time reiterating points which have been gone over many times already in syndicate and full group sessions. Taking the point that any training activity should end on a positive note, it makes more sense to devote time in the winding up session to discussing and taking decisions on future plans arising out of the activity.

Discussion

The discussion[61] is a common training vehicle which is useful for the presentation of ideas and plans, particularly when issues have to be clarified or expanded and the views of groups of people have to be ascertained. The discussion leader requires skill in planning, careful preparation, encouraging the involvement of individuals, controlling the debate, summarizing the results of the meeting and ensuring that suitable action is taken.

The objectives of the meeting need to be clearly established and the necessary information gathered in advance. Part of the planning process is to decide who should be present, since a good deal of expensive time can be wasted by people being required to attend all the time when they only have a tenuous, or limited, interest in the topics being discussed. It is suggested that there should be a skeleton membership for the full period of the meeting, and co-opted members should be called as and when required.

Having established the membership of the discussion meeting it is vitally important that a detailed agenda is sent out some time before the event. Lack of precise information about the subjects to be discussed can give rise to members misinterpreting them and arriving at the meeting having briefed themselves for the wrong topics. Needless to say, this results not only in the inefficient use of time but can also be highly de-motivating. When all members know in advance the precise purpose of the meeting and the rules which apply, they start on common ground. If they know the meeting is purposeful, they will be motivated to contribute towards a successful outcome, thus improving the prospects of a practical solution to the problem.

For the discussion leader[62] to be successful, he must be able to handle the debate in such a way that useful contributions are optimized and inappropriate offerings limited. This calls for sensitivity not only in being able to identify practical and workable suggestions but also in being able tactfully to reject the less acceptable ones without offending the contributors. Members should not be allowed to digress from the matter in hand and should be encouraged to be brief. There is a tendency for some groups to go on debating an issue long after everyone has agreed on a course of action. Another time-waster is the practice of some members to carry on private discussions during the debate and this should again be curbed diplomatically.

Following the discussion, the leader needs to record the outcome of the meeting and ensure that everyone is clear about what future action has to be taken and who has to take it. This last requirement often means that the leader takes on the role of progress chaser between meetings, but this is necessary because failure to follow up the items actioned in one meeting will lead to time being wasted in the next.

A symposium is a form of discussion meeting. Commonly used by professional bodies, it usually consists of a collection of papers given by a number of speakers. The contributions normally deal with discrete topics within a common theme and are straight lectures, not allowing any immediate feedback in case it may prejudice the talks of future speakers. It is not unusual, however, for a panel discussion to take place at the very end under the leadership of a trainer or chairman, who determines the way in which questions may be put to the speakers.

Team training

In the mid-1950s, when the writer moved from a local government environment to an industrial one, his naively held beliefs as to how manufacturing firms operated were rudely shattered. The books he had consulted led him to the view that management was a team effort and everyone employed was working towards clearly identified corporate objectives. In reality, not only were these objectives completely unknown to a large proportion of the employees, including some managers, but it was quite normal for departmental chiefs to shut themselves away in separate boxes 'doing their own thing' and having little contact with the world outside their departments.[63]

Although over many years this outmoded approach to management persisted in some companies, there has in general been a growing awareness that the contributions of individuals to corporate goals have to be not only optimized but co-ordinated if these organizations are to be successful, or indeed survive. People have become alive to the fact that, whatever advantages there may be in giving managers and their subordinates freedom in working out how they should do what they perceive to be their individual jobs, activities which do not promote the organization's objectives, directly or indirectly, are a luxury which is simply not justified. Insularity breeds such luxuries, and it is manifestly unjust that the efficient employees in organizational terms should have to bear the burden of the inefficiencies of others.

It is, of course, widely known among training managers and specialists that problem-solving in groups is generally more productive of solutions than problem-solving by individuals (see p. 121). It should follow, therefore, that there are benefits to be reaped by work groups operating in teams and capitalizing on their combined resources as they work together to meet organizational goals. This policy should prove to be in the interests of the business as a whole, and it would appear to have other desirable by-products. For example, by removing the traditional communication barriers between individuals or departments, it should widen their horizons and enable them to see more of the total action. The effect on morale could be considerable. Much industrial unrest and conflict arises from people being ignorant of management's intentions. Opening up the communications networks and encouraging greater involvement in company operations must surely be to everyone's advantage in the long run.

If management and other work groups are encouraged to work together in teams, it is logical to train them as teams.[64] One of the criticisms of training individuals in isolation is that when they return from a training programme fired with enthusiasm to put into practice what they have learned, they often encounter indifference, or worse, they are flatly denied the opportunity or facilities to implement any changes. The training then is largely abortive, unless the individual is soon promoted and is able to exercise more personal freedom in the way he operates. Training in a team context enables problems to be directly work-orientated and decisions to be taken jointly by those people who have a vested interest. This helps to ensure greater commitment to making decisions work. It also gives individuals confidence that the day-to-day decisions that they are taking in the workplace are not in conflict with the philosophy of other members of their team. The quality of decisions can be improved since more information can be produced and more options explored. Mistakes made by individual team members will more readily come to light and be eliminated, and where decisions require a variety of actions from members, these may be more fairly allocated.

It should not be thought that team work or team training is in fact a panacea for all ills in problem-solving. There can sometimes be difficulties.[65] These may centre around the composition of the team. A team made up of people with largely similar characteristics may be less effective than one with differing philosophies, experience, skills, etc, since the homogeneous group will tend to have a narrower view of problems. A mixed group may give rise to more serious in-group pressures and will call for greater expertise from the trainer in handling them. For example, in a team which comprises employees at different organizational levels, there may be a danger of individuals trying to pull rank in order to have things their own way.

As with seminar groups (see p. 108), the desirable size for a team may be between four and six, and one of the dangers of having a greater number is that the team may tend to sub-divide into smaller groups and so disrupt the problem-solving process. Team achievement could also be adversely affected where individuals were permitted to leave the group before the allotted project time expired in order to attend to pressing problems in the workplace.

Team development tends to go through certain identifiable stages before it can be considered productive. Initially there will be a certain amount of confusion in which each member tries to orientate himself and establish his position with respect to the others. In seeking to apply themselves to the task the team members will continue in a stage of uncertainty, whilst searching for support from anyone who is prepared to offer it. Lack of confidence in their ability to carry out the task often leads them to attack it or the trainer and in extreme cases may even give rise to a total withdrawal. This uncertainty is also characterized by conflict within the group, though this should not necessarily be seen as destructive. Frequently conflict is a positive agent which enables people to resolve differences of viewpoint effectively. As the team gradually becomes accustomed to working together on a common task, the individual members begin to appreciate the support they are getting from each other and the first signs of a cohesive group emerge. Trust is built up between them and they come to value each other's knowledge and experience, thus giving each other greater confidence. The final stage, which is commonly termed 'maturity', arrives when the team has established its structure and *modus operandi* and its members are working effectively together.

Needless to say, the trainer will usually be able to identify these stages in a team's development by observing the behaviour of its members, and he should resist the temptation to interrupt the process unless specifically asked for help and guidance. This may not happen, particularly with management groups, since assuming adequate briefing and basic information are given in the first place, the aggregated experience and knowledge present in the group is usually sufficient for it to reach a rational solution to the problem. Frequently the difficulty is not lack of knowledge or expertise but lack of the ability to use it. The team concept of training helps people to test their experience and ideas against those of other members of the group and so check their acceptability. This process thus enables them to decide which aspects of their knowledge are usable and which may have to be rejected or at least shelved until customs or practices change.

Patrick Suessmuth[66] has made some interesting observations on the monitoring of sound levels in groups in order to identify the stages reached in their deliberations:

- ☐ the start-up stage in which the sound level quickly peaks and then flattens out
- ☐ the thought-collecting stage during which there is comparative silence, which the trainer is advised to respect. Intervention by him at this point would be disruptive and would restrict progress
- ☐ the main working stage, in which the sound builds up to a high level and fluctuates for a fairly long period, when the information is being gathered from individual members and consolidated
- ☐ the finishing stage where there is a sharp drop in noise level and any subsequent rise is likely to be mere chatting. When this stage is reached the trainer should check that the task has been completed.

When introducing team training into an organization, the trainer has a mammoth selling job to do. The first hurdle will be to get the active support of the top management (see Chapter 9). However, once obtained, it will provide a springboard from which to integrate the methods gradually throughout the organization. If the management are seen to go along with the idea to the extent of involving themselves in the process, there are better prospects of support at lower levels. This is only one of the prerequisites for success, however, and the ultimate activity has to be worthy of the effort that has gone into selling it. The following suggestions may be helpful in getting the required co-operation:

1. Make it clear to everyone concerned that the problems to be worked on will be real organizational problems and not generalized hypothetical examples. The training, although carried out off-the-job will be part of the members' everyday work.
2. The composition of the teams should be such that they have the basic expertise to carry out the project and the authority to implement their findings rather than having to take them through lengthy procedures of obtaining higher agreement.
3. The activity should not be open-ended. To underline the real life nature of the project, target times should be established and adhered to where possible.
4. The importance of each member's contribution should be stressed and absences from the activity, except in dire circumstances, discouraged.
5. The effectiveness of the team should be monitored and the results communicated to members and examined. It is important that group effectiveness, and thus corporate effectiveness in the organization, is optimized at the earliest possible time. Competition which may be counter-productive is therefore undesirable.
6. The team should be treated as a group rather than as individuals. Where any rewards or sanctions are necessary or desirable, these

should be on a team basis.

7. The activity should be organized within the rules of any other business activity, eg objectives should be clearly defined, budgets of time and cost prepared, suitable resources made available, means of dealing with the results understood.

Some training managers have tried to introduce team training into their organizations relying on one specific method or technique. Those with an organizational or systems orientation have chosen, for example, management by objectives[20] on the assumption that if everyone is shown how to set targets they will work together for the common good. Others who are more behaviourally biased have put their money on, say, sensitivity training (see p. 129), expecting that the enhanced insight and awareness in individual members will improve the effectiveness of the team. Neither of these approaches of itself is likely to provide the desired result. The likelihood is that a judicious combination of both approaches will improve the prospects of making some progress towards team and ultimately organizational effectiveness. One pilot study using this combination of techniques has been described by Iain Mangham.[67] A consultant was invited into an organization in which a particular department employing eight people had been re-organized in the interests of better consultation and employee involvement. The success of this operation had encouraged the management to introduce training aimed at greater and more far-reaching participative management.[68] Team training was therefore seen as a first stage.

The process was introduced by means of a simple questionnaire, the results of which were shared by common consent. It explored the views of each team member on how his team handled its objectives, conflict, etc, and surprisingly brought about widely differing responses. These were examined and explanations sought for the variations. Initially the actual team's problems were disguised, references being made to difficulties experienced by other groups. The scepticism about team work and the feeling that conflict should be avoided were eventually overcome, however, and members gradually became more open and honest with each other, trust being developed to the point where they were prepared to discuss their real problems in the working group.

The next stage in the study consisted of a practical team exercise in which members were not able to communicate verbally with each other. It provided a bridge to finding solutions to group problems through the use of delegation and shared responsibility and led to discussions on job enrichment and job enlargement[69] as means of optimizing group performance. This was followed by another simple exercise providing members with the opportunity to bring their work-related problems out into the open and discuss them. The results of this session and the actions agreed were committed to paper and circulated to members for their confirmation and commitment. Subsequent training followed established management by objectives[20] practice, concentrating on defining the role and objectives of the group in the previous discussions into the future work programme. The final session was one of consolidation and making sure that the results were in no way conflicting.

Although only anecdotal feedback was used to measure the usefulness of the programme, members were in no doubt that it met its objectives by obtaining commitment to the continuous review and improvement of departmental performance through team work. Other observations included a noticeable increase in morale and a wider recognition of the value, both from the individual and the organizational point of view, of members working closely together.

The benefits of team training are unlikely to be felt in the short term. In the long term they will be forthcoming so long as team work is not seen as the magic wand which on its own will convert an ineffective department into a successful one. New problems arise if a highly effective team is created within an organization in which other departments are relatively ineffective. This can only lead to frustration and counter-productive rivalry which will militate against the achievement of the desired objectives. To be most profitable, therefore, team working needs to be compatible with some form of organization development.

Organization development (OD)[70] is often wrongly described as a technique handling change. In reality it is a strategy which depends for its operation on the use of a number of techniques, most of which have been developed individually over many years and are familiar to training managers. The justification for OD, seen by many as being surrounded in mystique, is that organizations are in a constant state of flux but, because of the preoccupation with production and profits, their management, systems, procedures, techniques, etc do not change in sympathy with the needs of the business. Companies can multiply their sales volume, change their product mix dramatically and even transfer their activities to a totally different business sector, without any significant change in organization structure, in administration or in the training of their employees to satisfy the changed requirements. Growth of the business can cause confusion, reduce morale and create friction and conflict, introduce more routine, formality and managerial remoteness, increase controls, perpetuate existing systems and practices to the point of making them unmanageable, and so on. This clearly gives rise to gross inefficiencies and a deficiency in the resources, skills and attitudes required to meet the new challenges.

The pioneers of OD were behavioural scientists and naturally their approach centred around the human aspects of running an organization and keeping pace with change. This may explain why it has tended to mystify some training specialists. In the last ten years or so, however, the skills of the OD consultant have tended to become less specialized, technical and organizational factors having assumed at least equal importance with purely behavioural factors. Employees working in groups are developed in such a way that they are helped, through greater involvement and understanding, to satisfy both their own and the organization's needs within the constraints and influences of the changing internal and external environment. For the training specialist involved with OD the accent is on development rather than simply training. He is committed to creating a learning climate enabling employees to develop themselves in the work situation, optimizing the application of their life experience, rather than simply using the knowledge or skills acquired through conventional training. The latter is sometimes criticized for its lack of relevance when it is carried on outside the work situation. Employee development in the OD context, however, is at the heart of the organization's activities and in the more enlightened businesses will attract as much attention from the management as technical or other organizational factors. Ideally, work is a continuous learning experience, a way of life which broadens the employee's horizons, is directly related to organizational goals and is dynamically geared to change.

This approach is reflected in the IPM's 'A boost for continuous development (ABCD)' campaign launched in 1984. The Institute's most important statement on this subject was contained in its *Code for Continuous Development: People and Practice*, published in October of that year.[71] After a good deal of useful work by its National Committee for Training and Development, it launched a six part *Continuous Development Learning Pack* in the autumn of 1987. It is hoped that this work will continue to stimulate greater interest in the idea that employees have to be developed throughout their working lives if they are to keep pace with the constantly changing needs of the business.

Case study

The case study method has had a substantial following in training in the years since the war, its greatest exponent being the Harvard Business School. The object of the case study is to present trainees with a realistic business situation, giving a considerable quantity of background information from which they are expected to analyse, and compute the outcome of, a series of events, or provide solutions to specific problems. Sometimes the information is purely fictitious and is concocted in order to make points in a fairly convincing way. More often, and more appropriately, the case study is a summary of a documented real-life situation in which a named organization has found itself. The actual outcome is usually known to the trainer and he is thus able to compare or contrast the trainees' findings with it. Since the true outcome may not be the most expedient, however, it is more profitable for the trainees to explore the various options that might be available rather than seek the 'right' answer. When dealing with management decisions, for example, it is quite unrealistic to assume that there is only one acceptable answer to a complex business problem and it would be undesirable for the trainer to suggest to trainees that decision-making can be so tidy. Nevertheless, there are many trainers who offer trainees neat packaged solutions to case studies when there is no hard evidence that those solutions have been proved the most successful in practice.

Case studies[72] are normally examined in small syndicate groups, and the points already made about these groups apply equally here. It is not unusual for each group to be given a different question to study in depth, so that more ground can be covered in the full group session and duplication is minimized. Many case studies dealing with the practical problems of specific organizations are available from a variety of sources, but the use of these does of course restrict trainees to studying situations which are not always easily related to their own problems and indeed may never be repeated elsewhere. There are therefore advantages in using case studies derived from the experiences of the group's own organization, where there is first-hand information about its successes and failures.

One variation on the case study is the 'action maze'. This is a programmed case study in which the initial issue of information is restricted to that necessary for the trainees to arrive at their first decision. In a similar way to the multi-choice questionnaire, a number of alternatives are given from which the group has to select the one which in their estimation is most appropriate, having studied all the data. When they have made their choice they obtain further printed information from the trainer, enabling them to check their solutions against the 'preferred' answers and to examine the effects of their decisions. The information also leads them into the next set of decisions, which are produced in the same manner. The number of decision sequences will depend upon how many specific issues the trainer wishes the group to explore.

'Incident process' is a further example of the case study approach, its main objective being to sharpen up the trainees' questioning skills. In this method the trainer does not give the groups sufficient data on which to make valid decisions. After due consideration of the available facts, they then have to request such information as they deem necessary to make a judgement. This type of exercise encourages trainees to scrutinize data carefully, to formulate the right questions to elicit further information and to interpret such information before taking decisions. It is therefore a very suitable vehicle for developing the skills required for dealing with industrial relations and disciplinary problems.

Practice in the use of the Socratic method of question and answer is also useful in handling health and safety and other investigations, in most interviewing situations, and in problem-solving generally. This dialectical method is attributed to the Greek philosopher Socrates, although he himself did not commit his experiences to writing and we have to rely for evidence on the written work of his pupils and others. The story goes that after being told by the Oracle that he was the wisest man in Greece, Socrates modestly refuted this and set out to discover who really was. By skilful questioning of other Athenians, giving nothing away himself, he ascertained that they claimed a level of wisdom which they did not in fact possess. Both he and they knew nothing, but whilst they were unaware of the limitations of their knowledge, he was fully conscious of his. He thus had one piece of information which they did not have and he therefore had to concede that he was the wisest man in Greece! W L Reese records in his *Dictionary of Philosophy and Religion* that Socrates' vocation in life was comparable with 'a gadfly, causing the lazy steed of Athens to bestir herself', or 'a midwife helping others to give birth to their ideas'.[73] The method is now widely practised by trainers and teachers and is characterized by their use of patient questioning to bring the trainee or student to a point where he can recognize a true conclusion without actually being told that the conclusion is in fact true.

One of the criticisms levelled at case studies by trainees is that they are bombarded with volumes of information which bewilder them and can introduce considerable stress. In other types of training they often complain that they do not have sufficient data on which to base any useful decisions. In the case study it is helpful to inform them that they may have more information than they need, and as in real life, one of their first tasks should be to reject those facts which are inappropriate or irrelevant.

Since the case study is based on actual events it should provide an ideal vehicle for training in decision-making. Whether it does so or not depends very much on how it is handled by the trainer, how flexible he is and how sensitive he is to the real needs of the group. However realistic the data being used, the training environment, being off-the-job, introduces an artificial element. There is the risk, therefore, that participants will treat the whole experience with detachment and will not enter into the spirit of an activity which can and should have a practically based outcome. The trainer's briefing for the exercise should reflect the reality of the situation and its importance to the organization. He should refrain from introducing hypothetical factors or arbitrary viewpoints into the syndicate discussions but should only dispense true facts about what actually happened in the case. In the final full group session, where the trainer is seeking alternative solutions to the problem, hypothetical outcomes are valid and should be explored. If examples can be provided as to how such solutions were arrived at in similar cases, so much the better.

Role play

Role playing[74] requires the acting out of parts in situations as close to those arising in the real job as possible. It essentially consists of an interview or a series of interviews, each participant having been given a brief specifically relating to his role and the particular set of circumstances to be enacted. The way he carries out his brief depends upon how he sees his role and how he believes the particular situation should be handled. He develops a strategy as to how to approach the task and tries to anticipate the reactions of the other party or parties. Some role playing develops into a negotiating situation and thus provides the opportunity for exploring the skills required in this activity.

Whatever the purpose of role playing exercises, it is important that they reflect the true working environment of the participants. In other words, not only should the everyday conditions be reproduced as far as possible but the roles should be acted out within the limits of existing managerial and supervisory authority and the constraints of organizational systems, procedures and policies. Acting for the sake of acting is purposeless. The over-confident love to demonstrate how clever they are, the more reticent suffer dreadful traumas. And herein lies one of the problems of role playing. It can be stressful for many who are afraid of making fools of themselves in public. Because it involves some practical demonstration of their abilities it makes them feel rightly or wrongly that they have much to lose in prestige and reputation. Their self-esteem is under threat. It is for this reason among others that it is advisable not to carry out role playing exercises in isolation or at the beginning of a training programme. Participants need to get to know each other and get used to working together before they are required to carry out this type of activity. Once the barriers are down and they are relaxed and no longer care what they say to each other, they will be willing and able to embark on role playing, and indeed will be eager to do so. Because of the satisfaction derived from such practical learning activities, it is common for participants to rank these among their most pleasurable and profitable training experiences. It is helpful for role playing to be carried out in small syndicate groups rather than in full group sessions. The pressures are very much less and for this reason learning is less likely to be inhibited. If it is considered advisable that some role playing is undertaken in a larger group, and indeed some participants request this, the experience gained in the more private environment of the syndicate room will remove most of the psychological difficulties.

Where role playing is embarked on in syndicates, the trainer should respect the group's privacy unless they ask for help and guidance. There is no reason why what goes on in the syndicates should not be discussed in a later full group session, but in the interests of removing the barriers to learning the small group activity should preferably not be directly monitored by the trainer.

A variation on role play is 'reverse role play'. This arises when two participants have reached what appears to be an intractable situation in their discussions and they are asked by the trainer to change roles. This move serves to bring home to each trainee the need for him to understand and respect the other man's point of view. It can be a salutary exercise for dealing with someone who delights in putting another on the spot, although the trainer should be on his guard against giving the impression that the ploy is used for disciplinary purposes or to cause embarrassment. It should be seen as a training tool to improve negotiating skills and it does, of course, emphasize the importance of understanding the feelings of others.

Simulation (and business games)

Simulation, as the term implies, is a combination of case study and role play.[75] Whilst the case study normally deals with the analysis of a historical set of circumstances, the simulation attempts to reproduce a present-day situation to be played out in a lifelike way.

A good deal of information is given about an imaginary organization and about external factors affecting it. Participants are allocated or volunteer for roles within that organization or as consultants to it. They therefore work as a team on specific business problems. Decision points are built into the programme in a similar way to the action maze, the effects of the trainees' decisions being fed back to them, so influencing their future strategy and the next set of decisions. This continuous check on progress makes a simulation a much more satisfying and stimulating experience than other off-the-job training methods. A weakness of many training programmes is that the participants are required to make business or other decisions in isolation and they seldom know what would be the consequences of those decisions in real life. The simulated exercise helps to remove that frustration.

It is increasingly common for simulations to be computerized (see computer-based training in Chapter 7) and this has distinct advantages. It provides participants with training and practice in the use of computer terminals on problems which are directly work-related and also enables them to obtain almost instant feedback on their decisions. The time scale of business activity can thus be greatly compressed in a practicable training period. Unfortunately, this does introduce a degree of unreality into the process and could conceivably give rise to impatience back at work if the results of decisions were not instantly forthcoming.

Where a simulation involves a number of teams in competition with one another, it becomes a 'business game'. A good example of this is where the teams represent different companies competing in a common market or markets. Although some such 'manual' games exist, they demand a good deal from the trainer who has to compute and feed back results to the teams. This often means that time is wasted in waiting. Furthermore, the model is likely to be unrealistic because it would be impossible to build in sufficient variables to simulate a real-life situation. To some degree this problem is overcome by the use of a computer programme. It nevertheless requires a good deal of skill and business know-how to produce a programme which cannot be criticized for failing to reproduce the complex interactions of a real business.

As in other situations, participants should be encouraged to identify with their roles by behaving naturally rather than by trying to put on an act. This applies particularly to simulation where every effort is made to reflect reality. There is little pay-off in training terms for play acting. It merely becomes a diversion from the main purpose of the exercise.

Brainstorming

Brainstorming is a practical exercise to stimulate creativity in a group,[76] and is a very useful training technique. The fact that the term brainstorm retains for some people connotations of violent mental disturbance may present the training specialist with an initial difficulty of persuading them that this is a technique which can be used for the organization's benefit, and that it does not involve any psychological stress which they would wish to avoid.

Brainstorming is based on the fact that it is possible to generate more ideas collectively than the sum of the ideas which would be produced individually. This arises from the interaction which enables one member to trigger off new ideas in another. Chain reactions are sometimes set up which ultimately turn an apparently ludicrous idea into a practical one.

The process of brainstorming demands discipline in order to overcome the temptation in most people to pass judgement on ideas as soon as they are revealed. The subject of the session having been decided, the members are required to commit to paper as many ideas as possible for dealing with the problem, without attempting to evaluate them. They should let the ideas flow freely and write them down even if they at first seem impractical. After a suitable period of time, each member reads out his list and the other members are asked not to criticize, however wild they feel a suggestion may be. A combined list is produced and the group is then encouraged to evaluate each item. The cross-fertilization that takes place at this stage leads to the development of new ideas which may or may not be directly related to the original ones.

How the process develops from this point depends on the purpose of the exercise. It is usual for the aggregated list, which is now devoid of impractical suggestions, to be rated and arranged in order of acceptability. When the technique is used for value analysis,[77] the cost of implementing each idea is estimated and this may influence the order in which items are placed.

A variation on this technique involves the use of large boards, at least four feet square, which are supported vertically on either a wall or a movable stand and on which papers may be fixed by means of mapping pins. A generous quantity of pieces of paper, of different colours and approximately 8 x 4 inches, is supplied to the participants. Each idea is committed to one piece of paper and at the end of a specified period of time the papers from all the team members are pinned to the board. The team discusses the contributions, eliminates duplication, re-words ambiguous or inaccurate statements and removes irrelevant or unacceptable ideas. At this point cross-fertilization between members may generate further contributions which are added and agreed.

The next step in the process is to group the ideas in order to be able to produce a suitable structure with headings. A member of the team leads a discussion which results in the papers being re-arranged on the board in new groups, and headings are provided for each group on paper of a different colour. A logical sequence for the various subjects is then established and the total project reviewed.

This technique is extremely useful for generating ideas. Some examples are for incorporation in a report, for establishing guidelines for courses of action, for designing training programmes and for writing books or manuals. The writer used it to effect in his own department when trying to arrive at unambiguous titles for new training programmes. It has the advantage of optimizing the creative abilities of any number of people with a vested interest in, and contributions to make to, a given topic. Further assistance, in order to treat the topic as comprehensively as possible, may be obtained by circulating the team's product to interested parties for comment.

It has been suggested that brainstorming, if it is to be effective, requires discipline. There are, of course, barriers to thinking in a creative way. Some may unwittingly impose restrictions on ideas by looking at things, as it were, through a narrow tunnel. They may fail to challenge the obvious or may assume that there can only be one answer to a problem. Some are inhibited by the prospect of being ridiculed if they disclose what is in their minds. Others are too eager to assess the value of an idea or pass judgement upon it. When these constraints are overcome, training in the brainstorming technique can be extremely rewarding, not only to the individuals themselves but to the organization which is constantly seeking new ideas and approaches.

Fishbowl

A useful exercise for enabling teams to study group processes is the fishbowl. It is usually carried out with two teams. Team A is assigned a topic which it is required to discuss for, say, 30 minutes. The task is unstructured and the team can elect a chairman or leader if it so wishes or alternatively can cover the topic in a free discussion. Team B is seated around Team A and observes the process. Its members are not free to interrupt the discussion, but when it is finished they are given about 15 minutes in which to criticize and comment on Team A's performance in *process* terms only. Team A does not have the right to reply or even to comment on any criticisms at this stage.

The roles of the two teams are then reversed, Team B being given the topic to discuss and Team A taking up positions around Team B as observers. After Team A has given its judgement, the two teams come together in a full group session and notes are exchanged on the processes which were observed in the two parts of the exercise. The areas covered may be, for example, the team's interpretation of the task, how its resources were shared, the decision-making process used and the interpersonal relationships developed in the group.

The discussion topic used in fishbowl is sometimes centred around how the team sees its own development in earlier exercises. For reasons of reducing stress in what could be a traumatic experience for some, the exercise would not be at the beginning of a training programme, but rather in the middle or towards the end. The team would therefore have had the opportunity to build up group cohesion over a number of previous exercises.

Group exercises

Until the 1960s group training methods tended to follow a fairly consistent pattern of formal inputs by experts, followed by discussion either in full group or in syndicate sessions. The discussion groups addressed themselves in a structured way to questions posed by the speakers and rigid time limits were set on reporting back for 'judgement' of the results by the specialist, who was seen to be the authority on the topic examined. Even the reporting-back had a formality about it, geared more towards complying with a set of rules and conventions than towards optimizing learning.

As the training profession developed in status, and the work of behavioural scientists attracted more attention, approaches to training began to emerge which caused something of a revolution in methodology. How to optimize learning became the key factor and different means of achieving this end were explored. Management training exercises appeared on the scene, pioneered in the United States by Professor Bernard Bass of the University of Rochester among others and further developed in Europe by the European Research Group on Management (ERGOM).[78] These exercises involved responding to a number of simulated management situations and the results from a large number of managers and students in both America and Europe were fed into a computer and analysed. The data collected provided useful information on the varying responses of different people to the same management situation. It highlighted cultural differences of an international nature and also differences between industries, types of company and levels within an organization.

Clearly different people saw things in a different light depending on their knowledge, experience and the environment in which they lived and worked. The value of this in training terms was immense. Rather than rely on an expert to provide a model answer, ie reflecting his own personal experience or that of a limited group, it was possible to examine the knowledge, beliefs, attitudes and views of a widely differing group of managers and so weigh the different options that were available to solve a business problem. This enabled a group to make full use of its own resources, provided enlightenment for those who approached their problems with tunnel vision and generally improved morale and self-confidence.

The group exercise as it has since developed for training purposes is a written syndicate task which provides clear instructions on the objective, the procedure to be adopted and the approximate timing. The objective can vary considerably. It may involve, for example, learning a technique, skill, procedure, system or policy. The exercise provides an ideal vehicle for developing team work, for problem-solving, decision-making and examining and interpreting data. The procedure usually involves studying the information provided and/or answering the questions posed firstly as individuals and then by syndicate discussion arriving at group responses. Where there is wide disagreement within the group, members are advised to try to persuade the others by reasoned argument rather than to settle readily for a majority answer. They are told that the value of the exercise is not so much in the answer as in the thorough exploration of the issues underlying the question. Preoccupation with seeking the 'right' answer when such does not exist is discouraged.

The trainer role is a relatively passive one.[79] He should not assume that he is welcome in syndicate discussions unless the members say so, and it is advisable to establish this at the commencement of a course. He is a resource on which the groups can draw but he is not an authority in any autocratic sense. He supplies the vehicle for their discussions but they are responsible for their own learning. They are free to manage that learning in whatever manner they agree will be most effective. They are not obliged to appoint a chairman or even a spokesman unless they feel that this will further their objectives. When they report back to the full group they can present their case as a number of individuals and not through a spokesman if they so wish. This freedom and flexibility of working can be a little unnerving for groups experiencing it for the first time. They have been used to being dependent upon a trainer giving the orders, telling them what to do and what not to do, controlling the timing and so on. What they often do not realize is that whatever the trainer does, there is no guarantee that he will achieve learning in the group. In the end they themselves will determine the degree of learning, and indeed, if learning takes place at all.

Flexibility in timing is important. Since what is discussed in syndicate groups should be what is important to its members and to their development, they will be selective about the areas in which they concentrate. This inevitably results in more or less time being spent by different groups on a given exercise than that allotted in the programme. It is counter-productive in both learning and morale terms if a valuable and fruitful discussion is cut short simply because the programme says so. The participants know that one of the reasons why they are provided with off-the-job training is that they may have the opportunity to stand back from the pressures of their jobs and examine problems in depth and without interruption. Trying to reproduce the real work time constraints therefore conflicts with the requirements of this type of training.

The full group sessions provide the opportunity for the groups to compare their findings in a wider debate. They agree in advance on the way in which this will be done and they are discouraged from looking to the trainer for chairmanship or for arbitration. They are free to request an input from him if they feel it would be helpful. If he thinks that anything vital may have been overlooked, he may tactfully suggest that there might be some benefit in their examining that aspect. Any intervention that he makes should be advisory and supportive rather than authoritarian. At the end of the session he will usually provide handouts which either reflect his own views and/or those of the organization, or give a summary of research which may have been done in the area of the subject which has been discussed.

Group exercises take a variety of forms. In fact, there is probably no limit to the number of variations possible. The choice clearly has to be made on the basis of what is appropriate for the objective to be achieved and some vehicles are more suitable than others for a particular need. The important point to be remembered is that the means chosen must stimulate groups to explore the topic in depth, using all the resources at their disposal. This demands a very clear definition of the objective of the exercise and what is required of the groups. They must be able to relate their knowledge and experience to the problems and although they need to be stretched they should not feel that the goal is unattainable.

One exercise which is widely used in education and is of considerable value in the training field is the multi-choice questionnaire. As the name implies, this consists of a number of questions or statements accompanied by three or more alternative answers from which the participants select the most appropriate in their considered judgement.

The writing of such questionnaires requires some skill and a knowledge of, among other things, the misconceptions which people have about the particular subjects treated. If it is necessary to provide an easy option because any or all of the other statements may have validity, it is probable the question and/or answers have not been properly formulated. The system is most effective if each statement or answer is so worded that it produces serious discussion and is not simply rejected arbitrarily. One of the problems encountered with this type of exercise is that participants treat it as an examination paper or test, and if everyone comes up with the same answer without discussion the group is content to move on to the next question. They may, of course, arrive at the same answer for widely differing reasons and failing to examine these may defeat the whole purpose of the exercise, which is to explore issues and to challenge beliefs, attitudes, experience etc. It is important for the trainer to brief the groups carefully on how they can get optimum benefit from the exercise and to discourage them from treating it in a purely mechanistic way. The multi-choice questionnaire is a very suitable device for introducing a group to the subject to be studied and establishing common ground on which the remainder of the course can be built. It assists participants to warm to the subject and to start to build up the right relationships to achieve cohesive working groups.

An example of one of the questions in an exercise using the multi-choice questionnaire technique is:

Why is employment legislation considered necessary?

(a) to fall into line with EEC countries
(b) to strengthen the hands of the trade unions
(c) to create a climate of sound and fair practice in industrial relations
(d) to give the government greater control over the industrial relations scene
(e) to protect employees.

Each of the responses deserves some discussion even where untrue or not entirely valid, but only one, that is (c), is sufficiently comprehensive to answer the question satisfactorily.

A variation on the multi-choice questionnaire approach is the exercise which invites participants to consider certain statements and to respond by stating whether they believe them true or false. This clearly reduces their options and it is imperative that the participants are required to substantiate their answers in the ensuing full group discussion. It is unprofitable from everyone's point of view if their responses are arrived at by pure guesswork or the toss of a coin.

Another exercise which can be extremely productive in homing a group in on the major subject to be covered in a course and in bringing out their views and attitudes about it is the open question. In its simplest form this type of exercise may merely consist of inviting consideration of the question, 'What do you understand by (the subject)?' followed by a further question, 'What are the implications for you as (managers, supervisors, accountants, scientists, engineers, salesmen . . .)?' Such questions encourage the groups, even when comprised of total strangers, to open up in the privacy of their syndicate rooms and often to expose the problems that really worry them. They seldom have such an opportunity to be frank and honest about their difficulties at work, and the syndicate discussion, if security is assured, provides that opportunity. Enabling them to 'let off steam' at the outset in this way helps to highlight the factors that inhibit their decision-making. Having released their pent-up emotions, it is then possible for them to concentrate on the real issues. The groups are usually asked to produce the results of their discussion on flip-chart displays, which facilitate their being challenged by the other groups in the later full group sessions.

The use of this type of exercise illustrates how important it is for the trainer to create the right climate for learning to take place. It is very rare for groups not to be inhibited in some way in the training room by constraints which frustrate their efforts at work. The trick is to get these problems out into the open as soon as possible, not only in an effort to find ways of solving them but also to remove the frustration which may prevent learning from being accomplished.

Mini case studies are useful in focusing the attention of groups on specific problems requiring the exercise of judgement based on experience. Often solutions will be produced intuitively rather than by a sound appraisal of all the facts and implications, and this gives the trainer the opportunity to highlight the pitfalls of operating in such a way. Unlike the case studies dealt with on pp. 116-18, which provide vast quantities of information, mini case studies describe a situation in one or two paragraphs and certain assumptions usually have to be made. Due to the shortage of hard facts, solutions will also tend to be qualified in some way, and will therefore be varied, enabling a number of approaches to be examined and compared.

Although it is quite common for a number of unconnected mini case studies to be used in a training programme, there are clearly advantages in linking them where this is possible. It adds to the realism, for example, if the situations are chosen from one department or from the same company, division or plant. In fact, designing a whole course around a single organization or identifiable part of an organization has its merits, because participants come to identify themselves with the business and are more easily persuaded to enter into the spirit of 'running it'.

The use of group exercises when training mature, and particularly experienced, groups has advantages over other methods. The major problem of resistance to training due to arrogance on the one hand or lack of confidence on the other is largely overcome. When trainees can be shown that they are being treated as adults, will not be preached at by someone who thinks he knows it all, will not be embarrassed by exposure of their possible lack of knowledge and will take their fair share of responsibility for the conduct of the training programme, they will respond in such a way as to make the whole exercise more worthwhile. Furthermore, learning by discovery and testing their ideas against those of other participants is likely to be much more lasting. The increased self-assurance developed in the process enables them to use their knowledge and experience to more profitable effect in the workplace.

Newcomers to these methods may be sceptical and critical of them on the basis that the trainer is opting out of his responsibilities and is simply leaving the group to their own devices. This is very far from the case. If anything, this type of training is more demanding of the trainer than the direct teaching kind. Frequently the latter may result in trainees going away feeling that they have not learned much from the experience, but, since the trainer has done what appears to have been required of him, they blame themselves for not having been more attentive. When they have a joint responsibility they are determined to make the most of the opportunity and any conditions that might arise which place constraints on their learning will be vehemently attacked. The trainer thus has the task of creating conditions which not only provide the most suitable vehicle for learning but which are also acceptable to the trainees. The utmost care has to be taken in writing the exercises. They have to meet the training objectives and be seen by the participants as meeting their own goals. They must encourage the deepest penetration of the topics discussed within the limits of the aggregated knowledge and experience in the group. In the full group sessions the trainer must be prepared to supplement the efforts of the groups with appropriate additional information and guidance once they have exhausted their own resources. Handouts also need to be well written and readable, encouraging participants to use them as reference sources in their future work.

Workshops

The term workshop has come into popular use in recent years and is often loosely used to describe any form of participative off-the-job training. It is, however, more appropriate to confine its use to describing a method of designing training activities around identified work problems in order to find solutions to them in the training room. The objective is to obtain contributions from all individuals who are affected, and thus to optimize the resources available to solve the problem and agree future action. The workshop differs from other group methods described only in so far as it is set up to tackle specific operational problems and is therefore an extension of the work situation.

Sensitivity training

Sensitivity training, T-group (training group), study groups, group dynamics and group relations training are some of the terms used to describe laboratory-type training which sets out to promote more effective interpersonal relationships in an organization.[82] The goals are:

- ☐ to increase awareness of one's own behaviour and how it is received and interpreted by others
- ☐ to develop sensitivity to the behaviour exhibited by others and be able to diagnose the causes of that behaviour
- ☐ to improve one's skills in handling problems at work by understanding and managing the behavioural factors and constraints.

The technique relies for its effectiveness on creating a climate in which participants are willing to be frank, open and honest with each other and are prepared to explore in small groups facts about themselves, their backgrounds and their inner feelings without inhibition. Because the focus is on personal behaviour and discussion of one's (normally) private thoughts, sensitivity training has given rise to considerable controversy among training and non-training staff alike. Unfavourable criticisms have naturally been levelled at it by those who are prejudiced against any form of behavioural training, but other critics have been genuinely concerned about the adverse psychological effects T-group training has been known to have on some participants. This fear needs to be put in perspective. There have been instances in the writer's experience, for example, when trainees have suffered some kind of mental disturbance even when the course (not T-group) has been one in which every conceivable effort was made to create a relaxed atmosphere and reduce threats and pressures to a minimum. In other words, any kind of training situation could prove harmful to a trainee who already has psychological problems. This fact leads one to sound a warning that where employees have a previous history of any such difficulties, this should be taken into account before they are considered for participation in group training activities.

Because of the dangers that may be inherent in the study of emotional factors as distinct from job knowledge and expertise, it is imperative that T-group trainers have a high level of skill in the use of this technique. This is certainly not a job for amateur experimenters, but one which demands special training in advanced skills.

It is generally believed that sensitivity training is unstructured and not in any way under the control of the trainer. It is true that there is normally no specific agenda or agreed procedure, and the trainer does not control the group's activities directly. Nevertheless he is usually there all the time and acts as an observer and facilitator, indirectly guiding the group's deliberations and helping them towards an understanding of themselves, their colleagues and the group processes.

The interactive element is a key feature of T-groups. Whilst in many other types of group training, the accent is on the study of organizational problems *per se*, in T-groups another dimension is added, that of the observation of participants' behaviour and the analysis of their feelings. Those feelings will have a profound effect on how an employee approaches his job, in fact how he develops his relationships with other people generally, and understanding them is essential if objectives are to be achieved. The participants are therefore encouraged to study the behaviour and question the feelings of other members whilst submitting freely to scrutiny of themselves by those members. They discuss how the behaviour of one affects that of another, and how their conception of the way others see them differs from reality. A certain amount of experimentation takes place. Individuals try out different behaviour patterns on their team mates to see the effects that they produce. This eventually leads to insights as to how they need to behave in order to achieve the desired results in others. The interesting thing is that the trainer is seen as one of the group and is therefore equally open to examination by the course members. He may come under fire from anxious participants because they misunderstand his role and accuse him of trying to 'measure with blunt instruments'. The climate of openness and trust created encourages them to say what they really think about each other. They know that the exercise is a temporary one and that they are not under any threat of long-term repercussions since everyone is a party to the same contract. They therefore enjoy a certain freedom, although this does not remove the anxieties that arise from revelations about themselves. These anxieties are to some extent cushioned by the help and encouragement they get from colleagues, and frequently T-groups become highly cohesive. This may of course have adverse effects if they return to the real world of the workplace and discover that similar support is not forthcoming. Perhaps this is a good reason for sensitivity training to be carried out in actual workgroups and not with employees from different sectors of the organization. The trainer should however be prepared for the possibility of having to cope with greater conflict between work colleagues than with a group who do not already know each other.

We have stressed the behavioural bias of sensitivity training. One training approach which combines the benefits of this technique with the specific business needs of an organization is Grid Organization Development (GOD).[26] This incorporates the well known Managerial Grid concept[83] which relates a manager's concern for production or output with his concern for his subordinates (see fig. 20). Various managerial styles may be identified by assessing these two factors. For example a 9 : 1 manager is motivated almost solely by the task, with minimum regard for the people who have to produce the output, whilst a 5 : 5 manager tries to give equal weight to the needs of both. There is therefore an implication that the 'ideal' manager has a 9 : 9 rating, being highly skilled in optimizing employee satisfaction and commitment with organizational performance. Reddin[56] expanded the grid three-dimensionally to include a measure of effectiveness, which was a function of the organization in which the manager worked. The style used, in his view, was not important so long as it was compatible with the organization. Although it is not the purpose of this book to join the debate as to the importance of leadership style, the writer feels from his experience in both manufacturing industry and the public

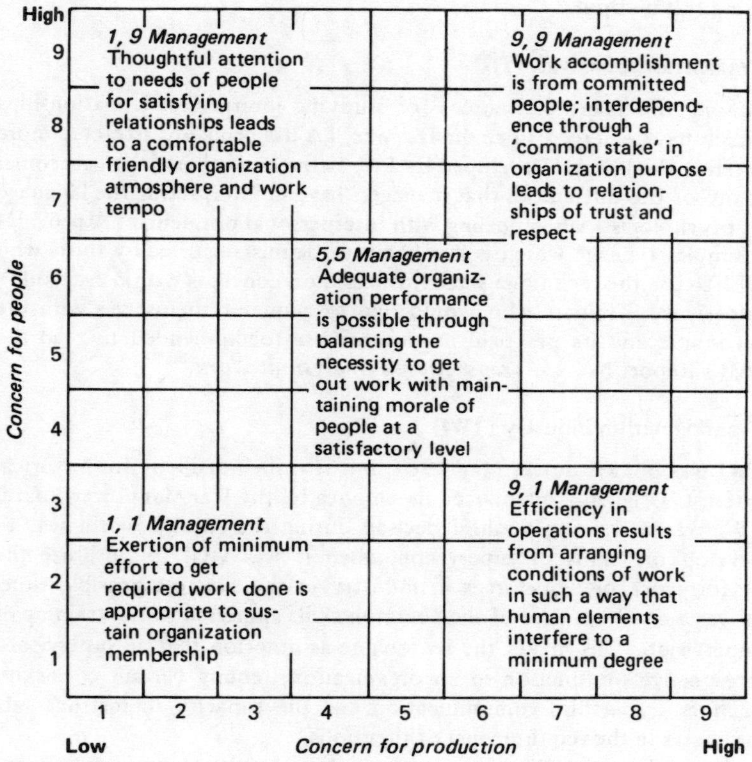

Figure 20. *Blake and Mouton's Managerial Grid*

sector that one of the key factors is employee preference. If the work-group favours an authoritarian style, and there are many that still do, that would appear to be the most promising style to achieve results with that particular group. A good deal of behavioural research seems to ignore the individuality of groups.

GOD is an attractive training approach since it incorporates sensitivity training into a structure geared to the corporate strategy of the organization. It therefore goes to the heart of OD (see p. 115) by developing team work to the point where its contribution to meeting the organization's short and long term goals is material, and it becomes an essential ingredient of management.

One example in the mid-1960s of the introduction of GOD into an organization has been described by George Clark in 'Managerial Grid training: an application in ICI Pharmaceuticals Division'.[84] In addition to a description of the scheme, its operation and its results, there are useful guidelines, based on ICI's experience, for anyone interested in using this method.

Transactional analysis (TA)

Among the many techniques for studying interpersonal relationships which have emerged since the last war, TA has probably attracted more interest than most. Developed by Eric Berne and others,[85] it overcomes many of the difficulties that managers have in interpreting the language of psychologists when dealing with interpersonal problems. TA provides a simple language which is less likely to be misconstrued by those who wish to use the technique since it is based on concepts within everyone's experience. Trainers who would like to acquaint themselves with the technique and its practical importance are recommended to read the IPM's Report No. 23, *Transactional Analysis at Work*.[86]

Training within industry (TWI)

TWI was phased out in May 1984, but it is included here for historical interest. Originally introduced in America by the War Manpower Board, TWI was a training method devised during the second world war to develop the skills of supervision when it was vital to optimize the performance of workforces in industry in the shortest possible time. It was a good example of the common skills approach to the training of supervision. This makes the reasonable assumption that all supervisors, irrespective of function in an organization, require certain core skills such as leadership, communication and the capacity to instruct subordinates in the requirements of their jobs.

In the UK the TWI service was provided by the Manpower Services Commission (see p. 226) which was able to offer both public and in-plant courses run by their own staff, or instructors' courses enabling an organization to mount its own programmes internally.

Supervisors often had their first taste of supervisory training through TWI courses. Whilst many professional trainers will say the programmes did not go far enough, they could nevertheless be a reasonable first step for employers who wanted to introduce basic supervisory training at a minimal cost. Experienced supervisors' were often resistant to training, believing that having been promoted into such a responsible job they were expected to have the skills already. TWI could be a fairly painless way of easing them into a situation where they began to realize that they could learn more about the skills of supervision or perhaps re-orientate their thinking concerning them. It could therefore be something on which to build more sophisticated training.

The courses used a discussion leading style which helped to move the group towards certain conclusions. Supervisors were encouraged to exchange their experiences with their fellow trainees to lend weight to those arguments and in this way they began to realize that their knowledge of and approach to dealing with their day-to-day problems did not differ markedly. Where a practical skill was involved, such as instructing a learner, each supervisor was given individual tuition and practice in carrying out the required task using a planned and proven method.

One of the problems encountered in off-the-job training of this kind is that the trainees may find it difficult to relate the tasks presented to them to the jobs that they are responsible for in the workplace. It is desirable, though not always practicable, with a group from a variety of functions, to provide examples which are exactly equivalent to those encountered at work. There are however advantages in using examples common to everyone's experience and demonstrating a method or system which can be used in any set of circumstances. Training is a systematic approach to learning and helps people to orientate their knowledge around common sets of principles.

This approach was therefore adopted by TWI with a certain degree of success over a period of about 40 years. Supervisors trained under the scheme were not recommended to carry checklists around with them to refer to every time they had to undertake a task. They were persuaded to conform to a tried pattern, however, by memorizing these prompts in the interests of consistency and removing the risks of omitting something vital from their instruction.

Television, film and slide presentations

The reader may be forgiven for making the assumption that these training methods should be listed with those in which communication is largely one-way. They were included in this section because it was considered important to highlight the fact that they should *not* be used in isolation. As visual aids to learning they should only be used as accessories to the main training activity, and should never be relied upon to substitute for it. They can be extremely valuable in providing an additional visual dimension to a programme to underline the message in an agreeable way.

It is not sufficient for a trainer to show a TV programme, a film or a series of 35mm slides and then sit back and assume that learning has taken place. It is highly desirable that the aids used should be associated with a task, and if the trainees know in advance what that task is they are more likely to see them as something which requires their undivided attention and not as an entertainment. Having said that, there is no reason at all why the programme should not be pleasurable. Indeed, if one enjoys an experience one is generally more receptive to learning from it. But however entertaining the visual aids may be, it is often necessary to point out that there are appropriate lessons to be drawn from them and the trainees should be looking for and making due note of them. Small syndicate discussions of the relevant issues following the showing stand a better chance of success than trying to generate a discussion in a full group session, since there are fewer opportunities for individuals to 'hide' in the smaller group.

Where aids of this kind are used[87] to supplement training programmes and to reinforce learning it is essential that they are operated skilfully. The slightest hiccup, however small, can prove a major distraction, such that the following discussion centres more on what went wrong with the operation of the equipment than on the subject matter of the programme. (See Chapter 9 on the use of visual aids.)

The value of demonstrating a process or activity by means of models should not be underestimated. People in general relate more readily to visual stimuli than to the spoken or written word and showing them a component or a piece of equipment brings the subject to life for them. This is particularly true where practical skills are concerned but again it is important that models are used carefully and are properly integrated into the programme.

Field trips

The point has been made in the preceding section that visual stimuli in training can often make a greater impact than verbal or written information. For this reason the value of factory, office or other visits to provide visual reinforcement of information given by other means should not be overlooked.

Unfortunately this method is often avoided either because it is seen to be too much of a disruption to the unit concerned or that it is of doubtful value in learning terms. It is too easy for field visits to be equated with external visits in the eyes of the host unit and so they are not treated as part of a training programme. Most visits tend to be arranged purely for interest and the visitors are nearly always people from walks of life which are remote from that of the host.

The purpose of including field trips in this chapter, therefore, is twofold. First, training specialists may like to be reminded of the value of such visits in terms of reinforcing information and providing atmosphere for trainees who would otherwise not get to know what another environment looks like. The second reason is that in arranging such a visit, every effort should be made to organize it *as a training activity*. This means that objectives have to be set. Trainees are not told that they are going to visit a certain department or establishment because it will be interesting (although it is hoped it will be) but with a much more specific purpose, the outcome of which is seen by them as an integral part of their training. They should be clear about what they are expected to get out of it and should also understand that there will be some sort of follow-up which will check their learning. Those managers, supervisors or other employees who will have contact with the trainees during the visit should also be carefully briefed so that they know what the objectives are and what their role in the activity will be.

The size of the visiting group must be chosen with care since too large a group will result in less effective transfer of information. There are no hard and fast rules about this because it has to be related to the size of the particular section, department or establishment, the space available, the noise level, the people who will be imparting information, and so forth. As a rule of thumb, the recommendations made in earlier sections about syndicate groups may be helpful, although the final answer must be dictated by local conditions. The important thing is that, as with any other type of training, each trainee must enjoy conditions conducive to learning. He should not be adversely affected by the size of the group.

Junior management committee

Many people would argue that there is no better way to learn than by experience. The problem is that this is too often a way of opting out of the responsibility of providing a trainee with the tools and guidance to enable him to learn the job in the most efficient and effective way and so bring him up to experienced worker standard in the shortest time possible.

There are, however, certain types of training in which learning by experience, and often being thrown in at the deep end, so to speak, can achieve satisfactory results, providing there are adequate safeguards. One of these is the junior board, or management committee. The essence of this training method is that young managers or potential managers are appointed to a junior management committee which is set up as near as possible to mirror the structure of the top management committee in the organization. Roles are assigned and procedures agreed. Projects or topics are allocated to the committee on which decisions and recommendations are required. Trainees have access to their own bosses, the management development adviser, the training, or any other, manager for guidance and they are able to obtain such information as they may need in order to deal adequately with the specific problem. Some decisions may be implemented after agreement with the interested parties but most tasks will have been allocated by the top management and will therefore require their approval before implementation.

Clearly the value of such training depends upon the degree of responsibility that the top management is prepared to delegate to the junior committee. Sometimes it falls into disrepute when the projects allocated are trivial and of no real value to the organization, but in the main a management will not agree to such an activity being set up unless it is prepared to give backing to it. Because of the real-life nature of the problems tackled, this method of gaining experience can be very profitable, giving trainees valuable practice in running meetings, problem-solving and decision-making.

Job rotation

Most organizations suffer to some extent from the problem that people employed in certain functions become somewhat isolated and are not always aware of what is going on in other areas. In fact, they may not even know what is supposed to go on in other functions, which is even worse.

One training method which seeks to deal with this problem is job rotation. This provides an employee with the opportunity to work for specified periods in a variety of different jobs, gaining experience in a wide range of activities. This is on-the-job training and to be effective must be carefully planned and executed. It is not sufficient simply to hand the trainee over to another department and assume that he will receive adequate training and experience. Someone, preferably his boss, needs to have overall responsibility for the programme and, in consultation with the training department, should agree a detailed plan of experience in advance. The supervisor or manager in each department should be prepared to coach the trainee in the requirements of the job and should ensure that he is given appropriate assignments, under supervision, and not simply odd jobs to do. It is desirable that the assignments increase in complexity. This not only stretches the trainee and adds value to his training and experience but also maintains interest and motivation.

Job rotation is not always readily accepted by managers and supervisors. This arises from the fact that it is embarrassing to them to lose an experienced worker to another department and at the same time to have to allocate time to the training of a newcomer. The only way to deal with this is to make it part of company procedure and part of everyone's job description. However sympathetic one may be towards the managers who have to put in that much additional effort to operate the system, they must be shown that it is in the long-term interests of everyone in the organization, including themselves.

In-tray exercise

One way in which training can reflect the realities of the job is by means of the in-tray exercise.[88] This provides the trainees with a typical day's post, both internal and external, which has to be processed to the out-tray. They are required to study all the documents, decide priorities, allocate time and carry out, or if this is impracticable simply indicate, whatever action is deemed necessary.

To add to the realism of the in-tray exercise, other features of normal working, such as interruptions from telephone calls or from unexpected visitors, are often built into the programme. This places time constraints on the activity and can therefore give rise to additional stress. Trainers need to be aware of the symptoms so that action may be taken if it proves necessary.

Frequently the day's 'post' is the same for all participants and at the end of the exercise the ways in which different trainees dealt with the same task are compared or contrasted. There is merit, however, in making the exercise more interactive by allocating roles to the participants and arranging for the action required by the documents to involve more than one trainee.

Transcendental meditation (TM)

Transcendental meditation is a technique which seems to have an increasing following worldwide. There is justification in regarding it as a training technique since it is claimed that it influences the way in which an employee approaches his whole life and therefore his job.

The essence of TM is that it helps people to reach a state of complete relaxation without any deliberate control on their part. It merely requires 'about 20 minutes twice a day . . .' when 'the mind is allowed to settle down into a state of complete rest.'[89] There is nothing sinister about TM. No religious or moral commitments are expected and it does not involve any mental or physical effort, or any kind of skill which might make it more suitable for some people than others. Whilst it appears to be a perfectly simple device and does not demand too much from the employee, personal tuition is recommended by the exponents of TM in the first instance and periodic monitoring thereafter in order to obtain maximum benefit from the technique.

One researcher claimed that in a limited survey of 42 managers there was evidence of increased job satisfaction, improved performance in the job, reduced employee turnover and better interpersonal relationships. The conclusion was that it achieved these benefits essentially by the reduction of stress and it should therefore enable the full potential of employees to be exploited.

Coaching

One of the major features of training is the transfer of information from those with knowledge and expertise to those who need to acquire it. It is a tragedy that a good deal of that knowledge and expertise throughout an organization does not get passed on, but is often jealously guarded by those who feel that their positions will be threatened if they disclose it to others.

It is part of the job of anyone who has responsibility for the work of subordinates to ensure that their employees are suitably equipped to carry out their work adequately. Apart from the obvious need for job knowledge, there is a requirement for help and guidance to enable subordinates to find solutions to problems which face them in the execution of their work. They must have a mentor who is preferably one step up in the hierarchy, who is able to advise on the ramifications and difficulties of the job and who is knowledgeable about the interfaces of that job with others in the organization.

The main advantage of coaching[17] as a training method is that it is an on-the-job activity and therefore can be totally relevant. It involves boss and subordinate in a regular dialogue about the department's work and so can reasonably be expected to have a favourable effect on both work performance and morale. It would appear to have everything going for it and yet there is frequently a reluctance to get involved in it. The excuse given for avoidance is usually lack of time, but one suspects that the reasons are more likely to be lack of confidence in the ability to carry it out and a fear that getting too involved will mean more problems to solve. Since it is in the interests of bosses to ensure that their subordinates are effective and can work with the minimum of supervision in meeting the needs of the organization, training specialists should see to it that managers and supervisors are trained in the appropriate skills and encouraged to use them. Coaching is a perpetual activity and provides managers with an ideal opportunity for self-development.[27] It enables them continuously to appraise their subordinates instead of relying on one or two interviews in the course of a year. The progress of the work in their departments can therefore be more easily monitored without subordinates feeling that they are being closely supervised. If handled skilfully it enables a climate of trust and confidence to be built up.

Using coaching as a training medium is also fully justified on the basis that no other training programme can effectively deal with all the day-to-day problems of work. A constantly changing activity brings forth problems on a virtually continuous scale and these cannot be stored up to be dealt with on some future training programme. The machinery for handling such problems therefore has to be available at short notice and the objective is to match the needs of the job and the organization with those of the individual. Tasks are allocated and explained, problems clarified and solved. Expertise and information are passed on and reassurance and encouragement given where necessary. Guidance is provided on such matters as cost effectiveness and the management of one's time.[31] Coaching also goes hand-in-hand with delegation, since a boss needs to satisfy himself that a delegated task has been properly carried out.

The training of employees in the skills of coaching has to concern itself with a number of factors. Clearly, since it involves interactive skills, there has to be a substantial behavioural element. The boss has to know what motivates his subordinates and what influences their attitudes to, and performance in, the job. He therefore has to pay attention to his leadership style which must be appropriate to the subordinate he is coaching. He has also to create a learning climate and to encourage his employee to be honest, straightforward, information-seeking and questioning. He needs to be a good listener, must show understanding and be seen to be fair in all his dealings with his subordinates. This clearly demands a much closer boss/subordinate relationship than frequently exists.

Other methods

The following methods do not readily fall into the previous categories and have therefore been listed separately. In general, whilst there is overall supervision in each case, the method relies upon self-activation and self-discipline in order to achieve learning.

Programmed learning

The term programmed learning or programmed instruction is used to describe a number of techniques involving prepared training programmes which are entirely trainee-centred.[90] This means that the trainee directly controls his own learning, the time that he embarks on the training process and the pace at which he progresses through it. He can also decide where the course takes place since the material and/or equipment required is easily transportable. In view of the self-contained nature of the programme, the full-time involvement of a trainer is not necessary.

This system has a number of advantages:

- ☐ assuming computer terminals are not involved, it can take place anywhere where the conditions are conducive to private uninterrupted study. This makes training schedules more flexible.
- ☐ the time of the staff is not taken up. It is only necessary for the trainee to have arm's-length access to a trainer in the event of anything going seriously wrong. Nevertheless there is good management control because all the ground has to be covered.
- ☐ the trainee is able to check his progress continuously and correct errors as they arise. He has to be totally involved and he obtains immediate feedback. The degree of reward in reaching the right answers is greater in this type of training than in many others.
- ☐ he can work at his own pace. He does not have to keep up with the rest of the group.
- ☐ the programme can be illustrated to aid understanding.
- ☐ provided the programme is professionally produced, he should normally have no problems of interpretation. Personal difficulties

that may otherwise occur in the relationship between trainee and instructor do not arise.

- ☐ it can be better sequenced than any other training programme because it demands greater care from the programmer in analysing and presenting the material.
- ☐ there is a built-in revision mechanism which aids learning.
- ☐ it is possible to stop the programme and start it again at any time without loss of continuity. That is, the trainee knows precisely where he left off and can review the last part of the exercise if he so wishes before proceeding.
- ☐ with the book system there is a permanent record of everything that happens in the learning process.
- ☐ where video equipment is used, it familiarizes the trainee with the operation of such equipment.

The disadvantages are:

- ☐ it is an impersonal system. The trainee is normally isolated and would therefore have no dialogue with anyone else. This would make clarification of points not properly understood more difficult than usual.
- ☐ it requires discipline and motivation to work at a reasonable tempo. If the subject is not particularly absorbing, progress may be slow.
- ☐ it assumes that the trainee has acceptable reading and comprehension skills. Educational limitations could prove a drawback.
- ☐ the programme may be written on a 'one-track' basis and not allow for the exploration of a number of options. It therefore tends to be more suitable for the teaching of concrete facts than for the discussion of ideas and management problems or for behavioural subjects. For this reason it may not stand on its own but have to be used alongside other methods.
- ☐ programmes are costly to produce.
- ☐ learning objectives have to be precisely defined (which could be interpreted as an advantage!).

Programmed learning can be achieved in three ways, by means of a book, a teaching machine or a computer. The much greater versatility of the computer (see computer-based training in Chapter 7) has meant that teaching machines have been largely superseded, although a few are still in use. In each case the learner is taken through a prepared text or programme in small easily assimilable steps. He is permitted to move on to the next step only when he has satisfactorily answered the questions relating to the current one. In the book programme the model answers appear on the back of the page being studied or on the following page and are therefore not visible until the page is turned after the trainee has written in his responses. If the trainee's answers are correct he is instructed to pass on to the next section.

Frame 21

The identification of your own training needs is the responsibility of

(a) the Training Department .... Turn to Frame 22
(b) your manager or supervisor .... Turn to Frame 23
(c) yourself .... Turn to Frame 24

Frame 22

You have said that identifying your training needs is the responsibility of the Training Department. You are not quite correct, although this is popularly believed. Which of the following statements do you think is correct?

The Training Department

(a) can provide or obtain advice and practical help on all training matters .... Turn to Frame 26
(b) knows what skills and knowledge I require in my job .... Turn to Frame 27

Frame 23

You have decided that your boss is the person who should decide what your training needs are. You are right. He is responsible for seeing that you satisfy the requirements of your job in meeting organizational objectives and is the best one to assess what knowledge and skills you require

.... Turn to Frame 28

Frame 24

You have taken the responsibility for your training into your own hands. This is very commendable but is not acceptable. The person who is accountable has to know what the knowledge and skill requirements of your job are.

Is that

(a) the Training Manager? .... Turn to Frame 27
(b) your boss? .... Turn to Frame 23
(c) anyone else? .... Turn to Frame 25

Frame 25

You have rejected both the Training Manager and your boss. You are right so far as the former is concerned since he can only learn what skills and knowledge you require in your job from someone who is accountable to the management for it.

Do you feel that that person is

(a) yourself? .... Turn to Frame 24
(b) your boss? .... Turn to Frame 23

Frame 26

You are quite right in saying that the Training Department can provide or obtain advice and practical help on all training matters.

Who do you feel knows best what skills and knowledge you require in your job?

(a) yourself .... Turn to Frame 24
(b) your boss .... Turn to Frame 23

Frame 27

You say that the Training Department knows what is required in your job. This is unlikely. It would be a tall order for them to know every job inside out.

On reflection, who do you feel is more likely to have this knowledge?

(a) yourself .... Turn to Frame 24
(b) your boss .... Turn to Frame 23

Figure 21(a). *Seven frames in a typical branching programme*

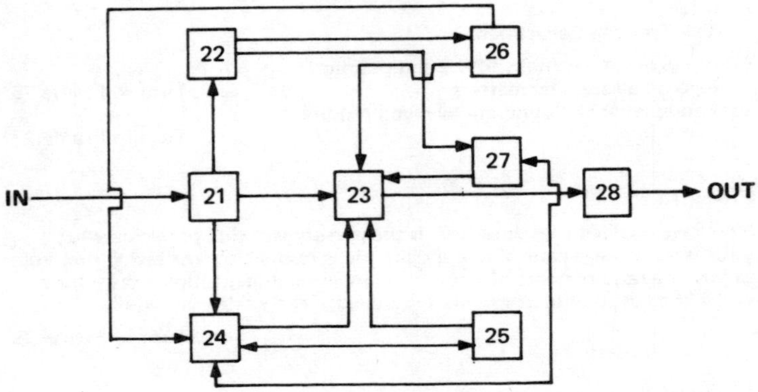

Figure 21(b). *The possible routes which can be taken between Frames 21 and 28*

If not, he is referred back in the text to revise the material he has not grasped. Each step in the process, usually on one page if possible, is termed a frame.

The process described above is known as 'linear programming'. An added refinement is called 'branching' and this provides additional frames or branches which may develop a theme or present the material in a different way for the benefit of trainees who fail to get the right answer. This helps understanding and also has the advantage that the trainee does not have to keep back-tracking over earlier material when he fails to respond correctly. The branching method usually offers alternative answers from which the trainee has to select the right one. If he does, he moves on to the next page; if he chooses one of the others he is directed to another page which explains where he went wrong. He is then tested again and proceeds as appropriate.

By way of illustration, fig. 21(a) shows what seven frames of such a programme might look like and fig. 21(b) indicates the paths that might be taken depending on the responses. This example, which deals with a very limited amount of information, clearly illustrates how complicated and therefore expensive a complete programme is likely to be. To justify the use of this method a substantial throughput of trainees needs to be assured otherwise the *per capita* cost would be extortionate. The programmes used with visual display units (teaching machines) or computer terminals follow much the same procedure. Each frame is called up on the display and responses are keyed in to the machine for comparison with the required answers. The appropriate new frame appears on the screen, indicating whether or not the response was correct, adding further information, posing new questions, giving new instructions and so on. Computer systems have the added advantage of offering the calculating capacity of the hardware. Equipped with a suitable program, the facility exists for manipulating data in a limitless number of ways so making it possible to incorporate programmed learning into much more sophisticated training programmes. The use of computers and some teaching machines can also be extended by linking them to subsidiary equipment such as tape-recorders, slide projectors or even working models.

Prescribed reading

A problem with training programmes is that they have to take place at a particular time which is not always convenient or most appropriate for some participants. These activities are often seen as disrupting the work programme rather than contributing to organizational effectiveness. It is not unusual, too, for the time limits imposed to restrict learning for those who are not as quick on the uptake as their peers.

In coping with such problems, we should not underestimate the value of self-development.[27] It is probably true to say that most people are eager to learn more, but are not too keen to disclose to others that they need to do so. One of the major constraints to their learning about their jobs by reading is the lack of knowledge as to which book, paper or journal would be suitable to provide the knowledge they require. They may not even recognize appropriate information when they see it. It may only be necessary for the boss to identify the sources to enable them to embark on a useful training activity which they can carry out at work, on the commuter train or in their own homes.

Prescribed reading may be used at any level in an organization, although it is more common with managerial and technical staff than with others, partly because reading is a skill which normally has to be used more by them in their day-to-day business activities. Whoever the learner may be, it is essential that certain safeguards are built into the exercise. First, the boss should take particular care to see that the material recommended is not only suitable in content terms but also in terms of the reading abilities of the learner. Bearing in mind that reading about one's job for work reasons requires a certain amount of self-discipline, it is unlikely to have the desired outcome if the reader is put off by the style or the degree of complexity. Second, there must be some follow-up during which the boss can review the learning which has taken place. This would take the form of a coaching session (see

p. 136) and it should not be made to appear like an examination. It should be a free discussion during which the views and feelings of the employee on the subject and the prospects of implementing what has been learnt, may be explored. In this way there is greater likelihood of prescribed reading becoming of lasting benefit to organization and individual alike. There is a danger that it may be conducted on an *ad hoc* basis without any reference being made to it in the employee's training record. If it is carried out in the way suggested, however, it is important that it be recorded as a practical and recognized part of his training.

One of the attractions of prescribed reading is that training costs can be kept to a minimum. At a time when there are severe budget restrictions on training, to the extent that some activities are eliminated altogether, this is a significant factor. There are skills, of course, which all managers are *expected* to have, yet no training help has been provided for them. Sometimes they themselves are reluctant to admit their shortcomings, although they will do so if pressed and will welcome any assistance that may be offered, particularly if it can be given in private. Areas such as interviewing, presentation and counselling are examples of what may be termed 'core skills'. With this problem in mind, the writer produces a series of self-help guides for managers. These are small booklets, of two or three dozen pages, which give advice and guidance on how such skills may be improved in the manager's own time and at his own pace.[25, 42, 44, 54]

Distance Learning

It is common, particularly with apprentices and junior trainees, for job training to be supplemented by further education at local establishments such as technical colleges. This sometimes requires day or half-day release from work each week, with or without pay, and it is naturally desirable that practical and academic work are suitably integrated. It is not always possible for employees to attend an external establishment for organizational reasons, because of country transport problems or because a suitable course is not available locally. One possible alternative is the correspondence course. Such courses are offered by independent colleges or schools which undertake to prepare the student for examinations and usually give a money-back guarantee if he fails after having completed the course to their satisfaction. Payment is made in full in advance or by instalments over the period of the course. All the work of a correspondence course is normally conducted by post and so suffers from a time lag between the student sending in work and receiving it back marked by the tutor. The dialogue which goes on between student and tutor is protracted, since there will be a considerable delay between either party asking a question and obtaining the answer. This can be very frustrating if the answer turns out to be unsatisfactory and the process has to be re-activated. Nevertheless, some correspondence schools have carried out sterling work in providing facilities for obtaining qualifications and acquiring knowledge which may not have been possible by any other means. It needs to be said, however, that success in correspondence courses depends for the most part on the tenacity of the student. He has to discipline himself to allocate a suitable amount of his own time to study on a regular basis and must set himself targets which he must be determined to meet. It is all too easy to put off until tomorrow what should be done today and it is in this way that many students starting correspondence courses fail to complete them. In an attempt to reduce this risk, some employers will only reimburse the cost of such courses when the students are successful in their examinations.

A highly developed form of correspondence course, introduced in 1969, is the Open University (OU) course. The term 'open' implies that the facilities are available to all UK residents over the age of 21 who are interested in furthering their education and knowledge in their own time. The topics studied may be work-related or simply connected with outside interests. No academic entrance qualifications are required and the curriculum is not restricted to the University's Bachelor of Arts or post-graduate degrees. In addition to the usual postal dialogue by means of written exercises, etc, the OU provides radio and television programmes which are fully integrated into the programme. It has a national network of study centres, based in local education establishments, at which evening tutorials, discussions, etc can be arranged and other opportunities for students to meet their course tutors and colleagues are provided at one-week summer schools. The problem encountered in correspondence courses of having to discipline oneself to pace the programme realistically is partly overcome by the need in the OU courses to listen to or watch certain scheduled broadcasts on radio or television.[91]

An Open Tech programme was introduced in the early 1980s and its strategic direction was the responsibility of a Steering Group set up by the MSC. The Group also had consultative and review functions and the Commision provided pump-priming finance to give the necessary stimulus in the scheme's early stages. This financial aid enabled projects such as the development of open-learning materials to be carried out by educational establishments, employers or training organizations.

The Open Tech programme set out to meet part of the third objective in the MSC's *New Training Initiative*[92] which was to widen training and re-training opportunities for adults (see p. 227). Specifically, it was directed towards technician, supervisory and management levels of skill. The methods of achieving its aims were more flexible than in any other form of training. It was 'open' to everyone, irrespective of formal educational qualifications. Every effort was made to reduce to a minimum any limitations as to time, location or the nature of the learning media used. Thus a trainee unable to attend a regular course at a technical college was able to satisfy the study requirements by some other means. Learning could take place at home, in a library, at work or in an educational or training establishment. The learning media might include books, tapes (video or audio), radio/TV programmes, programmed-learning packages or computers. Tutorial assistance could be provided by letter, telephone, face-to-face discussion where practicable, or computer or interactive video systems. Existing facilities, in whatever mix was considered appropriate in a particular case, were used and it was not then intended to set up a separate establishment on the OU or any other model. Clearly the scheme demanded for its success the closest co-operation between 'further education and training institutions, examining bodies, sector training bodies and their industries, employers and trade unions'.[93] The writer would suggest that it also required an ability and a willingness on the part of the trainee to adjust to any form of training which was appropriate and necessary in order to meet his requirements.

The Open Tech programme, during its period of operation which ended on 31 March 1987, provided well over 50,000 trainees with 30,000 hours of new open learning material. The scheme has been replaced with a new Open Learning Programme[94] intended to cover a period of at least five years. Maintaining the impetus given by the old scheme, it will promote the widest possible use of open learning methods in both industry and commerce. Local Education Authority institutions will also be encouraged to use these methods to the full when dealing with the needs of the labour market and further support will be given to the training of trainers[125] in the production and delivery of high standard open learning materials.

In September 1986 a new independent training company, the Open College, was formed. Limited by guarantee and registered as a charity, the College commenced operations in September 1987 and is expected to be able to cater for up to a million students on below degree level courses in the first five years of its operation, becoming self-supporting within three years. It will seek accreditation for its programmes from examining and validation bodies and will exploit new and existing open learning materials and methods, making use of other educational and training establishments and facilities, such as broadcasting, as appropriate. The concept has been well received and some of the larger companies are intending to set up their own fully-equipped in-house centres. These will provide employees with job-related training and access to sources of open learning materials, with suitable support from the company's managers and trainers.

Collection of materials suitable for use in open learning schemes is carried out by the Materials and Resources Information Service Network (MARIS-NET).[94] This organization, originally set up in 1983 by the MSC to provide information for the Open Tech programme, is now an independent limited company. It codes the data obtained from the suppliers of learning materials and feeds it into a computer system. A subscriber may access the database on behalf of the student seeking information on open-learning materials. In addition to owning and maintaining its own databases, MARIS-NET is a host system, creating databases for outside organizations such as the Institute of Training and Development.

The above and other trainee-centred methods, in which the trainee does not normally come into face-to-face contact with the trainer or teacher, are often referred to as 'distance-learning' methods.

Induction training

The major task of an employer when appointing a new employee, whether from outside the organization or by transfer from another section or division, is to integrate him into the business so that he begins to make a contribution at the earliest possible time. This does not merely mean training him in the specific skills of the job but also involves preparing him generally for his new responsibilities in the concern.

It was once believed that it was only necessary to show a newcomer the job that he was engaged to do and then set him to work. He occupied himself with his work within his own cocoon and did not concern himself with what went on outside it. In more recent years it has been acknowledged that employees should be better prepared to take their place as members of the community forming the organization. This means providing them with considerably more information about the business and their place in it. Most of the larger employers therefore regard properly organized induction training[95] as essential for all new entrants and some go so far as to arrange talks by the top management on the first day or soon after.

Induction training thus consists of two main facets, introduction to the organization and its activities and initial training for the specific job. The former is logically the responsibility of the personnel and training function, with assistance if necessary from certain functional specialists and trade union officials. The latter is a line responsibility, and managers and supervisors should be discouraged from trying to shift the burden on to the training department. The boss is better equipped than anyone to identify the requirements of the job and should therefore see to it that the training meets those needs. When trying to find the best means of satisfying the needs he can enlist the help of the training department.

The main ingredients of an acceptable induction programme are:

A Pre-engagement procedures

(i) *at interview*

- ☐ outline purpose and main requirements of job

- ☐ provide adequate information on terms and conditions of service, etc
- ☐ discuss accommodation arrangements
- ☐ answer candidate's questions
- ☐ check availability of candidate

(ii) *on acceptance*

- ☐ provide contract of employment
- ☐ inform new entrant's manager
- ☐ send joining instructions
- ☐ send employee handbook, safety policy statement, accommodation addresses or contact, etc.

B On engagement

(i) *The organization*

Acquaint employee with:

- ☐ organization's history, structure, activities, and provide written information for reference
- ☐ corporate objectives, policies, procedures
- ☐ documentation, obtaining necessary information for national insurance, income tax and personnel records
- ☐ terms and conditions of service (eg wages/salaries, pensions, holidays, overtime) and provide statutory written particulars within 13 weeks
- ☐ rules and regulations (eg absence/sickness procedures, general safety policy, fire procedures)
- ☐ grievance and disciplinary procedures
- ☐ industrial relations (eg management and union information, joint consultation)
- ☐ general services (eg wages department, cash office, surgery, canteen, staff shop, sports and social club, car parking, travel)
- ☐ career prospects and training opportunities
- ☐ accommodation arrangements

Arrange a guided tour of the establishment, introducing employee to the people he is most likely to have contact with in the course of his work. If there are too many for him to remember all at once he should meet a few at a time over a period of several weeks.

(ii) *The job*

- ☐ introduce employee to his departmental colleagues
- ☐ acquaint him with his workplace and the equipment, etc available for his use
- ☐ inform him of the departmental systems and procedures (eg job safety, security, office routine)
- ☐ issue tools, stationery, protective clothing where applicable

- ☐ check any personal problems
- ☐ provide initial job training (see p. 96 on one-to-one instruction)

C Follow-up

- ☐ check and reinforce understanding of rules, etc as appropriate
- ☐ invite questions of clarification
- ☐ monitor job performance and coach as required (see p. 137)
- ☐ review reasons for previous employee(s) leaving and take steps to see that it does not happen again!

It will be seen that induction training does not cease on the day a new employee joins the organization. It is important to think of it as a continuing activity since it is unrealistic to try to acquaint him with all he needs to know within a few hours. It is bewildering to say the least to join a new organization and there is a limit to how much information one can take in on the first day. Furthermore, conditions, systems, procedures, etc are constantly changing and one's knowledge of them therefore requires continual updating. It is useful to compile a checklist of the main items of information that have to be imparted and to record the fact as the requirements are satisfied.

Special problems of adult re-training

The rapid advance of technology over the last half century has created many problems for employers. For example, difficulties are experienced in deciding what the composition of the workforce should be in order to ensure that it is geared to the organization's changing needs. It is widely accepted that people will need to be trained for two or three jobs in their lifetime, and so employers are now frequently faced with the prospect of re-training adult workers in new skills. Unhappily this brings about a good deal of uneasiness and trauma and is not always successful, often because employers do not understand the nature of the problem from the older worker's point of view. Some valuable research was undertaken in this field by consultants of the Industrial Training Research Unit (ITRU) based in Cambridge, who were able to provide training managers with helpful guidance and advice when confronted with such problems.[96]

There is a popular school of thought that you can't teach old dogs new tricks. This saying is no doubt applied to the adult training situation because people do not take the trouble to find out why adults sometimes find it difficult to change their pattern of life and therefore tend to resist any change. Those who are concerned about the human aspects of work have identified reasons why adults can experience these difficulties and can provide evidence to show that something can in fact be done about it in a substantial proportion of cases.

Some of the reasons why there is reluctance on the part of older workers to be re-trained may be summarized as follows:

1. Having reached maturity after many years' experience, they consider it a retrograde step to start training all over again.
2. They fear the unknown, believing they will not be able to cope. There is a very real fear of failure which would bring their whole world toppling around them. They may well believe in the old adage mentioned above and it becomes a self-fulfilling prophecy.
3. They are proud of past achievements on which they have established their reputations. What opportunity will there be to build on past experience in the new role?
4. They fear the sÿstem which requires them to fill in forms, to answer questions, to be subjected to tests, to be equipped with physical attributes which they may no longer have (eg good eyesight).
5. They are anxious about the prospect of future competition with younger workers, having hitherto felt that they could hold their own with them.
6. They feel they will not be understood by the trainer and will thus be at a disadvantage when trying to acquire the new skills.
7. Accuracy is more important than speed to them and they think they may be forced to reverse their priorities.
8. They fear that the additional stress involved will make them ill and even shorten their lives. Will they have the stamina needed for the new work?
9. In extreme cases they may even be suspicious of the employer's motives, believing that the management is trying to find a way of proving them incapable of carrying out the required work so that they can be paid off.

These reservations and anxieties are understandable among loyal workers who over a period of time have settled themselves into a routine over which they feel they are the masters. The longer this period is the greater effect any change is likely to have on their morale. Their security and self-confidence are under threat, and it is important that training specialists recognize the need to exercise understanding in handling the problem. Some of the remedies suggested by the ITRU consultants were:

1. Where the change involves moving from one department or establishment to another, induction training should be carefully designed to take into account the special difficulties that an adult worker may have in adjusting to the new situation.
2. There are distinct advantages in selecting a trainer who is sensitive to the needs of adult trainees. The trainer/trainee relationship can be critical.

3. Course design should allow adequate time to cope with new concepts, anticipate possible physical problems including fatigue and make special plans to deal with educational shortcomings (see below).
4. Where training in the use of a new machine is involved, it is helpful to introduce the adult trainee to an associated activity in the first instance, enabling him to see the machine in action without having any responsibility for it.
5. Where practicable, enabling the trainee to talk to another employee with a similar background who has been trained successfully on the same job will give him some encouragement.
6. To reduce the fear of failure, final tests or examination may be abandoned in favour of monitoring progress on a continuous basis. It sometimes helps for the trainer to take the blame when things go wrong, at the same time indicating that he is confident of the trainee's success. Early success in adult re-training is of course highly desirable in terms of boosting confidence.
7. The method of achieving a satisfactory work pace should be carefully thought out. It will differ with the task, eg ease of learning and whether accuracy or speed is the more important. Pressure can be applied earlier when the task is relatively simple or when accuracy is not vital.
8. Arranging for trainees to work in pairs may reduce inhibitions in some instances. Indeed there are advantages in carrying out the training in groups with common interests. The shared experience reduces tension and aids learning.
9. Building on the trainee's previous experience is highly desirable because it helps him in relating the new learning to the old. This means, however, that before designing the programme the trainee's previous knowledge must be carefully checked.
10. Uncertainty is a de-motivator and should therefore be reduced to a minimum. The trainee must know in advance what is going to be dealt with in the programme and what will be required of him. He should also be taught in such a way that he fully understands the job rather than merely learning it parrot-fashion.

Educational shortcomings among trainees at any level can create problems for the training department. When they arise with adults they can prove a considerable embarrassment often requiring unique measures to deal with them. A training consultant from head office was invited into an engineering company in the mid-1970s ostensibly to sort out an operator training problem. On investigation he found that the shortcomings were with the supervisors rather than the operators and his report recommended a programme of supervisory training. The report was accepted by the management and he interviewed the supervisors in the process of producing a training needs analysis. He was alarmed to find that there were serious gaps in their numerical ability, in particular in regard to their being able to work with decimals and percentages. Before he was able to embark on the supervisory training programme he had to coach them in elementary mathematics. So that none of them would lose face, however, each was instructed in private without the knowledge of the others!

These are some of the actions that training specialists can take in order to overcome the problems inherent in the re-training of adult workers. Recognizing that these problems exist is more than half the battle. Managing them may not be as difficult as it appears and there are rich rewards to be reaped. Once the early difficulties are mastered, older trainees apply themselves diligently to the job and statistics show that they tend to stay longer in employment than younger ones. There is, however, another hurdle to be overcome and that is the transfer from training to the new working environment. Sometimes this phase is difficult because supervisors expect almost immediate integration into the skilled activity. When this does not occur, it is more likely to be due to social and psychological reasons than because of poor learning. Help in effecting the transference to everyone's satisfaction may be provided by the trainer who can give moral support to the trainee and who can become a short-term link between him and the supervisor.

Summary

The foregoing list represents a cross-section of the more common training methods which have been available to the training specialist for some years. The descriptions are of necessity brief, but further reading is suggested in the bibliography. The next chapter explores some of the more recent developments in training approaches.

There is a tendency for certain methods to be used with specific groups, eg apprentices, graduates, managers, salesmen, regardless of the aims of the exercise or the task. This arises from custom and practice rather than from any attempt to be objective. In general, the training of such groups has not been separately treated in this chapter since by so doing the impression would be given that there was one particular method or group of methods more appropriate than another in each case. It is strongly felt, however, that trainers should resist the temptation of being strait-jacketed in this way. They should keep an open mind about how different functional groups should be trained and, instead of assuming that a particular method is appropriate for a given group at all times, make the decision on the merits of each situation. This applies equally to cross-functional groups involved in, for example, training in industrial relations topics such as negotiating skills[97] (see Chapter 7).

The variables likely to influence the choice of training method will include the size of the group; its composition and the backgrounds of its members; managerial or supervisory style in the members' department; the training objectives and economic constraints. Whatever method is chosen, it is important that it meets certain criteria. It should:

- ☐ satisfy the training and organizational goals and the results should be measurable against them. The objectives should be directly work-orientated where practicable.
- ☐ motivate the trainees to learn by involvement. Adequate monitoring and reinforcement mechanisms need to be built into the programme.
- ☐ provide for ease of transferability of learning to the work situation.

Chapter 7

The Training Process – Some Areas of Recent Development

The training methods and techniques described in the last chapter have now been with us for many years. They have been developed in various forms, frequently being modified and tailored to suit particular situations and needs. The profession is, of course, constantly evolving, and training specialists seek to take advantage of any new technologies, methods or approaches which may promise to add to their effectiveness. Often what is offered as innovative is readily recognizable as something from the past simply dressed up in a new guise and described in a new jargon. Training staff should therefore be on their guard against offers of 'new' developments which may only treat them to 'the mixture as before', possibly laced with a new flavour.

In a number of areas, training can be justly said to be breaking new ground. While the foundations for such developments may have been laid some years ago, it is only now, in the late 1980s, that we can see real progress being made. In a rapidly changing world, one can only take a snapshot of what is happening at the time of writing and this could well be out of date in a matter of months. Specialists developing new ideas may sensibly resist telling the world about their activities until there is adequate evidence that their worth can be demonstrated.

The writer would single out the following areas in which training would appear to be making some progress currently:

Computer-based training

It was briefly mentioned in the last chapter (see p. 120) that the use of computer-based training (CBT) adds a valuable dimension in speeding up decision-making and so compressing the training time-scale. In recent years, micro-technology has contributed to reductions in the cost of computer hardware, opening up opportunities for promoting its use in the training area. Only a few years ago the cost of the computer equipment itself was beyond the means of the training department; most of today's cost is in the program or software.

Facilities for accessing programs may be provided by large computers, which are operated on a time-sharing basis, or by micro-computer.

Time-sharing requires a link-up of the terminal to a remote computer by telephone line. Difficulties may arise from unsuitable siting of the computer, unfavourable priorities, response delays or equipment breakdown. Sometimes it is possible to limit some of these problems by arranging the use of a computer exclusively for training purposes through a computer bureau. The micro-computer, however, has a distinct advantage over other systems: it offers a comprehensive facility on one's own premises. Computer, keyboard, printer and display unit can all be accommodated in a limited amount of office space and the complete system is under the user's control. All that is required is a modest electrical power source and suitable programs or software. The training department thus has immediate access to a valuable facility which provides both versatility and portability.[98]

Computer technology in business is now a fact of life, being increasingly used in the larger organizations where the implementation and running costs are more readily justified and absorbed. Smaller businessmen, however, are inclined to show reluctance to take advantage of new technological developments, not only from the point of view of economics but also because they are apprehensive about being caught up in activities which they do not fully understand. Indeed, as entrepreneurs who have been used to holding the business reins and taking all the decisions themselves, they feel that there is a risk that technology could take over completely. It is an important responsibility of members of the training profession to reassure them on this point. The managers need to be shown by non-technical people who do not have a vested commercial interest in the equipment itself that the computer is not something which will take over their thought processes or their jobs, but will only do what they command it to do. In this respect, its obedience may outshine that of some of their employees!

What can training specialists achieve by using computers in their own work?[99] The MSC has urged employers who introduce new technology into their organizations to ensure that they make full use of the computer's teaching and training potential. As with all training media, there must be a pay-off in terms of improved performance at economic cost, so it is logical to assess their applications against this criterion. For some years computers were seen as sophisticated calculators rather than as aids to decision-making. It is true that their facility for producing phenomenally rapid and accurate results where complex mathematics is concerned is of considerable importance. The removal of the drudgery in repetitive arithmetical tasks is certainly welcomed. More recently, however, many other training applications have been developed which enable computer technology to make more significant contributions to organizational effectiveness, with the added benefit of economies of scale. The more important of these applications are listed below.

Management of training

This book deals at some length with the overall management of the training function in business. The activities of planning, organizing, monitoring, assessing, recording etc are assumed to involve manual systems. All are extremely time-consuming and some can be quite complicated. Professional training managers who see the trainer or instructor role as the most important part of their jobs are only too pleased to be able to delegate as many of the organizing activities as possible to their supporting staff. The computer can be an extremely useful tool in controlling and speeding up these activities, thus reducing the administrative burden.

There are several ways in which computer programs can be helpful in the management of training. In a large organization the planning of the department's activities (see Chapter 4) and the management of all its resources, such as instructors, training rooms, equipment, training materials, stationery (see Chapter 9), can involve the control of a large number of variables. This is not always handled as efficiently as it should be and frequently becomes a fire-fighting exercise. Resources are allocated arbitrarily as the need arises and without regard for the effects such action creates elsewhere. A properly designed computer program can take the guesswork out of such decisions, planning the disposition of resources and providing an instant appraisal of their availability.

A trainee's progress through the system can also be more efficiently traced by the computer than by the more common manual means. Details of his educational and occupational background may be stored in the database ready to be retrieved at any time they may be required. This record can also include reports on his training progress, whether as part of a continuing programme or resulting from single modules of training such as technical updating. His future training needs can be fed into the system and the program designed to provide information on the most suitable means of satisfying them. Clearly, a program which provides such detailed data on all the employees trained or under training can also become the source of valuable statistics about the whole training activity in a given period.

Learning aid

Reference was made in Chapter 6 to the use of computers in simulations and business games (see p. 120) and in programmed learning (see p. 140). One of the refinements in the latter is the development of facilities for providing diagrammatic and pictorial displays in colour. These facilities are now being exploited to the full and enable much more sophisticated programs to be designed. To date programmed learning has in effect simulated the pages of a book, with a provision for student responses and for revision where the answers given are incorrect. The statements made and questions asked are standard and inflexible. The latest development is a so-called Socratic method (see p. 117) in which a more natural dialogue can take place between man and machine. This has led some people to credit the computer with human 'intelligence'. In fact it simply requires a more complex program, which of course demands the employment of more highly skilled programmers.

There have been some interesting new developments in the use of computers in simulations, too. Greg Kearsley, in his informative book *Computer-Based Training*,[100] describes a novel method of training technicians in troubleshooting and repairing electronic circuitry. Circuit diagrams are displayed on the screen and a light pen is used by the trainee to measure voltages at different points in the circuit. When faults are diagnosed, 'repairs' are effected by means of the light pen, this time employed as a 'soldering iron'.

Information source for trainees

There is nothing new in using a computer as a source of information. It is capable of storing a considerable quantity of data. With the increasing preoccupation of trainers with the concept of trainee-based learning, however, it is not surprising that this facility is being used more and more. Learners carrying out training tasks are able to access the information they need through suitable programs in the training room and elsewhere. The computer database provided by MARIS-NET (see p. 146) can provide them and other interested parties with detailed information about open-learning materials available.

Design of training programmes

Just as scientists and engineers can make use of computer-aided design when developing new concepts and products, so trainers can enlist the help of computers when designing their training programmes. The system lends itself to a high degree of experimentation with various ideas and approaches, with the advantage of instant modification where found necessary.

The discipline required in producing a computer program for a particular training application encourages precision in terminology and presentation which may not be present when designing a training programme manually. There is a temptation when writing course material in the traditional way to be unnecessarily unwieldy in the choice and use of language, making the process more complicated than it need be. The result could well be that the trainees become bored and consequently demotivated. Furthermore, the use of graphical and pictorial representation may not normally be fully exploited, because of the inordinate amount of time necessary to produce something acceptable. A computerized design system, if it does not entirely eliminate such problems, goes a long way towards reducing them. An enormous amount of potential training data can also be stored for retrieval as and when required. Searching for specific information in the database takes a fraction of the time needed to work through books and filing cabinets.

The degree of complexity of a computer program suitable for course design raises an important question. The trainer's own training and experience will have concentrated essentially on putting information obtained from practitioners into a suitable learning form. In no way can he be knowledgeable about every aspect of the business likely to be encountered in training. It is probably asking too much that he should be trained in the intricacies of computer programming, which is considered to be a profession in its own right. This suggests that course design has to be a team effort. Detailed information on the topics to be explored has to be obtained from the practitioners, a computer specialist converts that information into a suitable program and the trainer ensures that appropriate training principles are observed and that the outcome meets the agreed objectives.

Testing

A common use of computer programs in training is for test purposes. This application is mentioned here not because it is in any sense a new development, but rather because it is sufficiently important to merit inclusion. For this reason, it is constantly under review and subject to change. As stated earlier, a computer program can provide the basis for assessing a trainee's progress; that is, it can be employed to measure his performance against certain criteria. Those criteria can be incorporated into the program and the computer can carry out the laborious task of comparing performance of a number of trainees against them. The program can also be designed in such a way that it provides a means of selection for training, thus avoiding expensive mistakes in allowing trainees to embark on training programmes to which they are not suited.

By entering appropriate data into the database, tests or exercises may be devised. The correct answers are identified in the program and the accuracy of the trainee's responses communicated either to the trainee himself or to the trainer, as desired. Again, the use of pictorial representation has increased the sophistication of such tests, which do not have to be restricted to the written word. Pictures or diagrams may be used to test a trainee's capacity to identify certain objects, eg an electronic component or sub-assembly which has been shown elsewhere simply by means of symbols.

The flexibility of testing by computer is demonstrated by one of the more advanced forms of interactive testing, known as adaptive testing. Although the program may contain a large number of items designed to test a trainee's comprehension of certain principles, it is not necessary for him to work through all of them or even to satisfy them sequentially in order to demonstrate his understanding. His responses to a limited number of questions will show whether or not he has grasped the appropriate concepts to satisfy given training objectives. The process of testing can thus be speeded up considerably and can prove less frustrating for the trainee.

When evaluating a training programme, for example by the use of questionnaires, the collation and interpretation of information from a number of trainees can be an onerous task. Clearly the computer can not only lighten the load by reducing the sheer volume of work, but it can also be programmed to interpret the results more meaningfully by drawing attention to the interrelationships between certain responses.

Embedded training

One of the obvious applications of the computer is providing a program which teaches the learner how to use the equipment. Over ten years ago the writer adopted this device on a computerized sales forecasting course. The sales trainees were given instruction through the computer terminal on how to program the computer in the BASIC language. This had the dual advantage of concurrently teaching them about the system and giving them practice in using it. Nowadays it is common practice for suppliers of computer equipment, word processors etc to include embedded training in the contract of supply.

Do we need computer-based training?

From the above it may be felt that computer-based training (CBT) has a good deal to offer the training manager. Only the salesman is likely to want to convince him that it will provide all the answers to his training problems. It is dangerous, however, to assume that since it is based on new and ever-advancing technology it has to be good. It is equally wrong to avoid trying to evaluate it because it requires radical re-thinking which is somewhat daunting. Some training specialists will be inclined to evade the question by pleading that the cost of implementing CBT would be prohibitive. An honest and detailed appraisal of the alternative means of satisfying an organization's precise training needs is the only way of providing the evidence to support or contest this view. In some businesses, the introduction of CBT has saved money; in others it has cost more than was expected. How does one calculate the cost? If the system is more expensive in hard cash terms but leads to much greater efficiency and effectiveness, is this not an argument for considering it seriously?

It is not at all easy to compare the two alternatives. So much depends on how well the training operation is being carried out without the assistance of the computer. Simply computerizing a sub-standard system will not produce improvements, except possibly in the perpetuation of sub-standard work at a higher rate! Speeding up an already professionally-run activity and reducing the risk of error has a good deal to commend it.

However sound the basis of traditional training, it suffers from a number of drawbacks. Training people in groups leads to difficulties arising from different learning rates, so that at one extreme the less able are overstretched and at the other the more knowledgeable become thoroughly bored and frustrated. The training process can be very cumbersome, and indeed some of the material may be irrelevant for a large number of participants. The training specialist's task may be a burdensome one by reason of the sheer weight of work directed towards the organization of training as distinct from the training itself. The numbers of people who can be trained at a given time are restricted by the methods and yet the response from trainees may be limited by their inhibitions, even in a relatively small group. The methods themselves may not be suitable for reproducing real-life situations, so the training may lack relevance. There can, of course, be shortcomings in the trainer's capacity to train and in his ability to respond to change. Any change of itself demands a good deal of work with which the training department may not be able to cope.

CBT can be helpful in dealing with some of these problems. Training may be tailored to the needs of individuals, enabling them to learn at their own pace and removing any inhibitions about training which they may have. This clearly saves time, embarrassment and frustration, although it has to be said that it demands a good deal of time in designing the programs in the first place. They are, of course, available for future use without the need to engage the services of the training staff again to any great extent.Some bank staff are trained in this way, causing the least disruption to normal work by not having to involve other staff in most of the processes. The greater part of the organization of training can be taken over by the computer, thus saving the training department's time and allowing the staff to undertake more important work.

Simulations and business games are attempts to bring reality into training. This is only partially successful, however, because it is extremely difficult to feed back the effects of trainees' decisions (see p. 120). The computer greatly assists this process and improves the interaction which is so necessary if business is to be accurately modelled in the training room. This realism is, of course, enhanced by the graphical and pictorial representation that a computer program can provide.

Whereas in traditional training systems, coping with change is time-consuming, computer programs lend themselves more readily to modification as and when required. The results obtained from a computer program will, of course, only be as good as the quality of the programming, which will consequently need to have inputs of a high professional standard from several sources. The high cost of such an activity cannot be ignored. There are also difficulties in using advanced technical equipment in training. Suitable hardware has to be available when it is needed. It must be reliable and the computer and peripherals used must be compatible. The trainer must be fully versed in the operation of the equipment and must be aware of the problems that may be encountered as a result of his delegating some of his work to machines. They can introduce new frustrations for the trainee, who may expect them to have human intelligence. A good deal of work is currently going on to develop talking computers, but there is a long way to go before the results are acceptable for training purposes.

One further warning needs to be sounded: there must be a balance between the use of the computer and other methods or aids in training. If training staff go overboard for computerized methods in everything they do, there is a risk of de-humanizing the activity, which would be in direct conflict with the true training objectives. Much value is to be gained by allowing the widest possible cross-fertilization of ideas between participants, particularly when they are from different professional areas within the organization. The computer must not be permitted to interfere with that process.

Interactive video

When live radio and television programmes were first seriously introduced into education and training, they were used either to substitute for or to augment existing formal teaching methods. Radio programmes were in effect lectures in which the listeners were not able to see the speakers; television programmes were lectures with the addition of powerful visual effects. In either case, the programme was predetermined and there was no way in which a true dialogue could take place between the originator and the trainee. The best that could be done to encourage trainee involvement was for a trainer to lead a discussion after the programme and attempt to answer any questions. There was no possibility of interaction taking place when it was needed and likely to be most effective – during the programme itself. Thus the learner had little control over the content, sequencing or pacing of his training.

Programmed texts and teaching machines provided the opportunity for learning to be more trainee-centred. Their uses were described in the last chapter (see pp. 139-43). The trainee had the facility to feed into the system his own answers to set questions, and the system indicated whether or not they were correct. His responses determined the shortest route through the programme taking into account his own level of understanding of the subject. The quantity of data it was possible to handle by this means was limited, however, and there were no opportunities for extracting information which was not deliberately built into the programme. The first drawback can now be largely overcome by the use of computers; the second may be minimized by taking advantage of the versatility of video-recording equipment used in conjunction with a television set.

A link-up between a computer system and a video-cassette recorder (VCR) enables most of the functions of the more sophisticated teaching machines to be performed, but with added advantages. Whereas a teaching machine display offers a succession of fixed frames of text or graphics, the VCR is additionally capable of providing continuously moving images in full colour. The trainee's attention is more readily held and his interest sustained by the constantly changing scene. Furthermore, he may be familiar with the medium already from having used it in his own home. He is likely to feel more involved and confident, being able to access different sequences of the program as he chooses.

The combination of computer, VCR and television set represented a dramatic advance on earlier learning aids. Nevertheless, in a world which seeks perfection in technology, it does have limitations. A computer (mainframe or microcomputer) is capable of producing very high quality outputs, but these are digital in nature, whereas broadcast TV systems operate in analogue mode. The transfer from one to the other by conversion of the signal to a modulated radio-frequency waveform results in picture resolution losses and these place restrictions on the size and quantity of information that can be displayed. The quality of the fixed frame image may leave something to be desired, and accessing the precise frame required can be both time-consuming and noisy, and therefore distracting.

Application of laser technology has provided a major breakthrough in the development of video-recording equipment. The videodisc is a device which makes use of a modulated laser beam for both recording and playback. It was developed mainly with the domestic TV and music markets in mind but is adaptable for use in training in conjunction with TV cameras and receivers. Coupled also with a computer and suitable ancillary control equipment, it is possible to design and produce software for sophisticated training programmes. These may take the place of programmed-learning packages while also making use of, for example, broadcast radio or TV material, film, slide, teletext and sequences produced with a TV camera in the training room or elsewhere. All these may be placed under the control of the trainee himself, thus producing a truly interactive system.[101]

The advantages claimed for videodisc over magnetic tape (as used in the VCR) are:

- ☐ it is capable of handling more data
- ☐ the reproduced data is of higher quality (both moving and fixed frame)

- ☐ access/retrieval is both fast and precise
- ☐ it is quieter in operation
- ☐ it preserves its original quality, ie it does not wear out
- ☐ it does not damage easily
- ☐ it is more readily transportable
- ☐ its storage requirements are smaller and therefore less costly
- ☐ its cost per item of processed information is much lower.

A further technological advance which enables considerably more data to be handled, at the same time retaining the other advantages mentioned above, is the optical digital data disc. A disc of 30cm diameter can carry 16,000 million bits of digital information. This storage capacity would require 2,400ft of 2-inch (sic) magnetic videotape, the cost of which would be of the order of ten times that of the optical disc. A standard videodisc will carry 54,000 frames of television data and is directly compatible with other television equipment. As previously said, however, radio frequency conversion equipment is required if it is to be used with the computer. The digital disc is, of course, compatible with the computer and therefore is most suitable for accessing and recording very high density information from the computer database.

In summary:

- ☐ broadcast television programmes do not lend themselves to interaction between originator and trainee
- ☐ videotape, while adding a new dimension by providing moving pictures in full colour with some user control, has limitations in terms of precision of access and quality of display, even when used with computers
- ☐ computers provide routes to considerable sources of information
- ☐ videodiscs can handle the output from TV cameras or receivers directly, but require additional equipment when used with computers
- ☐ optical digital data discs are compatible with computers and are able to store very high density information obtainable from them with greater ease of access and at reduced cost. It is therefore preferable to use the more versatile professional equipment than to try to adapt domestic TV equipment if the full benefits of interactive video are to be obtained.

Clearly the latest technology offers practical advantages over earlier training aids.[102] There are better opportunities for using different instruction and learning strategies, thus introducing greater variety into the training process. Facilities may more easily be built into the programmes to continually assess the trainee's performance and to make modifications where necessary to meet his specific requirements. It is reasonable to expect him to be better motivated by his direct involvement in the determination of the content, sequencing and pacing of the project. It should nevertheless be realized that there are also problems in introducing the most advanced technology in interactive video. The initial cost of the wide range of hardware needed may be prohibitive for all but the largest organizations. Although the running costs may not be unreasonable, there has to be a substantial investment in software if the technology is to be fully exploited. This involves a variety of contributions from specialists, as pointed out in the section on computer-based training. Since the success of interactive video depends so much on the quality of the software, this investment cannot be skimped.

One final comment about the practical use of closed circuit TV equipment in training. If the intention is to employ it to monitor the performance of trainees in, for example, an interviewing or presentation exercise, it is extremely important to reduce the additional stresses that may be introduced. Having regard to the inhibitions created in a learner who finds himself in front of a camera which is going to record his every movement for future scrutiny, the time and manner of its employment needs very careful consideration. If the members of a group are not working colleagues already well known to each other, it is a tactical error to use television camera equipment on the first day of the training programme. It is essential that the trainees are given the opportunity to work together and to become relaxed in each other's company before this strain is placed on their relationship. So far as the manner in which the equipment is used is concerned, it is recommended that it is made as unobtrusive as possible and is not allowed to dominate the training activity. As with other kinds of training aid, if it is allowed to divert attention from the training itself, it is not being used properly and will be counter-productive. On an occasion when the writer engaged an outside contractor to set up some video equipment for a business presentations course, there was considerable preoccupation with creating studio conditions, including brilliant spotlights. The participants were so unnerved by these preparations that they refused to 'perform' and the exercise eventually had to go ahead under normal room lighting conditions, with all that meant in terms of poor picture quality on the playback.

Management self-development

When discussing the use of prescribed reading as a training method (see p. 143) the writer underlined the importance of self-development.[27] The suggestion was made that most managers were eager to learn and simply required guidance in selecting appropriate material. It is probably true to say that they have a natural impulse to further their knowledge, both of their jobs and their outside pursuits. Few are content to remain in one job very much longer than it takes them to learn it thoroughly. If the job itself is changing, there is still a challenge and they may not need to change jobs in order to get the stimulation that they seek. The significant factor is that they pride themselves on being able to learn from experience and self-help rather than from being taught by someone else.

Mike Pedler and Tom Boydell have made some interesting observations as a result of discussing self-development with a number of managers.[104] The effects of various experiences and events on their learning could be fairly clearly distinguished by whether or not situations were 'contrived'. Important lessons were more likely to be learned from 'non-contrived' experiences such as 'being confronted by a subordinate' than from 'contrived' situations such as, regrettably, 'planned training'. Pedler was quick to point out that this did not in any way rule out a more formal training or teaching approach, but merely questioned the methods themselves and any priority that they may be seen to have over self-development.

Managers' jobs have marked differences from those of other employees in an organization. The lives of non-managers tend to be dominated by planned situations in which the problems encountered have standard solutions. Managers, on the other hand, are concerned largely with unplanned events posing problems for which there are no 'right' answers. Furthermore, these events are usually of direct concern to the management as a whole, not just individual managers or departments. A different approach is therefore necessary when training managers, one that not only deals with the realities of a job which appears to have very few ground rules, but also capitalizes on the innate inquisitiveness and thirst for knowledge of the individual. Management self-development can make a significant contribution to satisfying these criteria.

In general, management self-development involves a group, although the activity does not necessarily have to deal with group problems. The purpose of the meeting may be to assist the self-development of one or more of the group's members seeking support and assistance from their colleagues. They may want to improve their own performance or to find answers to their own career problems. It may be that they only require endorsements of their own views on how to deal with a particular problem. Alternatively, the group may be task-orientated, studying problems and searching for solutions in connection with actual work situations. In either case, the group can be self-activating, or it can enlist the help of an 'outsider' such as a trainer or management development adviser. Should such a person be involved, he would normally act as a facilitator of learning rather than as a teacher or instructor. He may not be present at the sessions himself, but may be called upon to give his advice before or after them. This advice might be about the approach that a manager should take in introducing his topic to the group. It could have to do with the learning process itself; how to understand what is going on in the group; how to manage one's own learning, and so on. The members of such groups not only decide the composition of their group, but determine its objectives, its methods and when its activities begin and end. In task-orientated groups, permission may be required from top management, while in groups focusing on the individual this may not be necessary.

It is not difficult to understand why management self-development is becoming increasingly popular in business. It has a number of potent features in its favour. The managers involved are usually self-motivated volunteers whose commitment provides a sound basis for successful decision-making and problem-solving. There is an incentive to reach positive conclusions about real and pressing problems related to their own or their organization's progress. They are not bound by a rigid training framework, trying to accomplish too many things at once. Any time constraints are dictated by the project rather than the training programme. It is an activity which economizes on staff, a factor which commends it to managements with tight budgets.

Effective task-orientated groups engaged on work-based projects use an action-learning approach[105] to the solution of their problems. Reginald Revans has studied ways of improving managerial group effectiveness in various industries for over half a century, and his conclusions about the use of action learning in those groups are well documented.[106] His recommendations have been adopted by managements in such widely differing organizations as GEC, London hospitals and the mining industry. The Japanese acknowledged the influence of his theories when they introduced their Q-circles concept. Old as these theories may now be, they remain valid in business today and deserve wider attention.

The principle at the centre of action learning theory is, in Revans' own words, '. . . that learning stems from responsible experience, and is reinforced when that experience is shared with others . . .' This concept will be familiar enough, but he goes on to explain an important aspect of the proposition, which is that 'Action learning distils from that comradeship in adversity which seeks responsibility through action rather than avoids it through discussion.' The members of the management team, whom he very aptly styles 'comrades in adversity', are, by virtue of the relevance of their considerable aggregated and shared experience, the only people who can do very much to improve the activity for which they are responsible. The solution to their problems lies within their own experience rather than in the opinions of outsiders. If their organization is to progress and adapt to a rapidly changing world, they must be ready to learn from their own experiences and difficulties when they arise. They should also be as ready to learn from their employees as they would be in expecting their employees to learn from them.

Industrial relations (IR) training

A few years ago, industrial unrest in the UK tended to dominate the media, bringing home to everyone the seriousness both locally and nationally of management/workforce disputes. In some instances the action inflamed tempers to the extent that violence added an unwelcome dimension to industrial relations. Each side blamed the other in public for the state of affairs that existed. In the negotiating room the two teams had to try hard to reach a settlement often in an unhelpful climate.

Could anything be done to ease the process of management/union negotiations, to create more suitable conditions in which they could take place, and to bring about more speedy and lasting agreements? Clearly the prerequisite for an objective and civilized dialogue in the negotiating room is the establishment of working conditions in which managements and the workforce can communicate sympathetically and effectively on a day-to-day basis. If the only opportunity provided for speaking to each other is when the two sides are in dispute, they are surely starting from the wrong base. The debate still goes on about worker participation in industry, stimulated, for example, by the EEC and its Draft Fifth and Vredeling Directives:[107] whether such recommendations are accepted in total or only in part, there is little doubt that something needs to be done to improve working relationships. The Advisory, Conciliation and Arbitration Service (ACAS) itself warned in a report as long ago as 1983 that unless further action were taken as a matter of urgency, union/management relationships in many sectors might take on a more combative character when the economy improved.

It has to be conceded that improving the working climate of itself will not solve disputes, although it will certainly provide a more suitable background against which objective negotiations can take place. There is, however, another important factor over which training managers can have influence, and that is with respect to the training of management negotiators.[97] It is widely assumed that practising managers are competent to carry out the negotiating role without any formal training. After all, it is argued, they know the issues involved and what the management is trying to achieve. Yet lack of skill in analysis, strategy and the process itself can, and often does, have serious consequences. By their impulsive actions and the injudicious use of the wrong language, for example, they may create barriers to future progress. There is a growing acceptance of the need for managers to be trained in negotiating skills. The realization that the unions attach greater importance to the training of their own negotiators may have provided the necessary stimulus for such action to be taken.

The question arises as to *who* should be trained in these skills. Normally, negotiations are conducted by a select band of managers and/or industrial relations specialists. If they are the only people who are suitably equipped to consult and negotiate with the workforce, what happens if they are away for any reason when a critical situation flares up? Many months, or even years, of groundwork could be thrown away by the innocent actions of an untrained substitute negotiator. The risks are too high. In the writer's view, it is extremely important that back-up negotiators should be trained to the same level of competence in the face-to-face skills as the specialists.

The above arguments have been put forward with the highest level of negotiating in an organization in mind, that is the level at which plant or group-wide agreements are being made. Negotiations and consultations go on, however, at most levels in a business, largely between individual managers and shop floor representatives, and it would be wrong to assume that training for such activities was any less important. It could be argued that it is at this level that the true foundations for negotiations at the corporate level are laid. The training needs analysis is therefore widened to embrace anyone who is likely to consult with workplace representatives.

The essential elements of any training programme in negotiating are:

- ☐ the provision of detailed information about the organization's industrial relations philosophy, strategies, policies and procedures
- ☐ the process of preparation for a negotiating interview or meeting
- ☐ the skills involved in the negotiating encounter and
- ☐ the follow-up procedure.

A sound understanding of the concern's approach to industrial relations is considered desirable in order to provide the background against which negotiations will take place. It is possible to teach the subject in isolation with the aid of one of the many standard packages available. In order to give the training more relevance, however, there is merit in carrying it out in the organizational context in which the skills will be used. Indeed, it is highly desirable that the programme is designed specifically for, and attended by, those managers and employee representatives who normally have to face each other in the negotiating room.

The need for preparation before a negotiating encounter is self-evident. It can be both embarrassing and damaging to lose the initiative right at the start because one has not collected all the required facts. Unscheduled meetings, such as an unexpected visit from a shop steward, may have to be dealt with by an adjournment to gather information. In all other cases, the necessary facts should be ascertained in advance, and the training programme should clarify the various types of information that may be required, which may include existing agreements, data on terms and conditions of service of the employees to be discussed, the possible effects of certain actions or decisions and so on.

At the centre of the training is the study of established protocol and procedures and of the personal skills required in the negotiating room. Many of these will be common with those needed for other types of meeting or interview. There should be discussions on such matters as whether the management team should communicate through a spokesman and whether the chairman should call upon individual specialists as required. Considerable attention should be given to certain interpersonal skills which demand a high degree of discipline, such as putting the management's case in terms which are readily understood and cannot be misinterpreted; listening to other arguments without interruption; showing a willingness to understand and consider them, not rejecting them out of hand; demonstrating flexibility without necessarily making concessions; curbing one's natural impulses to respond to criticism with anger and indignation. When the theory has been studied in this way, it should be put into practice in role-playing exercises which reproduce the real-life conditions as closely as possible. In this respect it is useful to enlist the help of skilled union negotiators from outside the organization, rather than consider employing managers in union roles to which they are unaccustomed and in which their credibility would be in question. Some organizations use case studies, others provide exercises based on their own past experiences. The latter have the advantage that they are entirely relevant and that the outcome is known. It is profitable to be able to evaluate the actual outcome and to debate what the results might have been if different strategies had been used.

Negotiation training should not be seen as a once-and-for-all injection. Most negotiators will be prepared to concede that they make mistakes, or at least that they might have achieved more had they handled a particular situation in a different way. Trained groups should have the opportunity to meet again from time to time in order to explore such problems and also for the purpose of updating themselves on policy or procedural amendments. There may also be changes in the composition of union teams which may result in their adopting different strategies. The management response in such circumstances might be to discuss what modifications they themselves should make to their own approach. Negotiation and consultation with the workforce are dynamic activities which require continuous appraisal, often generating new training requirements.

It was mentioned on p. 168 that negotiations and consultations take place not only between management and trade union groups, but also between individual managers and employee representatives. Indeed, although the term 'industrial relations' tends to conjure up pictures in many people's minds of management/trade union confrontation, it should be seen more realistically as the total pattern of relationships in a company, including the environmental, organizational and behavioural influences on it. In this wider context, the management activities identified by the Oxford Centre for Management Studies when developing its IR training audit[108] were listed as:

- ☐ dealing with trade unions
- ☐ the application of terms and conditions of employment
- ☐ the implementation of communication and consultation arrangements.
- ☐ the organization and allocation of work
- ☐ the handling of employee grievances
- ☐ the implementation of disciplinary and dismissal arrangements
- ☐ the implementation of health and safety provisions
- ☐ the implementation of equal opportunity provisions.

The Employment Relations Resource Centre,[109] which was originally funded by the Manpower Services Commission but is now a limited company, offers a unique facility to anyone involved in, or who wants to know more about, the development of good practice in the broad field of employee relations. It has an extensive IR library and is able to provide information, audio-visual materials, advice, in-plant consultancy, internal and external training programmes etc.

The repertory grid in training

Psychology has provided training specialists with many pathways towards understanding human behaviour. Designers of training programmes are generally aware that their reception by trainees and their ultimate outcome depend to a considerable extent on how those trainees classify and evaluate their personal experiences and knowledge in their own minds. The classifications, or 'constructs', have a marked effect on their behaviour and how they deal with particular events in their lives.

The repertory grid emerged as one of the devices for studying this phenomenon as long ago as 1955 and it has enjoyed growing popularity in more recent years. It is mentioned here in the hope that trainers who have not yet considered its use will examine its potential as an aid to understanding their trainees' perceptions and so judge its possible value in improving the outcome of their training activities. The experiences of some of those who are committed to it are well documented and readers are referred to Mark Easterby-Smith's contribution to the *Management Development and Training Handbook* for detailed information on the technique and a useful bibliography.[110]

Graphology as an aid to selection for training

The mention of the study of handwriting as a serious contribution to training often brings expressions of scepticism from training specialists, matched only by their reactions to astrology. Graphology is a subject associated in most people's minds with a light-hearted assessment of their own personalities. When the findings are flattering, they are accepted readily; when they are not, the whole thing is dismissed as charlatanism.

In America and on the Continent, graphology has met with less resistance and cynicism than in this country and it is used widely for the analysis of personal problems. Although it cannot be truly said to be scientifically based, it deserves more serious attention if for no other reason than that those who practise it professionally are dedicated and ethical people who can provide uncanny evidence to support their claims. Through their own professional associations, they are concerned among other things with researching the subject in depth.[111]

Of greater interest to training specialists, perhaps, is the fact that more and more reputable organizations are making use of graphology in recruitment and selection and in analysing employees' suitability for promotion. One firm of graphology specialists has put over 250 character traits into a computer program.[112] Clients are asked to provide the age and sex of job applicants, together with 100 words or more of their handwriting. The company claims that the personality profile produced by the program is a valuable aid to selection, but concedes that it does not remove the need for the exercise of normal judgement.

If graphology can bring about improvements in selection methods, it can reasonably be expected to have an application in selecting employees for training. The process of probing the depths of personality for this purpose demands a high level of perception on the part of the training specialist. He has little to help him in arriving at his decision, which may be influenced more by subjective considerations than by objective analysis. Many embarrassing and sometimes painful mistakes have occurred in the past in assumptions being made about a person's suitability for a particular kind of training, especially that which may impose a high degree of stress, such as sensitivity training (see p. 129). It would be helpful to have some means of reducing the risks of repeating such mistakes. Graphology may be able to make a useful contribution.

Operator training methodology

The operator is a key employee in manufacturing industry. The standard of work he or she produces and the number of products which find their way into the market place depend to a significant degree on how well his or her training has been carried out. The quality of operator training varies enormously from company to company and even from plant to plant within large organizations. Sometimes it is arbitrarily assumed, without adequate evidence, that an optimum level of output or quality is being achieved and no consideration is given to the possibility of improving on that performance. Yet there may be considerable scope for such improvements, using suitable training methods.

Because of the repetitive nature of mass- or batch-production work, there has been in the past a common tendency to treat operators as automatons rather than as human beings carrying out repetitive jobs. This attitude has often been reflected in the way their training has been carried out. The approach seems to have been quite different from that applied to other types of employee. Clerical workers, for example, whose jobs have frequently involved routine and unvarying tasks, do not appear to have encountered this phenomenon to anything like the same degree.

The question has to be asked as to whether there is any justification for treating production workers differently from any others. It is true that they usually have to work to much tighter targets and output is vitally important for the success and survival of the business. The failure of, for instance, a clerical operation may not have quite as devastating an effect on the company's fortunes as the inability of the factory to produce the goods. Employee failure on the production line has an immediate impact on profits and losses. If the progress of a line is slowed down or stopped by an operator's action or lack of action, the resultant costs incurred are not restricted simply to that operator but are multiplied by the number of operators on that line and could be substantial even for a minor disruption. Are these not arguments for improving the attitude towards operator training? Can we not learn from our experiences of training other employees and apply similar principles to the production area?

Several years ago some experiments on this theme were made in the writer's company on the initiative of the group's operator training consultant. Unfortunately the results were not documented in detail because the move was part of the natural evolution of policy for the central training activity and was not then considered of particular significance at the time. The operator trainer asked himself why the philosophy of operator training should be any different from that of any other group. The department's management and supervisory training programme was proving very successful and he felt that certain elements of the trainers' participative approach to it could be relevant to operator training. After all, he argued, operators have to work as a team, so why not train them in such a way that they see themselves as members of a team rather than individuals? They had a natural inclination to be clannish, indeed the main reason many of them went to work was for companionship, so it seemed logical to capitalize on this. Instead of putting each new intake into the training school to be exposed immediately to the bewildering skills which they were to learn, he set up a discussion group. Six or eight operators sat on chairs arranged in a semicircle, the trainer occupying a place within the group, rather than 'up front'. A flip chart was provided and the operators were prompted into a relaxed discussion about the products with which they were going to be concerned: what they were, what they were used for, where they were sold, etc. Gradually the discussion was focused on breaking down the product into sub-assemblies and ultimately into components. To illustrate the various functions of the parts or sub-assemblies, analogies with things within the operators' experience were made and before very long the mysteries which had worried them as newcomers to the business disappeared. By this means they were gradually eased into the instructional process from which they learned their practical skills. The reactions to this training approach were favourable. The operators were agreeably surprised to be treated as grown ups, who did not have to be taught everything in a classroom, and as human beings rather than machines. Surprisingly, the semi-technical nature of the discussion did not worry them, because they were encouraged to relate everything to their own experience. They were grateful for the opportunity to learn where their particular part of the job fitted in with the general scheme of things and this gave them a pride in their work before they even reached the production line. One of the lessons learned from this experiment was that it was a myth that production workers did not really want to know what they were doing or why. The knowledge that they gained from the discussion group activity created unexpected interest in the job and contributed to a high level of motivation. One of the results of this was that they were able to think intelligently about their work and were later able to make valuable suggestions for improving the methods used.

The nature of many operator tasks is, of course, changing. Automation has eliminated some and substituted others which involve controlling and monitoring processes rather than manual ones. Although it may appear that the new jobs are far less demanding, in fact they require performance at a higher level of skill, and failure may have more far-reaching effects. For example, in a process industry, the whole costly operation may be brought to a standstill and people and plant put at risk by a single person failing to note and take action on changing conditions in his particular sector. Repetitive manual skills may thus have to be replaced by skills requiring a more intelligent approach to work of a non-recurring nature. An analysis of all possible causes of employee error has to be made in order to provide training which will adequately fit employees for these new tasks. The approach to operator training outlined above goes a long way towards easing the transition from a repetitive manual job to a monitoring or controlling one. If the employee really understands his job, he will more readily see the reasons for change and be more likely to go along with it.

Apprentice training changes

The traditional method of training craftsmen by indentured apprenticeship is rapidly disappearing. The concept of an indenture, a contract 'that binds apprentice to master' and which originally had to be paid for by the unfortunate parents, was an anachronism the removal of which was long overdue. Many 'masters' clung to the idea that the prentice needed to serve at least five years, ie until he reached the age of discretion at 21 (later changed by law to 18), before he could be considered suitably skilled to carry out a craftsman's or production worker's job without supervision. Learning by experience in this way was a very long drawn-out affair and depended for its success on the level of instructional skill of the craftsman alongside whom the apprentice worked and on the latter's determination to complete the apprenticeship and 'take up' his indentures. The advances in training philosophy and methods in the years since the war, stimulated partly by the recommendations of the Industrial Training Boards and the Engineering Council,[113] have gradually made the apprenticeship concept redundant. It is now being replaced by 'training agreements'.

The indenture agreement was a remarkably 'open' document. It specified the length of the apprenticeship precisely, but frequently said little, if anything, about what training the apprentice could expect. In spite of this vagueness, the skilled worker who could wave his indentures in front of an employer was more likely to get a job than one who could not. It was proof that he had completed a programme of training as, for example, a miller or turner, but it seldom identified the skills learned or the standards attained. By contrast, the training agreement is more likely to specify that induction training, basic skills training, specified skills modules and a part-time course of further education have to be completed to acceptable standards before the agreement may be said to have been discharged. The number and type of skills modules are usually agreed by management and union before the programme is commenced and a statement is made to the effect that the duration will depend upon how long the trainee takes to satisfy the requirements of the various modules.

The implications of these changes for the trainee are self-evident. He knows from the start of a training programme exactly what is going to be required of him, which may allay any fears that he may be used as cheap labour. The training itself will have to be more relevant, because the requirements of each module will have to be satisfied and suitably certificated before he can move on to the next one. This should help to ensure that he is given instruction on skills which are essential, with less attention to those which are simply 'nice to know'. There are also advantages in his not having to sit out a four- or five-year apprenticeship when he may be quite capable of acquiring the necessary skills in three years. The employer is bound to benefit also. Apart from producing a skilled worker earlier, the standard of training itself is predictably higher, with consequent effects on the quality of output. If the trainee has enjoyed the acquisition of new skills to a high standard within a reasonable period of time and there have been fewer frustrations along the line, it is reasonable to expect him to be better motivated.

Instructional systems development

Training systems fail to meet their objectives for a variety of reasons. The materials may be deficient in important features or may provide too much information of the wrong kind. When training fails to teach the skills required by employees to carry out their tasks effectively, there is cause for concern. There are also problems of consistency, for example when training manpower resources are supplemented by the part-time use of non-training specialists with appropriate 'technical' knowledge. They may not be familiar with training techniques or the production of training materials,[18] with the result that they develop their own, sometimes in conflict with the training department's philosophy.

A technique known as Instructional Systems Development (ISD) may be helpful in dealing with such problems and others by providing a co-ordinated approach to the training system as a whole.[114] It tabulates what steps have to be taken in each stage of the training process. It does not, however, detail how these steps should be carried out. Nonetheless, most training managers appreciate having checklists to guide them in their activities and ISD fulfils that need in so far as it provides them with prompts in working through the training system and developing training materials.

The various stages in the ISD approach used by the American services will already be familiar to training staff:

- ☐ *analysis* – training needs are derived in relation to the requirements of each task or job. Appropriate performance criteria are established
- ☐ *design* – objectives are defined, structure and sequencing determined, tests devised
- ☐ *development* – learning media and methods are selected and training materials developed
- ☐ *implementation* – the instructional plan is put into effect
- ☐ *control* – the programmes are evaluated and the system modified as necessary.

Some of the activities in the above stages are interrelated. For instance, evaluation is something which is taking place all the time and is not simply confined to the control stage. In the event of the training failing to meet the established objectives, it may be necessary to return to the analysis stage and re-start the process.

As will be clear from the earlier section on computer-based systems, there is considerable scope for the use of computers in conjunction with ISD.[100] While it applies to all stages of the process, the areas where it has created greatest interest have been in the design and evaluation of training materials and in testing.

Summary

In this chapter, the writer has briefly described some of the methods and approaches which have made an impact on the training profession since the first edition of this book was published. While few of them will be entirely new to training managers, the latest developments justify the attention of those who wish to keep abreast of what is happening in the training field. The references provided will help them to update their knowledge as necessary.

As stated at the beginning of this chapter, the technology of learning is continually changing. New or modified techniques and methods are being tested and applied by a profession which seeks to improve employee contributions by means of training to the highest possible standards. The importance of learning technology has been recognized by the IPM's National Committee for Training and Development, whose Learning Technology Group aims '. . . to collect, analyse and disseminate information in the area of learning technology which will be of use to personnel professionals in their jobs. The Group hopes to be able to produce materials for members . . . which will describe, demonstrate or employ innovatory learning techniques'.

Chapter 8

The Training Process – Measuring and Following-up Results

It is probably true to say that the biggest headache a training manager has is actually being able to measure and assess the effectiveness of the training which is carried out. Whilst he may be quite convinced in his own mind that the programmes he has designed will have the desired effect, and he will constantly be seeking evidence, however tenuous, to support that contention, he is likely to be hard put to it to be able to prove conclusively that the objectives are being met.

This puts him in a serious dilemma. He knows that he has the capacity, if given a free hand, to make a significant impact on the organization's effectiveness and he will be continually trying to persuade his management that he should be given the required support. They, on the other hand, will only be persuaded by hard facts and evidence of past success. If they have the choice of investing in something which can be evaluated and something which cannot, the dice are loaded very heavily in the former's favour. This is particularly so in periods of economic recession, in which businesses simply will not invest in projects which do not have a high chance of success. In a booming economy, when order books are full and profits are not too difficult to make, managements will take risks and many of them will pay off. When they do not succeed, the buoyancy of the business will cushion the effects. However, when orders and profits are hard to come by, the money for investment is in short supply and those risks are not taken.

Thus, without some tangible means of measuring the results of training, the specialist can be fighting a losing battle. It is a chicken and egg situation. 'Give me the tools to do the job.' 'Give us the proof that you can use them to produce what we want.' The longer we go on ignoring the fact that our effectiveness has to be demonstrated and proved if we want to gain support for our efforts, that support may not be forthcoming. We therefore have to apply ourselves urgently to the problem of finding a positive way of assessing our results.

No one would deny that by far the easiest type of job to evaluate is the factory job which is normally repetitive. The work study department can readily analyse the operation,[1] programmes can be designed to train employees in the tasks involved, targets can be set and the output, in terms of quantity and quality, can be measured. It is not at all difficult deciding how many acceptable units are coming off the production line in a given time or how many unacceptable units are being rejected. If the targets are not met, the reasons can be ascertained by observation and the training programme suitably modified if necessary. Trainees learning craft skills will be instructed in various manual and machine processes, the results of which are readily measured and compared with established norms. The dimensions of the article, the tolerances, the finish and so on lend themselves to ease of assessment.[10] Some jobs in the office may be similarly measured using organization and methods (O & M) techniques,[115] but these approaches may not be appropriate when dealing with, for example, managerial jobs which require conceptual thinking and the exercise of judgement in the choice of options and in the solution of problems. There are many more influences on a manager's job, some of them external to the business, which require him to initiate some appropriate action. Measuring the effects of learning in such circumstances is not at all easy.

There are different attitudes to training and thus to evaluating it.[22] Many still cling to the idea that any training is bound to be beneficial which, of course, is a myth and cannot be substantiated from the available evidence. Some training is, alas, ill-conceived, being derived from the whims of the trainer or the management rather than from the needs of the trainee or the organization. Even when an accepted system of needs identification is employed it may not necessarily be foolproof. It is possible for the reasons for an employee's failure to meet his targets to be misconstrued. Attitude training, for example, is an area in which false assumptions about training needs are common. Nevertheless, the view that evaluation, for whatever reason, is not necessary is reprehensible. The difficulties it poses should be seen by training managers as a challenge to them to find a way of proving that their efforts are worthwhile.

Another viewpoint is that since training is an investment, it should be possible to measure the results directly in financial terms. In other words, a certain percentage return on the investment is to be expected. If improving overall performance can be seen to reduce costs and/or increase income directly, then this argument holds and a value can be put on the return. Unfortunately, reality is not quite like that. Many of the pay-offs of effective training are indirect and in some cases intangible, such as increased morale which can have an effect on output, quality, labour turnover, absenteeism, safety, and so on. Bearing in mind the findings of the Hawthorne studies (see pp. 13 and 89), how can we measure improvements in morale and their effects? Much of our evidence is circumstantial and inconclusive.

If a satisfactory method of evaluating training performance can be found, there are benefits to be reaped by everyone. The organization is better equipped to meet its obligations and the management's decision to invest money in the activity is vindicated, encouraging it to continue to provide the resources. The employee himself is more fulfilled and is stimulated to put effort into his work and to seek promotion. His boss has everything to gain from having an effective work unit and is likely to be willing to release employees for training in the future. The training staff, of course, enjoy job satisfaction of a high order when they see that their efforts are producing the desired results. They can go from strength to strength applying the experience and knowledge they have obtained from successful activities. So there is no doubt that evaluation of training is a profitable pursuit from everyone's point of view.

Evaluation and validation

We have to distinguish between the meanings of the terms 'evaluation'[16] and 'validation'.[116] Evaluation tells us how worthwhile the training has been in respect of the total benefits accrued from it by the business. Before these can be fully assessed, the training has to be validated, that is, we have to ascertain to what extent it has met its objectives and the needs of the trainees. Thus with evaluation we are dealing with the total value of the training activity to the organization, not merely the achievement of its stated objectives. There may, for example, be social as well as financial benefits. Three types of validation[33] have been identified:

- ☐ internal assessments, to measure whether or not the objectives were met
- ☐ external assessments, to ascertain whether those objectives were realistically related to the original training needs analysis
- ☐ as used in programmed instruction (see pp. 139-43): the verification of a programmed text by comparing the results of a target population with established criteria.

Cost benefit assessment

It has been said that training needs to be seen as an investment and should therefore be measurable in financial terms. Economists created the technique of 'cost benefit analysis' to consider both the economic and the social effects of investment in the public sector.[117] Building a motorway, for instance, would not only have benefits in improvements in transport and therefore trade, but might also involve 'social cost' in terms of such factors as noise suffered by people in close proximity to it. Estimates of such costs and benefits to the community are perhaps more easily made in respect of public investment than in the private sector. Rightly or wrongly, the effects on the national economy of training in industry are less likely to occupy the thoughts of employers than making profits to the direct benefit of shareholders and the businesses themselves. Whilst some employers will say that they use cost benefit analysis to measure their training effectiveness, it is probable that they have adopted a more simplified method of assessment, possibly borrowing some of the more useful features of the technique.

There may be reluctance from both management and training specialists to use any form of cost benefit assessment in training, for different reasons. One of the main findings of a survey conducted in 1985 by the Industrial Society[118] was that roughly 65 per cent of a sample of 134 employers spent less that 0.5 per cent of their annual turnover on training and a further 23 per cent between 0.5 per cent and 1 per cent. With this level of investment, the management may not regard the introduction of such controls as of very high priority. Training staff, on the other hand, may feel that revealing detailed information on their activities will draw attention to the cost and make their jobs more vulnerable. Nevertheless, the case for measuring the cost and benefits of training is compelling, and if the training department is doing its job properly, surely it will be able to demonstrate that the benefits greatly exceed the costs.

The system of assessment used[119] will depend very much on what factors the management or the training department wish to take into account. It will thus vary from one organization to another. There are, however, certain fundamental points which need to be considered when designing the system:

1. It must be methodical and fully understood by everyone concerned with operating or interpreting it. Its objectives must be clear for every project.
2. Consistency is vitally important because comparisons will need to be made between projects. The same scales and units of measurement must therefore be used throughout.
3. Where quality as well as quantity is of importance, a realistic measure of qualitative features has to be found. This will be relatively easy for operator training but may be a problem when assessing the quality of management decision-making.
4. Opportunity cost should be considered. If a particular course of action is taken, what is the cost of not having taken some alternative action?
5. The benefits accruing from one project may be to the advantage of another, and this factor should not be overlooked. The calculation of a 'payback' period over a number of projects might be considered.
6. Any training board or other grants need to be taken into account.
7. Only those costs and benefits which have positive measurable *effects* on the organization's activities should be included in the analysis. If, for example, one of the 'benefits' of the training is to reduce the work to be done in another department, but that department does not take advantage of it by reducing its staff and/or its budget, it would be unrealistic to claim a saving.

Anecdotal feedback

There are serious weaknesses in *ad hoc* methods of evaluating and validating training. Some trainers run into problems when the managers of trainees want to know how their employees performed on a training programme. In the writer's opinion, this is an invalid question because the answer would be irrelevant. How a trainee performs on a course is no indication whatever as to how he will perform in the job, and the latter is the ultimate measure of the usefulness of the training. It is customary for trainees on off-the-job programmes to be reassured at the outset that no reports on their individual performance will be made. This reduces apprehension and creates an atmosphere in which they are free to say what they really think without fear of their comments getting back to their bosses. In this way, the open exchange of knowledge and experience is encouraged and predictably some will take advantage of it more than others. It would be unrealistic, however, to assume that their behaviour in such a low-risk environment would be transferable to the real work situation, where conditions may be more inhibiting.

Some training staff rely upon anecdotal feedback to assess the effectiveness of their training programmes. The assumption is made that if the trainee says the training was good and that he learned a lot it must have been satisfactory and the more people who say favourable things about it the better. This is a fallacious argument because the whole thing is subjective and the criteria for acceptability are not discussed. The reaction is often based on whether the trainee enjoyed the experience or not and it is not too difficult to make a training programme enjoyable. Furthermore, the question is usually posed at a time when the trainee is in a state of euphoria, with the prospect of going home after an absence of several days firmly fixed in his mind. The last day of a course is not an ideal time to attempt an opinion survey anyway, because the trainee will not feel in a position to make a reasoned assessment when lots of ideas are still buzzing around in his mind. He will almost invariably say, 'I need time to digest it all'. The trainer may try to strike while the iron's hot in the belief that if he leaves the questions for several weeks he may run the risk of discovering that the trainee cannot remember what the course was all about! Sometimes the effect of this action is to get responses solely from members of the more vociferous minority in the group, whose contributions tend to be somewhat negative. The majority may prefer to keep their counsel until they feel that they are in a position to be more objective.

Integration with overall design

One of the key requirements of any effective training assessment system is that it should be part and parcel of the total training procedure and not simply an appendix to it.[120] If it is not an integral part of the process there is a tendency for it to be skimped or even worse, abandoned, when time is limited. It is valuable at the outset of a programme to ascertain the expectations of the trainees. This may be done by designing a multi-choice questionnaire around the important questions which the training needs analysis has identified. The completion of such a document greatly assists the trainer to find out to what extent the employee's needs and those of the organization have been discussed with him before he came. It is disheartening to find that frequently no dialogue of any kind has taken place between boss and employee and the latter has merely been instructed to attend the programme without any reasons being given. He is hardly in the right frame of mind to apply himself seriously to the learning experience. Indeed, having resigned himself to having to attend, his personal expectations of the programme may differ substantially from those intended. The trainer has to pick up the pieces and try to establish what the objectives ought to be and how the employee should reasonably expect to benefit from the training. The training methods used can have a significant impact on the success or otherwise of his efforts. These are examined in detail in Chapter 6.

De-briefing by the manager

Coupled with this problem is the one of de-briefing which was mentioned briefly in the last chapter. The manager or supervisor who releases an employee for training should always concern himself with how the time is spent and to what extent the objectives are met. If the training falls short of what is required, the time to find out about it and to take action is immediately after the event. If this does not happen, the training may lose its value and the training staff will fail to obtain the feedback on the activity which they need. It is always difficult for a busy manager to find time, particularly on a Monday morning after an employee has attended a week's course, to sit down with him and discuss the events of the last week and their relevance to the job. But it is precisely because of the relevance to the job that this discussion is necessary. The training was an investment of time and effort and it is important to ensure that it was productive in terms of improved performance. The employee may well have returned with ideas as to how he may modify his approach to his work and he will want to obtain the agreement of his manager to implement changes. Such changes should be in the best interests of the department and the organization and should therefore merit the manager's attention. They may even help him or his other employees to do their jobs more effectively. He and his employees should see the post-training review meeting as part of his normal management duties. In other words, it should not be something which happens on some occasions and not on others, but should become a regular activity which everyone expects of his manager when he returns from training. It does not have to be a lengthy meeting. When the system is operating smoothly the employees will be able to anticipate the questions which will arise and be ready for them. If the implications of the answers are far-reaching and demand more lengthy consideration, an adjournment can be called to give both parties time to consider points of relevance. It is important that the first meeting takes place at the earliest opportunity after training so that the manager may make an initial assessment of the possible value of the training and also that the employee's enthusiasm is not dampened by lack of interest or action.

One should not ignore the possibility that the employee's performance in the job may exceed what is required as a result of training. Clearly it is valuable to have warning that this may happen and the post-training review meeting may well provide the signs. The nature of the additional skills or knowledge and the promotion possibilities in the organization will have to be considered in deciding whether or not training programmes should be modified to take account of this in the future. These decisions require close liaison between management and the training department.

The conduct of the post-training review meeting requires careful thought. If the employee returns from the training programme fired with enthusiasm, it is important to establish that his fervour is well-founded and not merely an indication of his having enjoyed his new freedom. If his cheerfulness reflects increased confidence in his ability to use his experience and knowledge to discharge his job duties more effectively, all well and good. But if he has simply not yet come down to earth to face the realities of his work, look out for withdrawal symptoms when he does! What the manager has to establish is basically two things. First, what did the trainee learn which is or will be applicable in his job? Second, did the programme meet the objectives agreed when the employee was sent on it? When the employee was nominated for the training, it was naturally expected of him to learn something, but certain minimum requirements should have been established from the needs analysis. Were these requirements met? If so, then it is merely necessary to monitor the situation for a period to confirm this. If not, manager and trainer have to get together to find out why and to take whatever follow-up steps are called for.

Transferability of training

If training carried out away from the job cannot be transferred effectively to the job, it will be abortive and a total waste of everybody's time. One of the difficulties encountered in achieving transferability is centred on the fact that the training takes place in artificial conditions which cannot accurately reflect the reality of the job situation. The premises, the people, the relationships, the tasks, in fact just about everything is different. However much the trainer tries to re-create the job atmosphere by for example devising exercises from real life, by role plays, simulations, etc, he will repeatedly hear the comment, 'Well, it isn't like this in real life, is it?' This proves a considerable barrier when trying to transfer the lessons of training to the work situation and this barrier varies markedly between groups. It appears that those who are able to conceptualize and relate ideas, however apparently remote, to their own job circumstances have the least trouble with this problem. They are likely to be managers and other professional people whose jobs require them to adapt theory and knowledge to constantly varying occupational situations in order to make decisions. There are many other people, however, who do not have the same opportunity to practise the application of concepts in their jobs and who would therefore find greater difficulty in relating training to reality. For example, the jobs of many supervisors are largely regulated by clearly laid down procedures and systems and do not necessarily call for the application of theories and principles. It is therefore helpful to know in advance to what extent the group can relate theory to practice and to design the programme accordingly. When one is aware that this could be a problem, illustrations and examples should be used which directly reflect the trainees' experience. For instance, if a group of sales representatives is role-playing interviewing situations, the examples will not be seen as very relevant if they are drawn from a factory environment, even though the principles used may well be the same. The exercise will have greater value if the examples used reflect the salesman/customer relationship. Thus, if identical elements exist in the training and in the employees' experience, the prospect of satisfactory transfer of knowledge and skill will be greatly improved.[52]

The secret of successful transferability is therefore not so much to do with the actual process of applying learning to the job as with setting up the training itself in such a way that the transfer is facilitated. One prerequisite is a willingness on the part of the employee to equip himself to do his job more competently, having conceded that there may be gaps in his knowledge or capability which can be filled by suitable training. The environment in which the training takes place must be sufficiently informal to protect the employee from embarrassment when any weaknesses are revealed. His relationship with the trainer should be one of trust so that he is not inhibited from seeking information or explanation. The training experience itself should as near as possible mirror the realities of the job. When handling the re-training of adults (see pp. 149-52) there is an added factor for the trainer to take into account. He needs to ensure that the manager or supervisor is fully aware that the older worker may take longer to become proficient in the new skill. If patience and understanding are shown during the early stages of transfer, the pay-off is usually worthwhile in terms of long-term loyalty and reliability.

Post-training assessment

It is quite common for post-programme questionnaires to be given to the trainees towards the end of a programme, although it has already been pointed out that this may not be a very favourable time to attempt an evaluation. Nevertheless, it is not entirely to be ignored if it is suitably linked in with the total training activity and is not seen as the once-and-for-all assessment. It is possible to relate it to the expectations questionnaire given at the commencement of the programme. Similar questions may be asked to ascertain whether or not the participants felt that the expectations they identified were in fact met. To assist them to recall their feelings about the various sessions in a lengthy programme, the writer has found it helpful to produce a form, listing the main activities, for use as an *aide-mémoire*. At the end of each session they can jot down a few comments which will enable them to marshal their ideas when completing the post-programme questionnaire. The latter, whilst mainly addressing itself to the questions previously asked in the expectations questionnaire, would also provide an opportunity for additional comments which would not otherwise be covered. Both questionnaires would be anonymous to encourage honest and critical responses. Examples of corresponding questions are given in fig. 22.

For the reasons already mentioned, some training specialists avoid any attempt at evaluation on the last day of a programme, and favour the idea of sending a post-programme questionnaire to the participants several weeks or months later. The theory is that they will have had time to consider the value of the training and will be able to comment more realistically on its effects with the benefit of hindsight. In practice, the success rate of receiving the forms back completed tends to be low and the progress-chasing necessary by members of the training staff time-consuming. Every conceivable excuse for not completing the forms is proffered, some of them being related to the absence of follow-up on the part of the manager as already described, thus thwarting any good intentions of the employee to put what he has learned to good use. Another common reason for non-completion is that the employee quite genuinely does not know what to report. He may not be able to say that he has used a particular technique or that he has changed his approach to dealing with a specific type of problem because the opportunities have not so far presented themselves for him to try them out. However, his work colleagues may remark that they have noticed a change in the way in which he conducts himself which has only come about since he attended the training programme. This is not an uncommon phenomenon. Training is one of the means of supplementing data in the trainee's memory store. This data will not necessarily be required immediately after training but it will be available to him to be retrieved as and when appropriate. When

NOP Data Company Ltd Programme . . . .
Pre-training Questionnaire Dates . . . .

3. I expect the training to

(a) be less useful to me than spending the time at work
(b) add to my knowledge and experience of my job
(c) help me to use my existing knowledge better
(d) provide me with answers from the experts
(e) confirm what I know already
(f) be infinitely boring.

NOP Data Company Ltd Programme . . . .
Post-training Questionnaire Dates . . . .

3. The training

(a) will be less useful to me than if I had remained at work
(b) will add to my knowledge and experience of my job
(c) will help me to use my existing knowledge better
(d) provided me with the experts' answers
(e) helped to confirm what I knew already
(f) was infinitely boring.

Figure 22. *Examples of questions in pre- and post-training questionnaires*

this happens, he will not concern himself with the source of the data he uses to make a decision. It will be used instinctively in the same way as knowledge gained from experience. But when all is said and done, if the employee's performance in the job is what we are seeking to improve, then his manager is the most appropriate person to make the judgement as to whether or not the training has had the desired effect. It may therefore be more appropriate for *him* to complete a questionnaire on his subordinate's performance.

There are a number of aspects of training for which questionnaires are appropriate feedback mechanisms. These are in the main associated with the training environment and the conduct and organization of the programme rather than with the value of the training itself. For example, they tell the training staff what the participants thought of the administration, the venue, the food and accommodation, the pre-programme information, the practical training arrangements, the exercises, the visual aids, the handouts, and so on. But are questionnaires of equal value when dealing with the effects of the actual training? This is doubtful, unless the questions are formulated by the managers of the employees attending, since they will have established their employees' strengths and weaknesses in the first place and therefore will have to satisfy themselves that the objectives have been satisfactorily met. Questionnaires have their limitations. On the one hand it is difficult to formulate questions which are sufficiently precise to get to the nub of the issue and on the other the use of open-ended questions leads to subjectivity, misinterpretation and ambiguity.

The project as an evaluation mechanism

What then is the answer? The criteria for valid assessment are that we have to be objective and we have to be able to relate results to actual performance in the job, meeting the targets agreed. A direct link therefore has to be established between training and job. Merely carrying out training out of context with the job will not meet the criteria. One way in which the requirements can be met is by means of projects which have to be carried out in the workplace following training.

Each project, forming part of the trainee's normal work, employs principles or techniques covered in the training programme and may require a certain amount of research in the job. Evaluation of the project will establish how effective learning has been and will indicate whether or not further training is necessary. It is useful, particularly when the training programme is of one week's duration or more, to split it into two parts separated by a period of several weeks. A project based on the work of the first part is set, to be undertaken in the job during the interval and presented for evaluation during the second period. This evaluation can involve the training group and the trainer as well as the trainee's manager. If the participants on the programme come from different departments in the business, there is an additional benefit in that each trainee broadens his knowledge of the various functions represented. It is assumed from the foregoing that all the projects are different and unconnected, but there is a lot to be said for relating them to each other, if this is practicable. It is logical to train people in their normal work groups or in cross-functional groups. Projects can then be designed in which each participant has a specific role to play. Project work offers distinct advantages where evaluation is concerned. It encourages commitment on the part of the trainee whereas questionnaires do not. It also requires research and an end result which are directly work-related and are of visible benefit to the organization.

Action plans

Another approach to the evaluation of training programmes, which follows similar basic principles to the project, is the practice of producing action plans. The trainees are briefed at the start of the programme to the effect that training is of doubtful value unless it is eventually applied to one's job. During the programme they will be acquiring new knowledge or skills and they should constantly be asking themselves in what ways they expect to be able to apply their learning. At the end of the programme they are required to spend some time considering, and discussing with their fellow trainees, in what key areas of their jobs they think they may be able to make changes. These changes, which must of course be achievable within the constraints known to exist, become targets which are committed to an individual action plan. The objective of the action to be taken, the timing and the names of the people who will be involved are recorded. The personal nature of the plan is stressed and the trainer will normally not be privy to it unless the trainee wishes him to be. This helps to remove any worries that the employee may have about his shortcomings being recorded and/or debated in public. However, it is important that he undertakes to discuss the plan with his manager and they jointly agree to take action on it. If they also agree that the training department's input would be valuable, they are free to call upon this additional resource.

For the action plan scheme to be successful, the most careful briefing is vital at the outset. There may be resistance to the idea that the trainees should use the last hour or so of a training programme trying to predict how they will use their new knowledge in the job. They will claim that they cannot see at that stage in what way they will be able to apply it. If the briefing and preparation are inadequate, the result is likely to be that they will grossly over-estimate the task and for that reason alone will have difficulty. The positive changes promoted by training do not have to be earth-shattering. In fact, a relatively small change can often give rise to far-reaching overall effects. Trainees should not therefore be looking for major upheavals in their knowledge levels or in their methods of working, but positive moves, however small, which can be seen to show promise of improvement in the way in which they carry out their responsibilities. It may be simply a question of becoming aware of a personal weakness in a particular area in which further reading may be all that is necessary. Or perhaps a skill that the trainee has used already for some time, eg interviewing, can be improved by adopting suggestions of a relatively simple nature which have emerged on the course. The important thing is that, in those aspects of the employee's job in which the training can be seen to offer improvement prospects, positive plans must be laid to follow up the ideas whilst they are still fresh in the trainee's mind. If this is not done, they may well be forgotten and the benefits of the training will be lost.

Performance review and targetting

The performance review system,[24, 25] which often forms part of a management development scheme, though may also be used independently, has already been referred to in Chapters 2 and 3. It was stressed that it will only be successful if the manager recognizes its importance and is trained to discharge his role within it with competence. It is not a role he enjoys carrying out, because he may believe that he is being asked to play god. This is an over-reaction, since he is not called upon to make judgements on good or evil in his subordinates, but merely upon their competence or otherwise to discharge their duties in accordance with organizational goals. This is clearly one of the major aspects of his role, as the management looks to him to produce results from everyone under his control. He is therefore not doing his job adequately if he fails to meet this obligation.

The evaluation inherent in the performance review system is centred on targetting results. If targets are not properly formulated in the first place it is unlikely that the results can be measured and so the process will fail. Some people try to equate targets with aims or goals, but neither of these expressions meets the case in terms of the precision required of a target. Since in our evaluation we seek to establish whether or not a target has been met, we can only do so if it is precise and therefore measurable.[16] The example given in fig. 23 illustrates the distinction between the terms used in the case of a field service engineer.

Field Service Engineer		
	General definition	*Example in field service engineer's job*
Aim	The general direction in which the job is pointed.	To know how to service the Company's products in the field.
Goal	Expanded aim – more specific and detailed.	To be able to evaluate customer complaints and rectify equipment faults.
Target	Precise, unambiguous and based on performance. Includes conditions.	To respond within x hours to every customer complaint received, evaluate it and rectify faults in accordance with the product service manual and return to customer within y hours in at least 80% of jobs. Effectiveness of work to be such that no re-work for the same fault is necessary.

Figure 23. *Definitions of aims, goals and targets*

From fig. 23 it will be seen that neither aims nor goals are adequate in evaluation terms. There is no practical way of checking whether or not they are satisfied, since nothing is quantifiable and no standards are mentioned. The target, however, specifies a response time, conditions laid down in the service manual, a turn-around time and the number of completed jobs satisfying these requirements as a percentage of the total. The standard of work to be achieved is measured by the need for re-work for each fault.

The following conditions therefore have to apply before a goal may be considered a true objective or a target:

- ☐ the end behaviour or outcome must be defined in language which is understandable and unambiguous
- ☐ the means of checking the end behaviour or outcome must be clear
- ☐ precise standards of acceptable performance must be indicated
- ☐ the conditions (eg information, facilities, constraints) must be stated.

By 'end behaviour' we mean the performance demonstrated by the employee at the end of the task. He must be quite clear in his own mind at the outset precisely what is required of him and how his results will be measured. Lack of precision in defining the required outcome, in establishing standards and in clarifying the conditions may result in misunderstanding and failure to reach the required targets. There are numerous reasons why targets are not met, some of which are external and unavoidable. Poor definition of targets in the first place is inexcusable.

When training employees in targetting skills, there is sometimes resistance to the whole concept. Those who do not wish to be tied down to a system requiring such accuracy will say that it is not practicable to arrive at detailed targets in specific jobs. For example, because of the empiric nature of research and development work, it is argued that targets cannot be predicted because it is not known precisely what the outcome of such work will be. The training manager's response to this is that if the management does not know where its employees are going, why are they being employed at all? Whilst we have to show some sympathy for the idea that creative work demands a certain degree of freedom and flexibility, there is no case for allowing that freedom to get out of hand. Management expects, and is normally entitled to receive, results from all its employees and therefore should have some means of ascertaining whether or not the results are being achieved. Targets can in fact be agreed for experimental work, because it is known in advance what the working group is trying to achieve. There may be more reasons why such groups are unable to meet those targets as compared with others, but those reasons can be identified when results are assessed and the necessary allowances made for factors outside the group's control.

If it is possible to target for results in this manner, therefore, it should also be possible to measure the outcome. Clearly, some jobs will be easier to assess than others. Where the results do not match up, it is important to establish why in order to decide what action needs to be taken. As already said, some factors preventing targets from being met are not within the employee's control and should therefore not be held against him, although lessons for the future may be learnt. He may not, for instance, have had any influence on factors external to the organization; internal policies, procedures, rules, regulations, systems, etc may have changed; sources of supply or service within the organization may have let him down; there may have been lack of adequate supervision or difficulties arising within the work group which were not of his making, and so on. It may be that the manager can take suitable action himself on some of them. Where the reasons for the shortfall in results are assessed as being within the employee's own control, a careful examination is necessary. Have the failures arisen because of a lack of understanding of what was required, because of a shortage of the required knowledge or skill, or because the employee has failed to adopt the desired attitude to the job? One reason for failure which should not be overlooked is the possibility that the employee is in the wrong job. If it is established that this is so, then early action must be taken to avoid a recurrence. The manager may therefore have to use all the skill at his command to arrive at the real problem, if necessary enlisting some help from the training department. Some coaching (see pp. 137-9) may well be necessary in order to encourage a change in attitude or to guide the employee in the way in which the work should have been carried out.[17] Any new targets agreed for the ensuing period should incorporate action on the identified shortfalls. In other words, if further training is seen as a means of ensuring that similar targets will be met in the future, that training activity should be the subject of a specific target for the next period. That target will be validated at a de-briefing interview and evaluated at the next performance review meeting, assuming the time scales are appropriate.

Records

One important feature of any evaluation or validation system is the maintenance of adequate records. It is impossible for anyone to rely upon his memory to provide the information for satisfactory assessments to take place. Just as it is vital for managers to record events for the purpose of disciplinary and grievance procedures, so it is necessary that every thought and action is committed to paper for future reference in evaluation procedures. Failure to do this may result in one falling prey to the 'critical incident' phenomenon, in which weight is given to an event close to the time of the assessment out of all proportion to its importance. In other words, one's judgement is coloured in a subjective way by a factor, favourable or unfavourable, which comes to light about the time that an assessment is taking place. This difficulty is less likely to arise if notes have been made on the employee's performance on a fairly continuous basis throughout the review period. Any factors then arising about the time of the interview would only receive the weighting they deserved.

At a performance review interview, the manager and his subordinate review the period just ended and agree plans for the future. These plans have to be clearly understood by both parties and therefore need to be recorded. It is advisable that nothing is left to chance but that the employee reads, and signs that he has agreed to, the targets specified. This appears to be a somewhat formal procedure but it is the only way in which there is a fighting chance of the plans not being misunderstood and it may be many months before any such misunderstanding becomes evident. Without meaning to imply that employees are likely to be basically dishonest about this, it does provide a loophole for them to question the targets when they fail to meet them if they were not properly agreed and understood in the first place.

The form which records for evaluation purposes should take is not critical and there is room for flexibility to enable them to integrate suitably with other personnel records.[127] They should, however, be:

- ☐ standardized throughout the organization
- ☐ confidential and therefore stored safely, but accessible to those who need them
- ☐ agreed with the employee
- ☐ comprehensible
- ☐ comprehensive though concise, providing information which will be used as a basis for action
- ☐ accurate, unambiguous and consistent
- ☐ integrated with career records
- ☐ realistic in terms of cost
- ☐ monitored by a training specialist.

Summary

This chapter has underlined the importance of following-up the results of training in order to ensure that it will have the desired effect on organizational performance.[121] Failure to do so can mean that the training is forgotten and ultimately proves abortive. This is a sheer waste of valuable resources. An added penalty is the adverse effect on morale when an enthusiastic employee finds that his new skills are not being used.

Finding a suitable means to validate and evaluate training, particularly in areas where the end results are not very clear cut, creates a problem. Effective transferability from training to job demands that the training itself is directly work-related unless it is known that the participants are capable of converting theory to practice in their jobs. The methods suggested satisfy the criterion that the measurements are made in the job rather than in the training. It is, after all, the performance in the job that matters and all evaluation systems should take account of this fact.

Without adequate records the process of evaluation can become a hit-and-miss activity with little continuity and a success rate depending almost entirely on the manager's memory. This is hardly the way to run a business.

Chapter 9

Training Resources

Training as an investment

An oft-repeated plea of the training manager is that his function's activities should be treated as an investment and not as an overhead. Although undoubtedly the general climate and attitudes have changed, in particular since the passing of the Industrial Training Act in 1964 and the advent of the Training Boards, there is still unhappily a body of opinion which sees training as an expense, even a luxury. There are a number of reasons for this. Undoubtedly one of them stems from the school of experience theory. Many managers will say that they did not have to be trained to get where they are today. 'Only apprentices and factory workers need training, because we want them to turn out good products . . . .' What they will not readily concede is that properly planned and executed training brings employees at all levels up to an acceptable standard of proficiency in their jobs over a shorter time scale than by other means. Learning from experience is successful only when certain conditions are satisfied. In order to be able to acquire knowledge and skills, the employee has to have:

- ☐ motivation
- ☐ capacity to learn and perform
- ☐ opportunities and facilities
- ☐ skilled guidance.

The first two may be satisfied if the incentives are right and the selection procedures are satisfactory. The last two involve an investment which there is often a reluctance to provide. Opportunities, facilities and skilled guidance to some mean merely a seat next to a skilled worker. It is hoped and expected that the employee will eventually become equally skilled by the process of learning by experience. Sometimes favourable factors will combine to make it work. More often than not the facilities are inadequate and the skilled worker, whilst first class at his own job, is unable to pass on his skills to someone else. Time and money spent in providing suitable facilities and training the skilled man in instructional skills would pay dividends for a long time to come.

It is a paradox that managers and supervisors cry out for output but say that they cannot afford the time for training their employees, when a modest investment in training could bring about an early and lasting improvement in work performance and consequently output.

Another reason for seeing training as an overhead is that although it may contribute to increased production as suggested above, in financial terms it is not regarded as a direct expense. Indirect expenses are, of course, highly vulnerable when economies have to be made and they are the first to suffer cutbacks. The value of benefits from training is not so easily assessed and this side of the account is therefore seldom calculated. On the credit side, some managements only consider the return from Training Board grants because the figures are easily identifiable in the accounts (see pp. 225-6). A fundamental change in accounting for the costs and benefits of training is therefore called for, and a step in the right direction would be improvements in evaluation procedures as suggested in the last chapter. If a financial value could be placed on the benefits of training, managements may begin to see it as an investment.

Top management commitment

The commitment of the top management in an organization is essential if the training function is to make its contribution to the success of the business.[122] Resources will not be forthcoming if those who hold the purse strings are not convinced of the value of the service. How can they be persuaded to support the activity?

Training departments have to prove their effectiveness in a tangible way before they can expect to get unqualified support from the top. The attitude of senior managers to training usually reflects their own experience in the past. If their previous experience has been in an environment where training was valued, and they themselves have benefited from it, half the battle will have already been won. Such managers will be conspicuous by their readiness to discuss matters of training interest with the training specialists. Those who believe in the school of experience will tend to be more remote and may not show the same interest in carrying on a dialogue with the training department. Yet it is a dialogue that is required in order to impress upon management the value of the training function. Some training managers are content to soldier on doing what they have an open authority to do without any contact with the top management at all, unless something goes wrong. Instead, they should seize every opportunity to show the management what the training department is doing, what success it is achieving and the ways in which the activity can be developed for the good of the business. If they are not already represented at the business planning stage (see p. 24) they should continually lobby for that representation, since without it they can hardly be said to have reached the starting post. Business is dynamic and constantly changing and so training managers are encouraged to operate in a proactive as well as a reactive way. In other words, they might sometimes initiate training action rather than simply wait for training needs to arise through some other agency. They are in contact with every department in the business and thus get to know a good deal about what is going on. They can therefore see scope for training, often on quite a wide scale, long before the needs are evident to other people. In organizations where parochialism among individual managers still reigns supreme, there are opportunities for training staff who, like top management, have the advantage of being able to observe the business as an entity, to discover ways and means of improving its overall performance. This may mean involving the directors and senior managers themselves, both as participants and as trainers.

One pitfall to be avoided when discussing training with management is peddling theories which have so far not been proved. Managers are used to dealing with realities and therefore the more facts that can be offered to substantiate one's claims, the better. Facts include failures as well as successes. Because of the difficulties often encountered in winning support, there is a temptation to overstate one's case and so increase the scepticism. It is far better to be modest and realistic about achievements and disasters, and to avoid exaggerating in order to win votes. Time should be taken to calculate the costs/benefits of each proposal and to estimate the penalties of not taking the suggested action. It should also be remembered that a senior manager's time will be valuable and this will limit the time in which he may have to be won over. This underlines the need to present a concise but convincing case. Knowing the man one is dealing with is extremely helpful. What are his own strengths and weaknesses, likes and dislikes, etc? What particular points does one have to concentrate on when putting a proposal to him? Often just one ally on the top management team can act as the training manager's mouthpiece and ensure that proposals have a sympathetic hearing. If one has to put one's own case, it is good policy to behave as a member of the management team. Little will be gained by going cap-in-hand to plead for resources or for that matter by adopting the pose of a door-to-door salesman. The aim should therefore be to demonstrate a positive desire to work in concert with one's management colleagues to promote business success.

Size of the training department

There are no hard and fast rules as to how large the training department should be in a given organization. The size and the composition of the function will be influenced by a number of considerations, such as:

- ☐ the management attitude to training

- ☐ the organization structure
- ☐ the track record of training in the past
- ☐ the cost
- ☐ the state of the economy and other external pressures.

The attitude of management to training has been mentioned earlier. There are several factors which affect it. History usually plays a significant part. At some time in the past the decision will have been made to appoint a training specialist. In most cases his continued employment would mean that he has an acceptable record of success, but there may also be instances where it has simply become custom and practice to maintain the function. While a prudent management will be carefully monitoring the performance of all its departments, there will be some who, recognizing their inability to measure results, may be content to assume that any training is a good thing.

There is, of course, no better way to convince management of the value of a service than by having a good track record. Where effectiveness has been demonstrated, firms have been more readily persuaded to accept the personnel function and with it the training function as an integral part of management, giving it the support it needs. The question may be asked, 'How does one establish a track record without having support in the first place?' This is certainly an obstacle, though not an insuperable one. It is possible to start in a small way, ensuring that whatever one does is carried out in a professional manner and will be met with the right responses from those involved. If influential people at different levels in the organization can be won round, by deeds not just words, a reputation can be built up which will not escape the notice of top management.

For some years another factor which undoubtedly influenced employers to maintain a training department was the presence of the Industrial Training Boards. The financial implications of the levy/grant system had the effect of encouraging some firms to carry out training to the Boards' recommendations, although the incentives tended to diminish over the years with the gradual reduction in returns possible. The practical help and advice available from the Boards was considerable, particularly for small employers who would otherwise have been fairly isolated from this point of view. Unhappily for them, some Boards have now been disbanded (see p. 226).

Management's recruitment policy will also affect the scope and responsibilities of the training department. ITB inducements notwithstanding, there are still employers who prefer to buy in skilled employees rather than have the problem of providing suitable training in the appropriate skills. This clearly reduces the scope of the training department, if indeed there is a training department at all in such circumstances.

The organizational structure will have an impact on both the size and the composition of the training department. The functions represented and the number of employees in each function will to some extent determine the type of training service which is necessary. The importance that management attaches to the training of functional groups will also influence the resources which will be allocated to them. For example, if an establishment is a self-contained manufacturing plant, its workforce will consist of a wide spectrum of functions. If over half the employees are assembly workers and only 5 per cent are clerks, the likelihood is that much more training attention will be given to factory than to clerical departments. In such an organization, the number of managers employed will be smaller than the number of supervisors, so that one would expect that training for the latter would be seen as more important than for the former. However in this instance, in spite of the numbers involved, it may be considered that management training has a higher priority for other reasons.

The relative proportions of trainees in the various functions in an organization will affect the cost of training. Where there is a predominance of management training, for instance, the cost is likely to be high, whereas clerical or on-the-job factory training may be much lower on a *per capita* basis. The external influences on costs, such as a declining national economy and adverse international trading conditions, will bring about closer scrutiny of the training department's activities in an attempt to keep its outgoings within acceptable limits. This may result in certain activities being suspended and full-time staff being replaced with part-time. In extreme cases, the objectives of the training function may well be re-written in order that the garment may be cut according to the cloth available.

Thus it is clear that the size and structure of the training department in an organization can depend on so many different factors. Any attempt to generalize about it would be challenged since, in a sense, every organization is a special case. Certain points can however be made. The majority of firms in the engineering industries, for example, are so small that they would not be able to justify a specialist training officer. Any training activities that go on in such businesses are instigated by line management and tend to be unco-ordinated. By the time the size of the concern reaches about 200 employees, the personnel role tends to emerge and with it some responsibility for training. It is not until the establishment exceeds about 500 employees that we see a significant increase in training officers employed. They appear in over 50 per cent of such firms, but many of them are part-time, often combining the role with other personnel duties. Whilst it is accepted that training is an integral part of personnel management, there is a distinct disadvantage in combining duties in this way. This arises from the fact that personnel activities include the inevitable day-to-day problems which cannot wait. For example: personal matters raised by employees require immediate attention so that they interfere with work as little as possible; action on collective problems brought by union officials cannot often be deferred; staffing emergencies resulting from absenteeism, etc must be dealt with immediately; and so on. Such preoccupations mean that the personnel-cum-training officer finds himself relegating apparently less pressing training issues to the bottom of the pile. In the long run, training is likely to be sadly neglected. For this reason, care needs to be taken when attempting to combine training with any other function. The priorities of the different functions have to be clearly defined.

The appointment of a full-time training specialist will be decided upon after considering the organization's total needs and after comparing the relative costs of setting up an internal function and using external resources. It is important that when computing the cost of having one's own training officer, the *total* costs involved are taken into account. These may be anything up to twice the basic salary paid, when national insurance, pensions contributions and the appropriate overheads are included.

An Institute of Personnel Management report on *The Industrial Training Officer – His Background and His Work*[123] was compiled from research carried out in industrial establishments in the south-east in the mid-1960s by the Department of Occupational Psychology at Birkbeck College, London University. The table reproduced in fig. 24 shows how many establishments out of a sample of 394 employed training officers. They are categorized according to the size of the establishment.

Size of establishment	*Number*	*Percentage with full-time training officer*	*Percentage with part-time training officer*	*Percentage with full-time or part-time training officer*
100- 249	98	5.2	17.3	22.5
250- 499	86	8.1	23.3	31.4
500- 999	117	21.8	28.5	50.3
1000-1999	65	34.8	16.7	51.5
2000-4999	24	45.8	25.0	70.8
5000+	4	100.0	0	100.0

Figure 24. *Percentage of industrial establishments in south-east England employing training officers in 1966*

The increase in the percentage of firms employing full-time training officers as the company size increases is predictable. The need for a full-time professional to manage and co-ordinate the function in the medium to large units is self-evident. The status of training in the company structure demands this if it is to be effective. What is perhaps surprising from the above figures, therefore, is that nearly 30 per cent of firms employing between 2000 and 4999 people in 1966 did not have a training officer at all and of those which did over 35 per cent had part-timers. The report indicated that practices varied considerably between different industries.

The writer has not been able to obtain statistics for the present time which would enable comparisons to be made with these figures. But for the recession in the years since the IPM report, an increase in the number of organizations employing training officers would have been very likely; things had certainly been moving in that direction. Instead, the inevitable cutbacks in the levels of indirect staff in many organizations resulting from economic pressures would have had the reverse effect and it is doubtful whether even the 1966 position has been maintained.

It is tempting to draw conclusions from such statistics that the training performance of organizations can be directly related to the numbers of training officers employed. This would, of course, be a false assumption, when in essence all the figures are telling us is that certain companies are at least playing lip service to the need for a formal training structure. It is hoped that the managements concerned are genuinely convinced that such a function is needed, rather than simply believing it is something which they morally ought to provide.

Some quite small firms which do not feel that they can justify an in-house training function will be able to satisfy their needs with the assistance of carefully selected outside consultants. Additionally, prudent managements will recognize that practically everyone in the business should be involved in training and will therefore see to it that their managers and supervisors are adequately equipped with the skills to be able to carry out their training roles effectively.

A 1987 BIM/CBI Working Party report on *The Making of British Managers*, resulting from a survey of 2500 companies the previous year, stated that 'Somewhat over half of all UK companies appear to make *no* formal provision for the training of their managers....' It also concluded that those employing between 20 and 99 people were more likely to fit into that category than the larger businesses. In spite of these depressing statistics, there are welcome indications in 1988 that more employers are beginning to recognize that training in general, not only for managers, is something which will help them to meet their commitments more readily in an upturning economy. Whether they are putting the function in the hands of the professionals, or simply tackling it themselves with the active involvement of their line managers, is hard to say in the absence of suitable research data. Recruitment advertising seems to suggest that there is no shortage of jobs for experienced training specialists, although the combined roles of 'personnel/recruitment/safety *cum* training officer' seem to persist, even in organizations of over 1000 employees.

Any move in the direction of improved training performance is, of course, to be welcomed. One of the encouraging indications of changing management attitudes towards training, with resultant benefits for their organizations, is the high standard of some of the 1200 or so entries in the National Training Award scheme in 1987, its first year of operation.[155] The award winners, and a large number of those who narrowly missed being award winners, clearly demonstrated that training contributed significantly to profit growth and cost reduction, to say nothing of other aspects of organizational performance. A useful spin-off of the scheme was the identification of what were deemed to be the good and the bad practices in training.

In organizations where the professional training role is combined with another role, the training officer is likely to be operating in the traditional sense, that is as an organizer rather than a practitioner of training. He will sub-contract the trainer or instructor role as and when required and the only practical support of a regular nature will be clerical. In other words, he will probably share a typist or secretary with another function or if he has his own secretarial support, only a proportion of that support will be directed towards training activities. Even when he reaches the stage of specializing in training full-time, he may have to share secretarial services with another executive. This raises the same difficulties of establishing priorities as already mentioned in connection with the personnel-cum-training officer.

As organizations increase in size, say over 1000 employees, we see separate training sections emerging, although they may still be part of the personnel department. The variations in the organizational structure of such sections are numerous. The training policy will dictate whether the training section will be essentially organizers and administrators of training or whether they will carry out some of the training themselves. In the latter case, specialist trainers may be employed. For example, if there is a substantial need for craft training, craft instructors may form part of the team. A significant requirement for management and supervisory training may mean that the training officer himself may be trained to carry out some of the required duties. In technology-based industries it is not unusual to find a training officer or instructor skilled in technical instruction. Where a significant amount of training is carried out by the organization's training staff, a sound administrative back-up is essential. The reasons for this are discussed on pp. 70-6.

In the larger groups of companies, it is common to have a two-tier training structure. Whilst each establishment within the group has its own training section geared to the specific needs of that establishment, a central training department exists at headquarters to determine overall group policy, provide professional advice and/or supply common needs training. The last mentioned service is justified where employees in different establishments in the organization have similar training requirements and it would be uneconomical or impracticable to provide the same facilities in each of those establishments. The cost of using external facilities can often be avoided if sufficient employees with the same needs may be brought together for a centrally organized training programme. The training department at group level can again take different forms. If it is purely a policy-making body it will consist of a small nucleus of training officers with a broad experience in the profession. Often some of them will have been promoted from establishments within the group. Where practical training services are provided from the centre, there will probably be a number of training officers and/or trainers, each of whom specializes in a particular functional area, for example: management, supervision, marketing, technical, financial, data processing.

The many permutations found in training departments make it difficult to generalize about lines of responsibility. For reasons already discussed, it is highly desirable for training to be represented at board or top management level. If it is not, there is a danger that top management will be cushioned from the activities and needs of the training department. Training directors are still quite rare but personnel directors have become much more common in recent years. Where personnel management is directly represented at the top in this way, the personnel manager reports to the director. The training manager may either be responsible directly to the director or through the personnel manager. In organizations where there are management development managers or advisers, it is not uncommon for them to form part of the personnel function and thus have close links with training, since certain aspects of training are essential to a management development system. Fig. 25 is an example of a training hierarchy.

Qualifications and skills of training staff

It has already been emphasized that training management has become a profession in its own right. It follows that there are qualifications which lay the foundation for a career in training. The two major institutions offering such qualifications are the Institute of Personnel Management (IPM)[15] and the Institute of Training and Development (ITD).[14] The IPM's membership examination syllabus is in three stages, one of the major areas in Stage 2 being 'employee development'. Candidates must be enrolled students of the Institute but they may choose the method of study which is most convenient to them, eg full-time, part-time or evening attendance at a suitable further education establishment, correspondence courses or independent study. The major qualifications of the ITD are the 'Certificate in Training and Development' and the 'Diploma in Training Management'. The certificate is a basic requirement for Associate Membership of the Institute. The diploma is seen as a major qualification in training and is normally required for corporate membership. Candidates studying for the diploma are required to be registered with the Institute as students and the method of study for

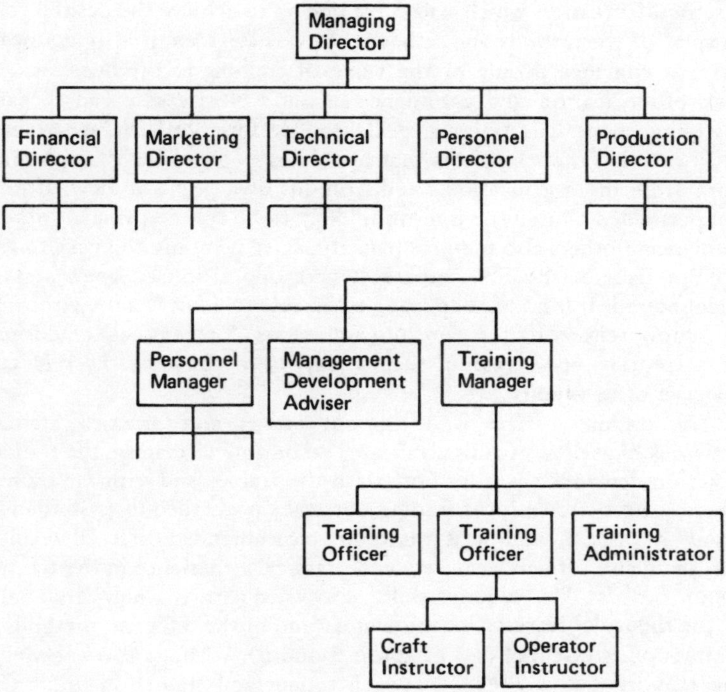

Figure 25. *An example of a training hierarchy in a manufacturing firm employing over 2000 employees*

both certificate and diploma qualifications is usually by attendance at an approved further education establishment. All the above qualifications include a work-related project.

It is clearly desirable for those who wish to make a career in training management to satisfy the requirements of either or both of these institutions. Not only does one acquire a broad working knowledge of the profession by academic study, but institute membership provides the opportunity for a wide exchange of knowledge and experience with others in the field. It also gives access to information through the libraries and information services, and enables one to contribute to the promotion of the profession at local, national and international levels.

Proficiency in training management requires practical know-how and certain skills and attitudes in addition to academic knowledge. In the first place, the writer firmly believes that entering the training profession should be a conscious decision, taken for the right reasons. It is not desirable that an employee should be channelled into training simply as a matter of expediency, that is, to fill a temporary void or to run down in a leisurely way to retirement. Success in training demands a sense of vocation which will drive one on to achieve the desired goals in spite of frustrations and setbacks. As we have seen, it is by no means easy to convince people of the value of training to the business, and lack of dedication and confidence in one's efforts can lead to early discouragement. The training specialist therefore needs to be certain in his own mind that the paths that he wishes to tread are the right ones both from the organization's and from his own point of view. If he is not persuaded himself, he is most unlikely to be able to persuade others. Convincing others also requires tenacity, since it is only too easy to give up the fight at the first setback. Where opposition to one's ideas is encountered, it is no use expecting to be able to achieve a breakthrough by simply reiterating the same old arguments. A means has to be found of presenting one's case in such a way as to convince the reluctant manager of its validity.

The training officer who has not carried out practical training activities himself is at a disadvantage. To be able to manage the training function demands empathy both with the trainer and with the trainee. There is no better way of finding out what is entailed in a job than by doing it oneself, and it is therefore recommended that all training managers and officers acquire some practical experience in the training room.[18, 124, 125] This requires skills of a varied nature. An understanding of the theory of learning, of motivation and of the different methods of instruction is essential (see Chapters 5 and 6). Without this knowledge the rapport that is needed between trainer and trainee in order that satisfactory learning takes place is unlikely to be achieved. Trainers need to be skilled in the use of training equipment. If they demonstrate when using visual aids that they do not have the required competence they rapidly lose credibility. It is always assumed that specialists are proficient in the use of the tools of their trade. In the trainers' case these also include other communication skills. They must be able to speak and write well, and they should be numerate. The ability to think in concepts is also important, since most training involves the development and application of ideas; the right balance must be obtained between theory and practice. The skills listed under the various training methods in Chapter 6 are all significant to the trainer.

No training officer can be expected to become a walking encyclopedia in the training room; he cannot be an expert on all the wide range of topics covered in training programmes. His role should be seen as facilitating learning by providing opportunities. If unable to supply answers himself when required, he should know where to go for them and be able to point the trainees in the right direction.

When building up a training function, the manager has to plan the human resources needed with a certain amount of skill. So often the structure of a growing training department develops in a random fashion without due consideration of the needs. It is important that the manager investigates the training requirements of the organization over the period of its medium- to long-term plan and computes staff needs accordingly (see pp. 24-6). It is dangerous to recruit staff on the basis of short-term requirements; before long one finds that the structure of the department is no longer appropriate to handle future demands. Usually, training departments are fairly small and it is therefore vital that the individual members are versatile and flexible. Large departments can justify specialists. Small ones need generalists unless the vast majority of the work entailed is specialized.

Rightly or wrongly, employees frequently look to training staff to set an example. Double standards should be avoided: if a training manager advocates a participative style in the training room he should be on his guard against abandoning such a style when running his own department; similarly, a trainer who impresses trainees with the importance of complying with company rules can hardly expect his own breach of them to go unnoticed.

In September 1976 the Manpower Services Commission set up a Training of Trainers Committee to 'consider the roles, relationships, training needs and current training of those staff who have specific responsibilities for training, and to make recommendations to the Director of Training on:

(a) the pattern of training for such staff
(b) the provision of such training
(c) appropriate means of its evaluation and, where necessary, of its oversight and approval.'

The committee produced two reports, the first in July 1978 covering those who 'have responsibilities for organizing, managing or advising on training'. The second report, published in 1980, concentrated on the 'direct trainers' or those who 'have a specific responsibility for directly helping people to acquire, develop and apply the knowledge and skills they need'. Training specialists are referred to these reports and to the MSC's later leaflet 'Learn how to learn', which provide helpful guidance for training both professionals and other specialist staff with a day-to-day responsibility for training. Guidelines for reviewing training arrangements are also given in the Commission's booklet 'Decisions about training'.[53]

The MSC pledges itself to continue promoting joint action, with its partners, on the development of trainers and educators. Among other things, they want to encourage the establishment of national standards in trainer training which, of course, entails identifying the gaps in their expertise so that the necessary steps may be taken to fill them. The setting up of networks of providers of such training, through which standards of competence and quality may be influenced, is seen as important. Special emphasis is also placed on encouraging trainers to make optimum use of open learning techniques and new training methods.[125]

The training administrator

A common response to the question 'Why do you want to do personnel work?' is 'Because I like people.' In reality, training, like all personnel management, involves a good deal of research, organization, planning and office routine and only a limited amount of direct contact with people. The training administrator who believes that she is going to spend most of her time playing the hostess will be very disappointed. Nevertheless, however limited this part of her job may be, the administrator's skill in dealing with people is as important as that of the trainer himself. One of the prerequisites of effective training is that the trainee is in the right frame of mind to learn. This means removing as many anxieties and uncertainties as possible, even to the extent of showing that the training staff are not to be feared! The administrator will often be the first contact the trainee has with the training department, either on the telephone, in the office or in the training room on the first day of a programme. She therefore has a vital role to play (see pp. 70-76).

It is often the case, particularly where the training department is small, that a typist or secretary is employed to carry out training administration duties as an addition to her normal responsibilities. This is fine, provided she is suited to the work and is adequately trained to carry out the requirements of the job properly. It is quite wrong to assume that a secretary or typist will automatically be an effective training administrator without any kind of preparation. The job demands a clear understanding of its importance and therefore of the high standards which are required if it is to make its true contribution to the success of the training function. The standards which appear to be acceptable in some office jobs may not be good enough in that of the administrator, since the most minor mistake can have disproportionate effects. Typing errors in exercises or handouts, for example, divert the attention of trainees from their learning and by giving them an excuse to talk about something else, provide them with a welcome respite from the tasks they have been given. The disruptive effect can be quite extraordinary. Furthermore, any sign of inefficiency or inaccuracy will undermine the confidence that the employees place in the department. The administrator's job is not for the amateur.

Another requirement of the administrator is that she is a self-starter. Her professionalism needs to be developed to the point where she is not dependent on anyone else to get things done. If external venues for courses have to be vetted, she should be competent to carry out that task without assistance. If equipment has to be hired for training purposes, she should be fully capable of assessing it and taking the necessary action. If trainees have problems of an administrative or personal nature before, during or after training, she should be able to handle them independently. The job of the trainer is training and he should not have to concern himself with administrative problems. He should be able to delegate such work to the member of staff trained and employed for the purpose.

Visual aids are normally the responsibility of the administrator and she has to ensure that they are properly maintained. It is also extremely useful if she is able to use the equipment. It is not at all difficult to train the administrator to set up and operate film and slide projectors, closed circuit television equipment, etc and so leave other training staff to concentrate on their dialogue with the trainees.[126] When equipment breaks down, this skill is particularly valuable, since the trainer does not have to suspend training to sort out the problem himself. When using television equipment, it is also very difficult to perform as trainer and camera operator at one and the same time.

The administrator often finds herself in charge of training records.[127] There is some logic in this, because she is in touch with all the training activities and is also responsible for the course nominations procedure. Record-keeping is more likely to be satisfactorily executed by someone who is thus involved with the total function than by someone employed solely for clerical duties. All organizational aspects of the training department's activities therefore revolve around the administrator. If the department is large enough to boast a training library, she will be responsible for it. If the organization is represented at careers conventions in schools, she is most likely to have to make the necessary arrangements. She will also have control over the stocks of training material and stationery. She will be accountable for all training administration procedures and should reasonably have some say in how they are set up.

To summarize, the successful training administrator will have the following qualities:

- ☐ a demeanour which will make her acceptable to employees at all levels
- ☐ high standards of office skill, eg typing, record-keeping, use of the telephone, stock control
- ☐ organizing ability and attention to detail: a self-starter
- ☐ an aptitude for trouble-shooting and for handling personal problems
- ☐ ability to set up, use and keep in good order all training aids
- ☐ mobility: should be able to drive a car and be prepared to travel at very short notice
- ☐ willingness to be accountable for many aspects of the job
- ☐ infinite patience and forbearance.

The writer has been taken to task by a reader for implying that the role of the trainer is a male preserve, while that of the administrator is a female one. This is neither intentional nor, in his view, desirable. He would like to see far more women becoming professional trainers, but remarkably few seem to come forward. Men are not unknown in administration and his own experience suggests that it is a first-class training ground for the would-be trainer, providing as it does an overview of the complete training function. The reality has to be faced, however, that more men than women are trainers and more women than men become administrators. In fairness, one reason for the latter situation may be that women tend to be more successful in the training administration role than men.

Budgeting

Budgeting is the concern of training managers in common with all involved in running the business.[16, 128] In earlier chapters, we examined training objectives and plans, showing how forecasts of future training activities were made. The budget is a means of expressing these forecasts in the form of an achievable plan. It can be in financial or in quantitative terms, is agreed in advance of the particular period of activity covered, and indicates what policy it is proposed to adopt during that period in order to meet the organization's goals. Throughout the period of the budget the actual results are closely monitored, say on a monthly basis, and the reasons for any variances from the forecasts are explored. The budget should not be seen as a bureaucratic irritation or as a strait-jacket leaving little room for manoeuvre. It does, of course, introduce an element of control, not only in corporate terms. The individual manager should welcome the discipline of preparing and managing within a budget as an aid to running his own department's affairs efficiently.

The management's attitude towards training is often indicated by the size of the training department's budget (see p. 180). Those training managers who can honestly say that their budget is adequate are few and far between. When budget allocations are made to training departments, as with other overhead functions, economic considerations often take precedence over practical ones. In other words, a sum will be allocated which the organization can afford rather than what is appropriate to the needs. This means that the training manager may have to fight hard for adequate funds to meet his training targets. Since as often as not he will have to accept a compromise, he also has to learn to live within his means.

Budgets need care in preparation. Underestimating requirements can be fatal, not only for the year in question but also for the future. It is not easy to go back and ask for more if the allocation is found to be inadequate, and once having established a figure for one year there will be opposition to increasing it for the next. For the same reason, underspending on one year's budget can result in a reduction in the funds available in future years.

The work of most training departments, in budgeting terms, is mainly concerned with expenditure. A profit and loss account is seldom attempted because of the difficulties of measuring results in terms of financial value. When training departments are said to have made a profit, the income side of the account is usually confined to Training Board grants, while substantial items of expenditure, such as trainees' salaries or wages and the costs of lost work output during training, are conveniently left out. If the training department operates as an internal consultancy or training centre, providing services to other parts of a large organization on a commercially viable basis, it then only has to concern itself with fixing its charges so as to recover its actual outgoings and, if required, achieve an appropriate margin. Its profit and loss account which will be an internal departmental document may then take the form of the example shown in fig. 26. No significance should be attached to the individual figures used, which were arbitrarily chosen by way of illustration only. It is assumed in this example that the central training department is responsible for the training board arrangements for the headquarters of which it is part, but not for those

The NOP Group of Companies	*Department:* Central Training
Budgeted Profit and Loss Account	*Year ending:* 31.12.1987

	1985 *Budget £000's*	**1984** *Actual £000's*
INCOME		
– from training services	180	162.3
– from training board grants (headquarters only)	1.8	1.2
Total income	181.8	163.5
COSTS		
– fixed (rent, rates, heat, light etc)	18.5	17.1
– maintenance and repairs	2.5	2.5
– telephone charges	7.0	6.2
– training wages/salaries and employment costs	79.0	74.4
– training materials	9.0	8.3
– stationery and photocopying/printing	5.5	3.8
– travelling (including car expenses)	12.5	10.2
– training of training staff	2.0	1.8
– staff expenses	4.0	3.5
– external venue costs	20.0	18.1
– external consultants' fees/expenses	5.5	4.1
– external liaison (schools, etc)	2.0	1.5
– training board levy (headquarters only)	–	–
– further education fees	7.0	6.4
– training awards	3.0	2.5
Total costs	177.5	160.4
Profit/(loss)	4.3	3.1

Figure 26. *Budgeted profit and loss account for an internal training consultancy*

of the group as a whole. The headquarters is exempt from levy (see p. 226) but is able to claim some additional grants for specific training.

The account shown is, of course, a summary which is built up from more detailed information under each heading. As previously mentioned, a budget may be in quantitative as well as financial terms. In this instance, the number of activities, eg training courses and programmes or consultancy projects, would have to be forecast in order to establish the charges which would have to be made to the client establishments. This is usually done on a trainer-day basis, the rate being calculated from the total number of trainer-days involved in the activity and the total costs which have to be recovered. Thus:

$$\text{Budgeted Rate per trainer-day} = \frac{\text{total budgeted costs of department + budgeted profit (if any)}}{\text{total number of budgeted trainer-days.}}$$

Where costs, such as external consultancy fees, are markedly different from normal costs, separate rates may have to be established for these special cases. The rates should also have a built-in contingency factor which to some extent anticipates the possibility of cancelled activities.

Having established the rate per trainer-day the total programme cost is easily computed and can be divided by the number of participants to arrive at a *per capita* charge. The difficulty that may then arise is that fewer participants than budgeted for may in fact attend. The immediate result is a loss of revenue. If the structure of the department's activities lends itself to this approach, a break-even analysis of each activity can be helpful here. This simple technique establishes the number of participants needed for a programme to be financially viable. Fig. 27 shows the basic principle of this form of analysis.

In drawing such a graph, the fixed costs line (a) is first established. These are costs, such as rent, rates, heat and light, which have to be met irrespective of the number of participants and can therefore be represented by a horizontal line. Variable costs (b) are those which increase with the number of trainees, eg stationery. They should be calculated for the maximum number of participants expected and a straight line graph drawn between the fixed-cost line at zero participants and the appropriate point of total cost for the maximum number, in this case 20. The revenue line (c) is drawn from the graph zero to the point of the total income which would be derived from the maximum number of participants. Where this line cuts the variable cost line (b) is the break-even point, that is the point at which a loss is turned into a profit. In fig. 27 this is at 13 participants. This form of analysis may be particularly useful nearer the time of a training programme when the costs initially budgeted for may have changed significantly.

By far the majority of training departments are concerned with expenditure-only budgets and do not therefore have to calculate charges to clients. Since they are not required to break-even or make a 'profit',

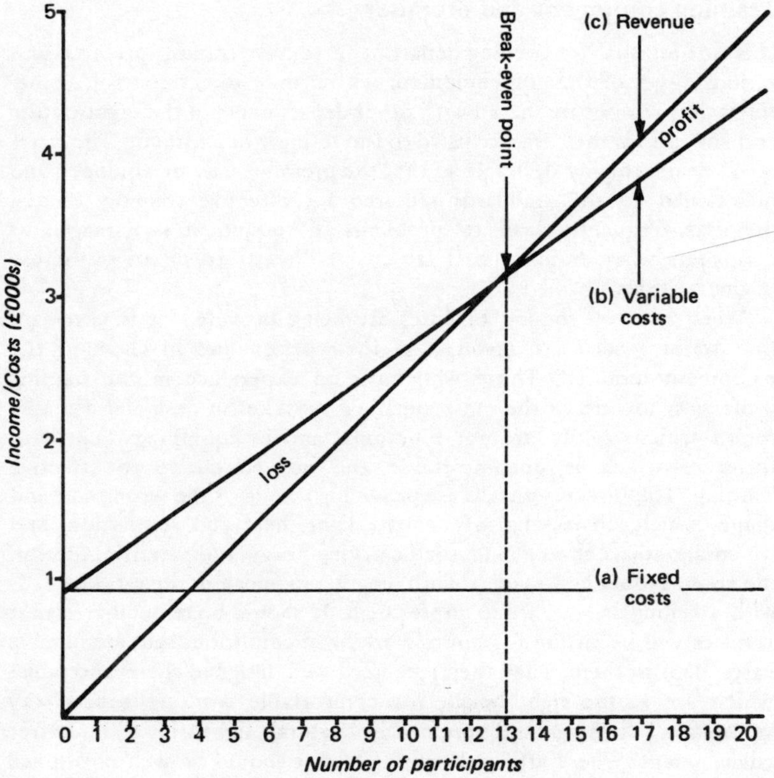

Figure 27. *Example of break-even analysis for establishing viability of training programme*

they may tend to take their budgeting responsibilities less seriously. It is, however, in their own long-term interests to give the matter their critical attention. Whether we like it or not, our efforts are measured in financial terms and we should be conscious of this and equip ourselves to cope with it. Budgeting is an important aspect of a manager's job and failure to carry it out satisfactorily will do nothing for his reputation and his future in the organization. There are many influences on whether or not a budget reflects reality, but that should not deter the manager from doing the best he can with the facilities available. Simply increasing the actual figures for last year by x per cent all round to reflect inflation is not budgeting. Each item demands individual attention and consideration of the factors that may affect it during the ensuing period. Even with such care and attention, forecasts will not be met every time, but they will be far more accurate than those arrived at by sheer guesswork.

Training equipment and premises

It is not unusual for training departments to have training premises and various types of training equipment within their direct control. Sometimes the premises are shared with other departments in the organization and sometimes they are exclusive to the training department. The latter is, of course, highly desirable so that the premises may be equipped and maintained to the standards required for effective training. Shared premises frequently lead to problems if equipment is damaged or disappears when training staff are unable directly to supervise the use of the facilities.

When new off-the-job facilities are being provided, it is necessary that training staff are involved in their design and in choosing the equipment required. Those who have no experience in the training profession can make the most appalling mistakes in designing training rooms which simply are not functional and in equipping them with furniture which is uncomfortable and not conducive to effective learning. The obvious pitfalls are providing rooms of the wrong size and shape, which are lacking in adequate light, heat and ventilation, and which are adjacent to a main road carrying heavy, noisy traffic. Ideally, the room should be square or with length and width in the ratio of 4 : 3, with a ceiling at least three metres high. It should be remembered that trainees will be sitting for hours working in conditions that are in most cases alien to them. They therefore need well designed chairs and tables which are at the right height for comfortable working, satisfactory ventilation, heating and preferably natural light, in a noise-free environment. Where artificial light is used it should be well positioned and provide adequate illumination. An absence of any of these factors can cause discomfort, fatigue and distraction from the learning process.

It is a mistake to install a telephone in a training room. The disruption caused by someone having to answer the 'phone during the training programme affects everyone in the room, and does not end with replacement of the receiver. People go on thinking about it long after the event, with obvious effects. Telephones should be located away from the training room and messages passed on to participants or trainers at appropriate breaks in the programme.

The training room should be equipped with a number of suitable power points strategically placed. It is not only restrictive to have to use one socket with adaptors to supply several pieces of electrical equipment. It also constitutes a safety hazard both from the point of view of overloading the circuit and increasing the risk of people tripping over cables. Sockets set in the floor can be useful, provided they are so placed that it is possible to cover them with tables or equipment.

Needless to say, on-the-job training facilities need just as much attention as those provided away from the workplace, but here we may find the requirements more difficult to satisfy due to the general working conditions in the department and the needs of the work activity. However, certain steps can be taken if one recognizes the effects that unsuitable conditions can have on learning. To summarize:

1. Trainees' concentration should not be impaired by physical discomfort caused by unsuitable furniture, heating, lighting, ventilation etc or by confusion due to bad housekeeping. A cluttered workplace should be avoided. All the tools, materials, aids, etc to carry out the work should be readily available and anything not so required should be removed.
2. Wherever possible, interruptions should be avoided. This may mean that telephone calls and non-urgent messages are diverted. The trainer should try to give the training his undivided attention (see p. 62).
3. The trainee should not be unnecessarily exposed to safety hazards. He should be fully acquainted with any hazards which do exist and know from the start how to avoid injury to himself and his colleagues and damage to equipment and premises.

Visual aids do not of themselves ensure the success of a training programme. Judiciously used they can add reinforcement, interest and enjoyment. Some trainers seem to think that the more visual aids they use, the more professional their presentations will be. In fact, it may have the reverse effect because the sight of a trainer darting about from one piece of equipment to another often distracts the trainees. They are so carried away by the speculation about what equipment he is going to use next that the training message goes over their heads. Furthermore, the trainer who relies so much on his visual aids is frequently the least well equipped to operate them. Equipment inexpertly used does little to help trainees' learning or the trainer's reputation.

Most training rooms are now equipped with blackboards, whiteboards and projector screens. These are often fixed along one wall of the room; whilst this removes the need to manhandle them each time they are used, there are disadvantages. It automatically establishes the operating end of the room, which the trainer may not favour. In some forms of participative training he may want to discourage a 'top table'. On balance, portable aids have the advantage that they can go where they are wanted and they can also be stored away or used by someone else. It is generally better to be able to adjust screens or boards to suit the group layout rather than *vice versa*. One example of adapting aids to the needs of the group is the development of the flip-chart and stand. This versatile aid is portable, may be used in confined spaces and has the advantage of enabling several groups to compare their presentations by placing individual sheets alongside each other on a wall, blackboard or a board specially designed for the purpose.

Setting up the equipment effectively is an essential part of operating it professionally. It is obvious that any image thrown on to a screen

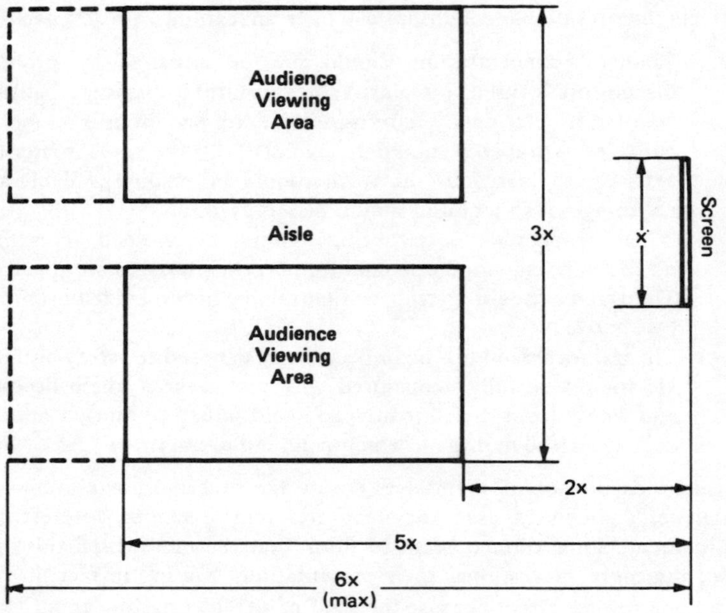

Figure 28. *Example of audience/screen arrangement for optimum viewing comfort*

should be readable by all trainees without straining. Yet many presenters do not take the trouble to check this out before the event. A common error is producing an overhead projector slide in minute writing which cannot be seen by the more distant members of the group. The screen size will limit the magnification obtainable and this should be checked before slides are produced.

Fig. 28 shows an arrangement of audience and projection screen for optimum viewing comfort. It assumes that the characters on the slides are of suitable size for the screen. The approximate distances shown on the diagram are important if the images seen by the trainees are not to be distorted or unclear.

Unless projection equipment is operated from a properly designed projection room, it is usually placed on a table or stand at waist or chest level. This means that the beam has to be fired upwards at the screen. If the screen is installed in a vertical position, therefore, the resulting image will not be square but trapezium-shaped and it will be impossible to achieve good focus over the whole of the picture. Fig. 29 illustrates how this effect is overcome by tilting the top of the screen forward. When installing fixed screens this facility should not be overlooked.

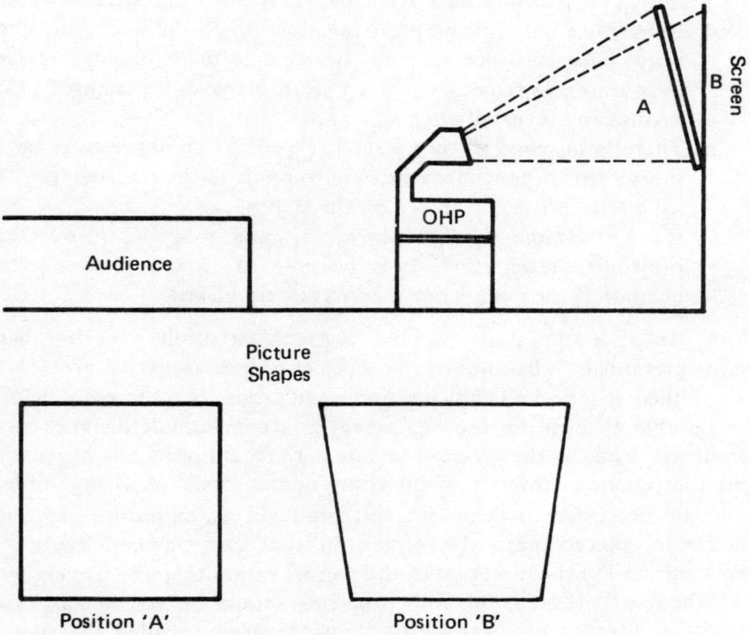

Figure 29. *The effect of using a vertical screen*

When using any visual aid it is important to remind oneself that it is a means of reinforcing learning and not a means of delegating one's presentation. It has to support what is being said but should never be allowed to divert attention from it. This means that it must be used in such a way that it integrates fully with the presentation without drawing attention to itself. Skill in its use is therefore essential. The following points are worth noting:

1. Transparencies should be graphic, making use of shape and colour, rather than just words. If written visuals are considered necessary, they should stand on their own but not be too complicated. They should list headings rather than give detailed descriptions. Whilst trainees are reading they cannot be giving the trainer's words their full attention.
2. Use spirit-based pens when preparing slides. It is then possible to write on the slide with a water-based pen during the presentation and wipe off these notes with a damp cloth afterwards without removing the original information.
3. Never stand in front of the projector or screen so that the picture cannot be seen.

4. Always switch off when the transparency has been dealt with. Do not leave a blank screen. An audience is easily mesmerized by it.
5. Remember not to leave more information on the screen than you want your audience to read. An opaque piece of paper placed over the transparency enables you to blank out unwanted information and reveal it when appropriate.
6. There is no need to turn your back on the audience to point to the screen. A pencil may be used to point to the transparency. Its silhouette will be projected on the screen.
7. Do not assume that you have to stand to make an overhead projector presentation. It is possible to operate from a sitting position if the equipment is conveniently placed.

The use of a film projector also requires attention to a few basic principles if it is to be unobtrusive. Projector noise is often a problem in a confined space when showing to a small group. It is therefore helpful to be able to position the equipment at a comfortable distance away from the back of the group, but this may create problems because of the limitations in the size of the room or the screen. A change of lens may be necessary to deal with this problem. An extension speaker is desirable, placed near the screen so that the trainees' hearing is concentrated in the direction of the picture rather than the projector.

Whenever possible, the film projector should be set up and made ready in advance of the time of showing. Having loaded the film, it should be run on until the leader has disappeared and the first frame of the actual film is in the gate. The focus and sound quality should then be adjusted. This will require running a few frames of the film and then rewinding to the first frame again, setting the sound level to zero. When starting the presentation, the sound should be slowly turned up until it reaches a suitable level. At the end of the film, the sound should be reduced during the credits and the projector switched off when 'The end' appears. If possible, re-winding the film and packing up the projector during a session should be avoided, even if the trainer has the time to do it. Trainees will be easily diverted from their work by such activities, which should preferably be left until a suitable break in the programme. A custom-built projection room has advantages here.

A training department which employs overhead projectors and flip-charts will have a good supply of pens for use with them. Both water- and spirit-based pens have a habit of drying up and causing frustration and embarrassment and it is recommended that they are always checked before use. Equally troublesome is the projector lamp which fails just before or during a presentation. Whilst this is usually unavoidable, it is important that a spare is always available and that the trainer or administrator, if present, can change the lamp with the least amount of fuss and delay. This is often the time when the trainer discovers that he does not know how to change the lamp or the fuse on this model!

As with motor cars, we cannot expect visual aid equipment to give trouble-free service indefinitely. If it is being used regularly, a periodic service by the manufacturer is called for, but in any event the user can avoid some problems by keeping the equipment clean and treating it with reasonable care. Cleaning kits are usually provided and these should be used at regular intervals in accordance with the instructions in the handbook. If the equipment is loaned to someone outside the training department, it is prudent to check it over before putting it into service again.

Closed-circuit television equipment with a video recording facility is being used increasingly in the training room. It is an extremely potent device requiring skilful operation. Programmes incorporating this technique tend to be dependent upon it and do not contain contingency plans to be put into effect should the equipment fail. Many a training activity has been ruined by a breakdown of equipment which has brought the programme to a standstill. The message is therefore clear. Ensure that the equipment used is of a high standard, preferably with standby facilities, as provided by some hire firms. Whoever operates the equipment must be fully competent to do so and preferably able to deal with minor faults. If it is possible to arrange things so that the programme can continue without it in the event of breakdown, so much the better.

One word about security. Many training programmes are 'private occasions' when trainees are encouraged to let their hair down without fear of information getting back to their bosses (or anyone else). Recording the training sessions on video tape is therefore a serious breach of this confidence unless the tape is wiped in the presence of the trainees concerned before the end of the programme. It may be felt that the next user will record over it, so no harm will be done. It is, however, difficult to resist the temptation, when it is known that there is something on a tape, to find out what it is.

The natural apprehension of trainees at being exposed to television recording should also be recognized. Although some trainers put groups in front of the camera right from the start of a programme, making the assumption that it helps them to get used to it as early as possible, the writer's experience suggests that this causes unnecessary trauma, particularly when the trainees do not already know each other. It is far better to give them the opportunity to become relaxed with each other in a risk-free environment before introducing the cameras. They are then much less likely to be inhibited by the prospect of having their actions monitored.

Visual aids[126] are tools of the training specialist's trade. As with any tradesman's tools, they need to be carefully selected. There is always a risk that one will be persuaded by sales talk to buy a particular piece of equipment only to find at a later date that it will not satisfy the real needs. It is wise, therefore, to carry out a good deal of research into what is available and what the various products can do before investing in capital equipment for training. Make a list of the functions that it will be required to perform and make certain that the product bought is capable of meeting those requirements. The cost has to be justified over the period of its working life. It is consequently important, too, that the equipment is properly used and properly cared for.

Training records

Whilst it is not proposed in this book to deal in detail with the types of records[127] which are required in the training department, it would be wrong to give the impression that they are not important. Information has to be available on the organization's policies, objectives and plans with respect to training and on the action taken and its effects. At no stage can anyone's memory be depended upon for reference purposes, but information must be adequately recorded and available to those who need it in order to meet the objectives of the organization.

When setting up a record system for training purposes, the following questions need to be asked:

- ☐ What is its purpose?
- ☐ What information is really required to meet that purpose? The temptation to include information that *may possibly* be required should be resisted.
- ☐ Will the system integrate with existing systems in the organization? Can duplication be avoided?
- ☐ What is the estimated cost of setting up the system? Is it justified in cost/benefit terms?
- ☐ Who will be responsible for keeping the records up-to-date? Is he or she competent to do so without supervision? If not, who will supervise?
- ☐ Who will be authorized to have access to the records?
- ☐ How will the records be used?

The need for a particular record sometimes shows itself when information that is required is not available from any existing source. The decision has to be taken as to whether a system to provide such information in the future is really justified. This is not an easy decision to take since it is seldom clear-cut. The guidelines have to be: is the information needed of vital importance and is the frequency of the need sufficiently high to warrant the setting up of a special system? It is uneconomical to operate a detailed system from which data is rarely if ever required.

Records are useless unless they are complete, accurate, up-to-date and the information contained in them is easily retrievable. The person responsible needs to be fully aware of the purpose of keeping them and the consequences to the organization of their not meeting these conditions. The data recorded is frequently privileged and should therefore be treated in the strictest confidence. It goes without saying that records should be in the simplest form possible consistent with their meeting the needs. Often information retrieval may be urgent and thus access must be achieved with the minimum of delay and confusion. Where coding systems are used, these must be simple and a key should be readily to hand.

Managing the resources – summary

The resources of men, materials, machines, money and time in the training department are considerable. It follows that they should be used wisely and to optimum effect. Those of us who have chosen training management as a career have done so as often as not because of the sheer personal satisfaction that we gain from the training activity. We should not, however, lose sight of the reason for it all. To survive and be successful, organizations have to be efficient and effective. Training is one of the positive ways in which this can be achieved, provided it is carried out with efficiency and effectiveness itself. Satisfying our own personal objectives will not necessarily be in the interests of the organization and failure to meet the needs of the business can only lead eventually to lack of confidence in the training activity and consequently lack of support from the top.

Managing the resources at his disposal requires the attention of the training manager to the following:

- ☐ his own training and professionalism
- ☐ representation of the function at top level in the organization
- ☐ the rational assessment of the organization's needs and the establishment of appropriate objectives, strategies and plans
- ☐ the identification of the roles of other members of the team
- ☐ the recruitment of adequately qualified supporting staff
- ☐ the promotion of team work in the training function
- ☐ the continuing appraisal of the development needs of the training staff
- ☐ monitoring the latest research affecting the training function
- ☐ the identification and implementation of training requirements throughout the organization using the most appropriate methods and techniques
- ☐ the constant validation and evaluation of the department's activities
- ☐ the control and efficient use of materials and equipment
- ☐ the maintenance of adequate records
- ☐ the management of time: his own and that of his staff
- ☐ realistic budgeting and the ability to live within one's means without loss of quality of the service provided.

Chapter 10

Influences on the Training Function

In this chapter we shall be considering the internal and the external factors which have some impact on the operations of the training department.

Internal influences

There is no doubting the positive effects brought about by success. Management expects a contribution from training which justifies the expenditure of money, time and other resources on it. If that contribution is realized, it sees the training department as a force to be reckoned with and one which deserves continued support and encouragement. If management is unable to see positive results, the function may lose credibility and support may no longer be forthcoming. The department may find itself ignored and eventually it may be re-formed, or in the worst case disbanded. Lack of professionalism may lead top management to be sceptical about the ability of training to carry out its role effectively. On the other side of the coin, an over-demonstrative display of confidence, characterized by over-zealous publicity for one's activities, will be viewed with suspicion and will most likely prove counter-productive. Managements, and indeed people generally, are more impressed with those who produce the desired results with quiet efficiency than with those who indulge in excessive self-praise.

It has already been suggested that trainers should seek to adopt a more positive approach to training, initiating change wherever this is seen to be desirable and deemed to be practicable. Clearly their ability to do so will depend to a large extent on their credibility at senior level. Management is unlikely to allow them to bring about far-reaching changes throughout the organization, or even listen to arguments for such changes, if they do not acknowledge their competence to handle such issues. The ability of trainers to promote a more proactive style will therefore be influenced to a major degree by their managements' confidence in them.

The management's attitude to training is usually demonstrated by its willingness to vote the necessary funds to the activity. In organizations where a management training centre exists, for example, the training department's contribution is usually valued. Introducing such a centre involves a good deal of initial research and evaluation and the financial commitments involved discourage the management from taking lightly the decision to provide it. Moreover, if they are prepared to make such an investment, the decision may be reasonably interpreted as an acceptance that the training department is sufficiently competent to assume responsibility for all aspects of management training.

It is fairly obvious that a dearth of resources is a serious demotivator. If training staff are unable to achieve their targets for lack of money or time, they become frustrated and disheartened. An unwelcome effect, too, is that other employees can either see them as lacking in competence to carry out their commitments or, if they know the true reasons, believe that the department has lost the confidence of the management.

Another indication of management's disposition towards training which influences the way in which the function operates is the priority given to it as compared with other pressing business activities. Where training matters appear towards the end of a committee's agenda, they are likely to be deferred when time runs out. If they continue to be given this low level of priority they may never be heard. Some training topics may be able to suffer deferment without too much harm being done, but the effect on others may be disastrous. While one deferment of a training item may be excusable, repeated delays can seldom be justified and may have ominous significance.

Managements are not always of one mind as to how a department's services should be viewed. Whilst there may be a majority view in favour of the function, there is often at least one dissenting voice. The extent to which the minority views affect the department's activities depends on the degree of influence the individuals can exert in the organization. One forceful manager may have a greater impact on what happens in a business than the combined efforts of several people who disagree with him. It should not be assumed, therefore, that the greatest influence always comes from a majority group.

The effects that the attitudes of other employees have on training should not be overlooked. Everyone will have built up his or her own image of the function, its individual members and its effectiveness from direct or indirect observation. These impressions will vary considerably according to the employees' experiences and prejudices. Where they have had favourable contacts with the department and have experienced training which they have valued, positive effects will result. If they can attribute an improvement in their confidence or in their skilled performance in the job to the training they have received, they will most probably be favourably disposed towards the training department and will want to continue profitable contact with it. The effect goes beyond them as individuals because they will not want to keep the benefits they have received to themselves but will want to share them with others. Furthermore, their managers will also be well acquainted with their improvements in performance. There is thus a cumulative effect which is bound to be felt by the training function. The managers will be motivated to make greater use of the facility and will no doubt be under pressure from their subordinates to do so.

On the negative side, an employee who has had favourable training experiences may become frustrated if he has expectations of promotion or of further training which do not materialize. Training frequently opens up new horizons for employees and stimulates them to forge ahead at a pace that the organization is not always prepared for. Managers must find ways of dealing with this problem, and their dilemma provides one reason why some of them are reluctant to release their employees for training. Their attitude can be misinterpreted by training staff as being anti-training when in fact they are simply afraid of the possible consequences of raising their subordinates' expectations without knowing how they can satisfy them.

There is sometimes resentment of the training department, particularly from people who have not had any direct experience of it, stemming from the fact that it is an overhead function which seems to go on spending money on activities with which those people are not in sympathy. The comparative freedom which members of the training department appear to enjoy may also be the cause of some animosity. It is not appreciated that absence from the office does not mean absence from the job and that training frequently involves working unsocial hours. The best way to dispel such ill-founded judgements and prejudices is to provide training experiences for the critics, but the resistance to participating in this way has to be overcome first. This calls for tact and diplomacy on the part of training staff, together with support from the managers concerned.

Recruitment policy is bound to have a marked impact on the training function. If the job entrant has come from an employer who did not rate training very highly, he may not value it himself to any great extent. The organization's policy in relation to training therefore has to be carefully spelled out to him. Employees who are not apprentices or craftsmen sometimes do not believe that training has anything to do for them. Unless someone convinces them that everyone in the organization can benefit from training, and examples are set at top level, they may persist in this view and thus resist any association with the training department. Adequate briefing of new entrants will help to establish a more favourable relationship with the function.

Misunderstandings about training abound among employees in an organization. Some of these arise from the total lack of contact with the function so that there has been no training experience on which to draw. Others stem from how the business is managed and the ways in which policies and procedures are implemented. For example, an employee may be forgiven for believing that training is not important if his manager fails to have any kind of dialogue with him on the subject either before or after a training programme. The employee's reaction to not being briefed or de-briefed, or not having any opportunity to discuss his training, may be to regard it as a welcome break from work rather than as a means of improving his work performance. The impression he gets of the training department in these circumstances will be quite different from the one intended.

The existence of managerial controls can have an influence on the status of the training department. If it is accepted practice to incorporate in training programmes any recent changes in systems, procedures, policies, rules, regulations etc, this will be expected by employees whenever any such changes occur. The effect in this case is a positive one. In the event of this practice not being adopted, however, the effect is likely to be negative, because the training department will be criticized for not keeping employees informed. In these circumstances, steps should be taken to ensure that such matters are regularly monitored and suitable action implemented.

The training department often has the responsibility of providing training for those whose job it is to carry out negotiations with workers' representatives and trade unions. It is sometimes said that whilst trade unions ensure that their shop stewards are properly trained to carry out their roles, managements neglect the training of their own negotiators, assuming that they are in control and know what they are doing. In these circumstances management and the training department come under criticism from employees for what is seen as ineffective handling of the consultative machinery, with consequent adverse results on industrial relations generally. The training department can clearly play an important part in developing the negotiating skills of managers[97] and indeed in improving the overall work climate. Where this has been successful, its role in industrial relations has been acknowledged and its reputation enhanced.

Employees expect to have reasonable prospects of developing their abilities and following career patterns which make full use of their experience, knowledge and skills. They see mobility in the organization as an important means towards that end. Managements which adopt policies which encourage mobility raise expectations which stimulate the need for training at all levels. There may therefore be pressure from the workforce to provide such training. Whether or not this service is forthcoming will reflect upon the training department's acceptability.

The overall climate in an organization is therefore seen to have important influences on the training department. In general, it is true to say that employees expect a business for which they contract to work to be managed in an atmosphere of openness and trust. They also like to think that the management has some concern for their welfare and development. Where these conditions are satisfied, a training department can reasonably look forward to being able to make its contribution to the success of the business. Most if not all of the influences will be positive.

External influences

An organization's reputation in the community, both nationally and locally, can have a marked effect on its business activities and on its employee recruitment. A business which has hit the headlines by reason of poor performance, industrial unrest, unfavourable employee conditions of service, scandals, malpractices, etc may find potential customers deterred from using its services or potential employees from applying to it for a job. This can apply to any kind of organization. The consequences of arbitrary redundancy policies are often not anticipated, for example, with the result that, when eventually the organization wishes to recruit again, it finds that its image has deteriorated and candidates do not come forward. This can result either in the business having to accept lower standards of intake with obvious implications for training, or in a requirement to re-train existing employees to cover for jobs which would have been done by newcomers if they had been available. The effects on training of an acceptable business image in the community, however, are far more straightforward. All other things being equal, employees of the right quality and in the right numbers can more readily be recruited, and there are fewer complications from the training point of view.

The race structure of the local community can be an important factor in some areas. Where a significant proportion of immigrants is employed in an establishment, there is often a need to provide language courses to ease their integration into the English-speaking workforce. The policy to provide such facilities sometimes introduces other problems. In one South London factory, the white workers complained to the management that they were being discriminated against because they did not have the same opportunities to learn languages as the coloured workers!

Literacy and numeracy are essential attributes for many employees in an organization, especially those in white-collar jobs. If standards are inadequate, it falls to the training staff to try to make up the deficiency. Although they may understandably feel that this is not part of their role, they will have to face up to the fact that any future training which needs to be done may well fail if the foundations are not properly laid in the first place.

The impact of government legislation on training has been considerable, in particular since the mid-1960s. This has been of two kinds: one directed specifically at training and the other, mainly employment legislation, which has training implications. The major training enactment was the Industrial Training Act, 1964,[9] which gave force to the government's intention to obtain improvements in both the quantity and the quality of training throughout industry, and to provide for a more equitable distribution of the cost amongst employers. To promote these policies, 23 Industrial Training Boards (ITBs)[10] were set up for the various industries, responsible to the Secretary of State for Employment. These included the Foundry Industry Training Committee, which was technically a committee of the Engineering Industry Training Board. In addition, the Local Government Training Board, a voluntary organization, and the Agricultural Training Board, responsible to the agriculture minister, were formed. There were also certain other bodies which had a statutory responsibility to provide their employees with appropriate training, such as the Electricity Council, the British Gas Corporation, the National Water Council, the Coal Board and British Rail.

ITBs were given statutory authority to impose a levy on employers within their scope and this was based on a percentage of payroll, ie of emoluments assessable to Schedule E tax. The levy raised by the Engineering Industry Training Board (EITB), for example, was 2½ per cent of payroll. The sum raised by this means, which was computed to be the approximate cost of training in the industry, was re-distributed to employers in the form of training grants, after deduction of the Board's administrative expenses. Criteria were gradually established over a period of years for training in various manpower categories, and firms had to satisfy these conditions in order to qualify for grants for those categories. Organizations with acceptable training arrangements over an appropriate number of categories in their establishments were sometimes able to claim over 100 per cent grants and so, theoretically, made a 'profit'. In practice, however, the cost of meeting the requirements would be far greater than the return from grants.

The value of the ITBs' services was in the practical and advisory aspects of their work, which were extremely useful to employers, particularly those who could not afford to employ their own specialists. The levy/grant system undoubtedly stimulated firms to pay more attention to training, although a minority sat back and accepted the levy as just another tax. In the early days of the scheme, the grant calculation system which developed was extremely complicated and working out one's entitlement was time-consuming. Indeed, the administration needed in an organization to comply with a Board's requirements became so cumbersome that resistance built up among employers in the early 1970s, many feeling that the system had satisfied its original objective and had outlived its usefulness.

In 1973 the Employment and Training Act was passed, amending the 1964 Act. One of its provisions was to enable ITBs to exempt employers from levy where they were satisfied that the appropriate criteria for training their employees were being met. A judgement had to be made as to what training was needed throughout the particular establishment and whether or not that training was being carried out according to the Board's recommendations. Importance was given to the planning of training, which included producing training plans linked to business and manpower plans, responsibility and accountability for training at a senior level in the organization and the provision of adequate expertise and resources to carry out the plans. Other conditions included the maintenance of suitable records, albeit fewer and less detailed than before, and access to them by the Board's officials at reasonable notice.

The ITB levies were gradually reduced over the years, and the current maximum is 1 per cent of payroll. This means that the funds available for re-distribution as grants have been severely cut. More and more firms who are still within the scope of an ITB are now able to satisfy the exemption criteria, which again limits ITB income. As a result of the government's sector-by-sector review of industrial training in 1981,[129] 16 of the 23 ITBs were wound up by March 1983. A number of new voluntary training organizations were established in their place, based mainly on employers' associations. The remaining seven boards cover the clothing, construction, engineering, hotel and catering, offshore petroleum, plastics processing and road transport sectors. If the Agricultural Training Board, which is responsible to the Minister of Agriculture, Fisheries and Food, is included with these seven, about 26 per cent of the country's working population is now within the scope of these statutory arrangements, compared with over half before the changes.

The 1973 Act also brought about changes in public employment and training services. An independent Manpower Services Commission (MSC)[130] accountable to the Secretary of State for Employment was set up, with the brief to run those services previously provided by the Training Services Agency (TSA) and the Employment Service Agency (ESA); to be responsible for Special Programmes for the jobless; and to co-ordinate industrial training generally, including the work of the ITBs.

We are only concerned here with the training activities of the MSC. The re-named Training Services Division (TSD) was made responsible for implementing the MSC's plans to 'support industry's efforts through:

(a) selective assistance to Industrial Training Boards (ITBs) and non-statutory training organizations under the 'Training for Skills' programme for action;
(b) development of its Training Opportunities Scheme (TOPS) and its Direct Training Services;
(c) its information, research and advisory services aimed at identifying manpower problems and promoting improved training standards and efficiency.'[131]

In the 'Training for Skills' report[132] the task group proposed 'an action programme to improve the amount and quality of training in skills needed by industry, discourage a "stop-go" attitude to training and prevent persistent shortages in skills from building up.' The report recognized the great diversity of need both between and within industries and concluded that an effective system for correcting skill imbalances and improving training opportunities for employees must take account of this and was 'more likely to be brought about through agreement than by new legislation . . . .'

To assist ITBs to carry out their responsibilities under this programme, the MSC provided grants directed towards 'meeting key skill needs and towards the reform of training systems, with special emphasis on resolving problems which are common to a number of industries (for example, training for micro-electronics and for computer software functions; training of instrument maintenance personnel; and training for design, development and maintenance engineering skills) . . .'

The TOPS scheme enabled adults to acquire new skills at colleges of further education, private colleges, residential training colleges (for the disabled) and government Skillcentres. Courses were made available in three categories: Skillcentre, which covered mainly manual and craft skills; clerical/commercial, such as shorthand/typing and book-keeping; and management level, covering management, executive and technological training. Training allowances were paid to trainees throughout these courses.

Direct Training Services to industry included Sponsored Training, which was tailor-made to the employer's needs, the Mobile Instructor Service for in-plant training, Instructor Training, Training Within Industry (TWI) (see p. 132) and International Trade Procedures (ITP) courses. The MSC was also responsible for a Youth Opportunities Programme, which offered young people up to the age of 18, who had been unemployed for six weeks or more, a chance of up to a year's work experience and training with an employer. Employers sponsoring candidates paid them a flat-rate allowance which was reimbursed by the MSC.

A White Paper, *A New Training Initiative – a Programme for Action*,[92] was published on 15 December 1981 and was hailed by the Secretary of State for Employment as containing '. . . the most far-reaching proposals for industrial training ever put before parliament.' It set out the following ten-point plan:

1. A new £1-billion-a-year Youth Training Scheme, guaranteeing from September 1983 a full year's foundation training for all those leaving school at the minimum age without jobs.
2. Increased incentives for employers to provide better training for young people in jobs.
3. Development of an 'Open Tech' programme to make technical training more accessible to those who have the necessary ability.

4. A working group to report by April 1982 on ways of developing the Youth Training Scheme to cover employed as well as unemployed young people, within available resources.
5. Setting a target date of 1985 for recognized standards for all the main craft, technician and professional skills to replace time-serving and age restricted apprenticeships.
6. Better preparation for working life in initial full-time education.
7. More opportunities for vocationally relevant courses for those staying on in full-time education.
8. Closer co-ordination of training and vocational education provision nationally and at local level.
9. A £16-million fund for development schemes in particular localities or sectors.
10. Examination of longer-term possibilities for more effective, rational and equitable sharing of the costs of training between trainees themselves, employers of trained people and the general taxpayer.

The Youth Training Scheme (YTS), which started in April 1983 and became fully operational in the following September, took the place of the Youth Opportunities Programme and other schemes of training and apprenticeship support for young people. It was designed '. . . to give school leavers a range of practical transferable skills to enable them to compete more effectively for jobs and to undertake further training in their adult lives'.[133] It catered for 16- and 17-year old school leavers and some older disabled young people. They usually followed a basic vocational programme lasting a year and combining a minimum of 13 weeks' off-the-job training (or further education) with planned work experience and training.

A new Technical and Vocational Education Initiative (TVEI) was also launched in 1983, designed to provide 14- to 18-year-old students with four years' technical and vocational education. Projects, although locally determined, had to conform to nationally agreed guidelines. The confusing pattern of qualifications available to young people came under scrutiny in the previous year, and the Department of Education and Science announced the introduction of the Certificate in Pre-Vocational Education (CPVE). Popularly styled the '17 plus', it offered further education of vocational relevance to 16-year-olds who chose to take up employment rather than higher education. It was designed to link in with existing vocational courses.

Disadvantaged young people aged 16 to 19 years who were not able to satisfy the entrance requirements for the above schemes could obtain help within the Community Industry Scheme. This provided up to a year's temporary work which was of benefit to the community and at the same time helped their own development. At the present time, up to 7000 places on the scheme are provided by Community Industry Ltd, a company with charitable status.

In Chapter 7, reference was made to the changes which were currently taking place in apprenticeship training and agreements. The MSC is committed to using its influence to modernize occupational training, not only in apprenticeship schemes but 'across the broad spectrum of employment'. One of the areas in which it seeks to make an impact is in working with further education authorities to remove some of the present restrictions on educational levels of entry to training programmes.

The Commission has taken on new responsibilities in connection with work-related non-advanced education. These were brought about by the Government's White Paper *Training for Jobs*[134], published in January 1984, which set out to provide training and vocational education which was more in line with industrial and commercial employment needs, especially at the local level.

For some time both the Department of Education and Science and the MSC have attached considerable importance to adult further education, training and re-training. In May 1982, the professional, industrial and commercial updating (PICKUP) programme was launched following the issue in late 1980 of the DES's consultative document *Continuing Education: Post-Experience Vocational Provision for those in Employment*. The scheme was designed to:

- ☐ '*encourage* colleges, polytechnics and universities to identify updating needs in their region and plan for ways of meeting them
- ☐ *promote* the development of new types of course, new materials and new ways of teaching so that updating needs can be met effectively and economically
- ☐ *build up* sources of information so that potential clients in industry and commerce can discover what is available, and providers can make the best use of available materials and avoid wasteful duplication of effort
- ☐ *tackle* financial and administrative obstacles'.[135]

In November 1983 the MSC submitted its proposals to the Secretary of State for Employment, following responses to its consultative document *Towards an Adult Training Strategy*.[136] The aims which resulted from nationwide consultation were to:

- ☐ 'secure and sustain the quantity and quality of skills necessary to meet changing needs and circumstances; and
- ☐ enable individuals, employed and unemployed, to undertake the training, re-training and continuing education that will give them the confidence, motivation and sense of responsibility as well as the skills, knowledge and experience which they need if the first aim is to be met; and to cope with the consequences of technological and structural change'.

Part of the new strategy involved launching a 'national awareness campaign' for adult training. It was argued by the MSC's chairman that failure to invest adequately in training would damage the country's ability to meet the challenges of new technology and foreign competition. In the interests of making its training schemes more relevant to local needs, it was introducing pilot schemes to:

- ☐ assist with the costs of consultancy for the definition of training needs
- ☐ improve the availability and quality of training for the management of small businesses
- ☐ give local grant aid to employers to modernize and extend the training of their workforce
- ☐ provide recruitment and training packages to speed up the filling of key vacancies.

The IPM rightly gave its wholehearted support to the campaign and was consulted with respect to its content. It pointed out that the key to the country's success in the past had been the skill and adaptability of the workforce. Technological change, however, would demand that individuals paid greater attention to their 'job-specific' training needs. Among other things, 'They need to know how to learn, to acquire the habit of learning, to recognize that learning will be a constant feature of their lives and to become more active in the learning process. The days of the passive learner are numbered; individuals need to become more self-reliant.'[137]

The main objectives of the Training Opportunities Scheme (TOPS), introduced in 1972, were to train unemployed adults in the skills needed for them to be able to obtain suitable employment. This end result was achieved on some of the courses but regrettably not on others. In its Corporate Plan for 1984 to 1988,[133] the MSC expressed its intention of continuing the same level of investment in the scheme, but of replacing the less effective programmes with new pilot schemes. These included: job-related training in areas where jobs were known to exist, eg in hi-tech industries; Open Tech programmes (see p. 145); training specifically designed to help unemployed adults, especially the disadvantaged, to improve their foundation skills and job prospects and to retain their employability.

The new Job Training Scheme for adults from 18 to 25 years replaced TOPS in April 1987, following pilot programmes in ten areas of the UK. It consists of a flexible, integrated package of vocational training and practical experience for periods of from 3 to 12 months, designed to meet known employment needs and supporting the creation and growth of business. The flexibility is achieved through individually tailored programmes using, among other things, open learning methods. Training in the new technologies and for self-employment are available for all participants.

Changes both in its structure and in its training provisions were outlined in the Commission's Corporate Plan for 1987/1991. The main organizational differences have already been mentioned on page 16 and an organization chart (Figure 1) was given on the following page. The stated role of the MSC for the period of the Plan in the light of these changes 'will be to contribute to efforts to improve GB competitiveness and to support employment growth and job creation by fostering the development of a better trained, more adaptable workforce.'

Working in close liaison with the new Employment Service, the MSC is committed to implementing the three guarantees for the unemployed announced by the Government in June 1987, viz:

- under 18s leaving full-time education and not entering a job will be guaranteed a place on the YTS Scheme;
- everyone from 18 to 25 years who has been out of work for 6 to 12 months will be guaranteed a place on the new Job Training Scheme, on the Enterprise Allowance Scheme or in a Jobclub;
- everyone who has been unemployed for over 6 months will be guaranteed a Restart interview every 6 months, with the aim of offering anyone over 50 years who has been unemployed for more than two years a place on the Community Programme, on the Enterprise Allowance Scheme or in a Jobclub.

In implementing the revised *New Training Initiative*, the Commission's objectives are:

- 'to develop occupational training, including apprenticeship, in such a way as to enable people entering at different ages and with different educational attainments to acquire agreed standards of skill appropriate to the jobs available and to provide them with a basis for progression through further learning;
- to move towards a position where all young people under the age of 18 have the opportunity either to continue in full-time education, or to enter training or a period of planned work experience combining work-related training and education;
- to open up widespread opportunities for adults – whether employed or unemployed or returning to work – to acquire, increase or update their skills and knowledge during the course of their working lives.'

The Commission's Vocational Education and Training Group (VETG) is responsible for all its VET provisions with the exception of the direct training services of the Skillcentres which are controlled by the Skills Training Agency.

All 16-17 year old school and college leavers, whether employed or unemployed, are now eligible for the YTS Programme. The scheme has been extended to two years for the 16 year olds, but remains a one year programme for those entering at 17 years of age.

The Enterprise Allowance Scheme, referred to above, has existed since 1983, and provides some financial assistance in the first year to unemployed people who wish to set themselves up in business.

Jobclubs were introduced with the objective of boosting the confidence of the jobless when seeking employment. They are given training in presenting themselves more favourably to employers both in writing and at interview.

In order to prepare employed and unemployed people for work involving new technology, assisted Access to Information Technology courses were introduced in 1985. These were evening or weekend programmes of up to 30 hours duration and were open to *anyone* from 18 years to retirement age. Those candidates already employed (or self-employed) were expected to make a small contribution to the cost of the course. The scheme was seen to achieve its objective of stimulating the setting up of new technology courses by colleges and other establishments and the sponsored scheme was due to be discontinued in March 1988.

The Wider Opportunities Training Programme is an adult scheme aiming to assist people who are out of work to improve their basic skills and so improve their work prospects. Individual training courses are designed to meet the needs of specific client groups and labour markets. They may include such skills as literacy, numeracy, English as a second language and special subjects for women returning to work.

In 1986, the National Council for Vocational Qualifications was set up.[157] Its role is to ensure that comprehensive practical qualifications are established which will enable a trainee's vocational knowledge and skill, and his ability to apply them in practice, to be checked against nationally agreed standards.

There are currently 60 Skillcentres in the UK, 40 of which serve inner city areas. Controlled by the Skills Training Agency of the MSC, they continue to provide a wide range of courses, largely geared to local needs, for the benefit of both employed and unemployed people.

Other government legislation, in particular that which seeks to regulate relationships in the workplace, has made its impact on the training function over the past 20 years or more. Enactments have included the Factories Act 1961, the Offices Shops and Railway Premises Act 1963, the Equal Pay Act 1970, the Health and Safety at Work Act 1974, the Trade Union and Labour Relations Act 1974, the Employment Protection Act 1975 and the Employment Protection (Consolidation) Act 1978, the Sex Discrimination Act 1975, the Race Relations Act 1976, the Employment Acts 1980 and 1982, the Trade Union Act 1984 and the Data Protection Act 1984. All these measures have implications for training, since they affect individual and collective rights of employees. This means that managers and supervisors in particular have to be aware of the provisions if they are not to find themselves in breach of the law. In many cases there are financial penalties for non-compliance, but it should also be realized that the publicity surrounding any court or tribunal case involving an employer and/or his employees can be very damaging. There is therefore a compelling need for training, not only in the main provisions of the law but also in the way in which it is being interpreted in the institutions administering it. Keeping up-to-date presents the training manager with a problem. The sheer volume of the legislation and the frequent amendments are daunting. Some publishers have, however, seen the need to produce *précis* of the acts in layman's language to assist managers to monitor the main provisions of the law. Croner's loose-leaf *Reference Book for Employers* which is updated monthly is particularly helpful in this respect and provides its users with much useful information about employment acts and regulations generally. Their *Employment Law* service is more detailed in that particular subject.[13]

The training of some groups of employees, particularly in the professional areas, requires a judicious mixture of practical and theoretical learning. Society has arranged things such that these two ingredients tend to be handled separately by different parties. Education is seen as the prerogative of schools, technical colleges, polytechnics and universities,[138] whilst the practical application of theory is largely regarded as the responsibility of employers. As the two are so obviously interrelated and interdependent, it cannot be denied that a close liaison between them is imperative. One of the most effective training courses to emerge since the last war is the sandwich course, which depends for its success on the careful integration of academic and practical activities, so giving meaning to the concepts to which trainees are introduced.

Liaison between training staffs and educationalists has made some progress in recent years. Recognizing the need for a joint approach to career progression, they spend more time now in discussing and agreeing syllabuses and training programmes than they did 25 years ago, to everybody's ultimate benefit. Schools and other educational establishments, and certainly careers services, are better informed about opportunities in the world of work through contacts with personnel and training specialists, both directly and through the medium of careers conventions and joint conferences. Although it has been found difficult to arrange exchanges of staff on any appreciable scale, there is evidence that this has been mainly successful where it has been tried in some areas. Works visits have their place in acquainting students with the nature of business, as do short attachments under work experience and vacation training schemes. All these activities have important significance for the training department. If improved liaison with educational establishments brings about a more integrated approach to training and helps to ensure that new employees are better informed about business, this can do nothing but good. The co-operation tends to be better where the educationalist has had previous experience outside education. Without that experience he may not fully appreciate the totally different tempo and way of life that characterize environments where people are striving to make profits, or indeed to survive. For this reason among others, there is predictably a close liaison between training departments and business schools and management training centres.[139]

The liaison of training specialists with professional institutions is equally important. Not only will their own institutions, such as the IPM and the ITD, have a strong influence on their activities, but other bodies representing accountants, engineers, etc[140] will from time to time make their presence felt. Their criteria for student, graduate and corporate membership will affect the education and training employees require to become professionally qualified. The availability of practical experience satisfying the conditions for corporate membership sometimes influences an employee in his choice of employer. Furthermore, the periodic statements and recommendations which are made by professional institutions cannot be ignored and often require a response from employers. The importance of the establishment of the highest standards and codes of practice for our professions demands close liaison between employers and the institutions.

Other external bodies, such as the Confederation of British Industry (CBI)[141] and the Trades Union Congress (TUC),[142] sometimes make recommendations at national level which in some way affect the activities of the training department. In representing the views of their employer or trade union members to government and other organizations, they may, for example, produce reports or policy statements which have to be incorporated in training programmes to bring managers and others up-to-date in industrial relations matters.

A similar role is also carried out at the local level by employers' associations,[143] some of which are affiliated to the CBI in the same way as certain trade unions are affiliated to the TUC. These associations have been formed mainly to assist in regulating relations between employers and unions, and they advise their members on, among other things, technical information, terms and conditions of service including wage levels, and on training matters. Local chambers of commerce[144] whose members are employers with the common interest of trade, provide a forum for mutual co-operation and shared information and can prove useful contacts for the training manager.

One way in which training managers may improve their liaison with outside bodies is by representation on their committees, particularly those specifically concerned with education and training. Technical colleges and other institutions of further education, for example, have advisory committees comprised of members of their own staff and representatives of the employers, their clients. These bodies provide opportunities for the valuable exchange of information of mutual concern and thus help to forge closer links between education and employment. Similarly involvement in some way with examining bodies such as the Council for National Academic Awards (CNAA), the

Business and Technician Education Council (BTEC), the National Examinations Board for Supervisory Studies (NEBSS) and the City and Guilds of London Institute (CGLI)[145] is not only useful but necessary in order that those who provide students for the courses are suitably represented when the future of such courses is being discussed. For instance, when TEC and BEC (later combined in BTEC) courses were proposed to supersede national certificate/diploma courses in technical and business studies respectively, joint working parties of educational representatives and employers throughout the country were able to study the proposals and make appropriate recommendations for consideration by the national bodies.

When discussing the external influences on the training department we cannot, of course, ignore the state of the national economy. The rise or decline of sterling and interest rates, government fiscal policy and particularly the public sector borrowing requirement all have an influence on organizations. In the public sector, manning levels may be directly affected. In business, remaining solvent and making profits are key issues on which the national economy will make a significant impact. A depressed economy requires critical examination of costs and gives rise to increased pressures to improve efficiency. The training department is at the centre of the efforts to achieve better performance and its reputation may rise or fall with its degree of success in producing positive results in a difficult period. Training managers are recommended to read the government's 'Economic Progress Reports'[146] which currently may be obtained regularly by post free of charge. They summarize the state of the national economy and the government's economic strategy, enabling readers to keep abreast of developments without recourse to Hansard. They also provide up-to-date charts, tables and statistics which may be used for training purposes.

Chapter 11

Review and Possible Trends

What is required of the training activity?

In Chapter 2 it was suggested that the aims of a training activity were essentially those contained in the IPM's definition of personnel management. The ultimate goal is organizational success, achieved through people. The training function is thus concerned with efficiency and effectiveness, which are influenced by human capabilities, relationships, job satisfaction and the concept of fairness in employment. To fulfil the corporate objectives, we have to establish what they are and the structure of the organization needed to meet them. The people we already have and the new recruits that we engage will not necessarily be able to satisfy the demands of their jobs in terms of skill and knowledge. Some may also adopt attitudes which are unproductive or even counter-productive.

The training department is therefore committed to influencing and developing employees' behaviour by appropriate means in any or all of the key areas of knowledge, skills and attitudes. The means will vary considerably according to the task and will be either instructional or experiential. The methods chosen must be appropriate to the particular task; the wrong methods may produce inadequate and sometimes damaging results. Measuring the results of training is vital in order to ensure that what is being done is effective and is meeting the organizational needs.

Finally, it is expected that, whatever training action may be decided upon at the corporate planning level, the training department will respond to the continually changing needs of the business.

What are the major ingredients for success?

What makes a training department successful? As with any activity which needs to gain full acceptance and also has to stand the test of time, it must be firmly based. It is not sufficient for a training specialist to be told 'Here's the job. Just get on with it.' The training function must be supported with commitment from those who are running the organization. Indeed, it needs to be an integral part of the running of the business, since training is a major factor in establishing the levels of effectiveness of components parts of the system, its people. If those who wield power in an organization do not recognize the value of training and consequently fail to give it the support it needs, it has little if any future. It is unable to demonstrate whether or not it can achieve success.

Training is only partly concerned with optimizing the effectiveness of its employees as individuals. The success of many organizations can be attributed to team work, not only at the top, but throughout the undertaking. Those firms which are able to operate as teams rather than as conglomerations of individuals are usually better able to agree their objectives and pursue them successfully than those whose members are steering their own courses in different directions. Normal conflict or disagreement may prove ultimately constructive: unrestrained obstinacy and inflexibility can frequently be highly destructive. The training manager who is able to achieve a team spirit throughout his organization can make a positive contribution to its fortunes.

Success breeds success, and it is therefore important for the training function to make an early impact in an organization. It is more difficult to establish credibility after a period of mediocre performance than it is to create a favourable image from the start. Once having gained a poor reputation, it is not at all easy to convince people that one is capable of better things. Often the more one tries the more difficult it becomes, because one's motives may be misinterpreted. For this reason, the practice adopted by some organizations of appointing someone to the post of training officer who is not suitably qualified to carry out this role is questionable. It is dangerous to assume that he can grow into the role, unless it is a supporting one rather than one with full responsibility. The person in charge of the training function needs to demonstrate a high level of professionalism from the beginning and so instil confidence throughout the concern. This will not come about if he appears to everyone to be wearing L plates.

In addition to the practical training skills that the manager has to possess to enable him to carry out his training role effectively, he needs to have a good knowledge of the organization. He has to know, for example, what the limits of his authority are and the organizational constraints or employee resistance that he may meet with in pursuing his objectives. Where opposition to his activities is encountered, bulldozing his way through it will not help his cause. Tact and diplomacy are called for in overcoming such difficulties and it is helpful to have warning of the problems in advance.

Professionalism is not only required of the head of the department. Quite apart from the skills of the trainers and instructors in the training room or on-the-job, every member of the team needs to show that the department is efficient and capable of carrying out its role competently. It is futile to expect employees to entrust their training willingly to a department which shows itself to be lacking in the ability to manage its own affairs capably. High standards are consequently expected of everyone who works in the training department. The penalty for not insisting on them is lack of credibility with adverse effects on the impact of the function on business performance.

Taking the argument a stage further, training staff should see one of their prime objectives as creating the conditions for employees *at all levels* to optimize their performance. This may seem a trite and often-repeated statement, but it surely has to be the ultimate goal. In this respect, lessons may be learned from Japanese industry, in which every employee, from manager to shop-floor worker, is exhorted to think 'quality' into his or her job. Even allowing for widely different national cultures, it should not be beyond UK management to move in this direction. In some areas, such as the motor car industry, there are encouraging indications that this is beginning to happen.

Being able to respond to the need for change is a matter of some consequence to training staff. Organizational performance can often be improved by adopting new methods and techniques. Changes in the law may affect the way in which managers and supervisors operate. Internal regulations, systems, work practices, etc may have to be modified from time to time. Training departments have a responsibility to monitor these and other developments in order to capitalize on new approaches to the conduct of business and to ensure that the introduction of changes in work practices can be efficiently carried out, causing the minimum of disruption.

One of the attributes of a successful training department is adaptability. Experienced training officers will agree that no two groups are alike, whether or not they are made up from people in the same function or at the same organizational level. Just as individuals have their own particular characteristics, so do groups. Their idiosyncrasies have to be assessed as quickly as possible and taken into account by the trainer in his handling of their training. Since a successful approach with one group or one individual may be quite inappropriate with another, the trainer has to be responsive to the specific needs of each trainee or group of trainees.

Effective evaluation of training performance is of itself one of the criteria for success. If it reveals weaknesses in the training carried out, it provides the trigger for remedial action which will bring the activity back on course. Conversely, confirmation that the training is adequately satisfying the needs gives the department confidence in its ability to meet its targets.

The cost/benefits of training is a factor of considerable importance. Simply providing a service to assist employees to meet work objectives is not enough. Managements will see training as most effective when the value of the benefits accruing from it equate with or exceed the cost of providing it. There may be a more cost effective way of achieving the same result. The possibility that there may be non-training solutions to problems should therefore not be ignored.

The factors which contribute to training success may thus be summarized as follows:

- ☐ top management support and commitment, preferably direct involvement
- ☐ the encouragement of team work, ie work achievement by co-operative effort towards defined goals
- ☐ high standards of professionalism; a sound knowledge of training principles and methods and an intimate knowledge of the organization and how it operates; a reputation established by a good track record in identifying and satisfying needs
- ☐ skill in recognizing the necessity for change and being able to handle it efficiently
- ☐ adaptability in responding to varying individual and group characteristics
- ☐ evaluation procedures which enable training activities to be monitored and if necessary modified
- ☐ recognition that training should be cost effective.

What is training's record?

It is almost impossible to generalize about the past record of training as a profession. Insofar as any improvement can be regarded as progress, it can be said to have moved forward over the past 25 years or so. In some organizations the movement has been substantial and these firms will continue to be in the van of training progress. At the other end of the scale, there are those which have been happy to recruit only skilled people and have made no contribution towards the training of any of their employees. They have grudgingly accepted a statutory duty to pay a levy to their Training Boards, but have firmly resisted the pressures to take on any training responsibility. Most organizations fall somewhere in between these two extremes.

The attitude towards Training Boards has varied considerably. On the one hand, there are those who have believed that these institutions have had nothing to offer them; on the other, there are those who have felt that they have had their money's worth both from the point of view of training help and the recovery of grants. It is not uncommon for training specialists to hold that training is about optimizing performance, not about maximizing grants. The argument is that they themselves should be the judges of what training is appropriate to the needs of their organizations and their training policies should reflect this. If their training arrangements satisfy the Board's requirements at the same time, so much the better, but they do not regard this as a priority. They do not always agree with the Board as to what criteria are appropriate in their particular situation and they often have problems with managements who cannot understand why the firm does not qualify for grants or levy exemption when a good deal of training is being done. Not surprisingly, the economic argument frequently wins the day, although it may be false economy if valuable resources have to be diverted towards meeting the Board's criteria rather than the organization's needs. Optimum benefit clearly accrues when these objectives coincide and most of the Boards' officers are committed to achieving this.

There is no doubt that the Boards have done valuable work for industry and consequently for the nation as a whole. A stimulus was badly needed in the mid-1960s and however unpopular the levy system may have been, it did provide that stimulus in a way that no other measure would have done. The record of achievement has a number of notable features such as:

- ☐ the development of craft training, in particular the first year off-the-job programmes and skills modules. Previously, although some of the larger firms were well advanced in their apprentice training arrangements, the standard in industrial firms generally was open to improvement. Both first year and module training were certificated on a national basis. The Hotel and Catering ITB also introduced craft achievement awards, the first of their kind in the catering industry
- ☐ the broadening of technician training to include manufacturing processes, purchasing and supply, which was a step towards keeping abreast with technology
- ☐ the improvement in the training of professional engineers
- ☐ the introduction of systematic training in the engineering construction sector
- ☐ the EITB's engineering fellowship scheme in manufacturing management which helped to create a new interest in this vital area
- ☐ the introduction of important research and manpower studies to improve the information systems on which decisions on training provision could be made
- ☐ the formation of constructive links by Boards between further education and industry, eg the Education and Training Advisory Council for the catering industry was introduced by the Hotel and Catering ITB. This liaison may not have come about without the Boards' initiatives
- ☐ the provision of incentives to employers to make greater use of further education facilities, particularly for the under-18s
- ☐ the promotion of adult re-training schemes to cope with changing skills needs
- ☐ the building up of a valuable source of training information on which employers could draw, compiled from the pooled experience of client and other firms and research sources

- ☐ the encouragement of a total strategic and systematic approach to training in an organization
- ☐ the creation of a number of training establishments specializing in the work of particular sectors. Examples were the Offshore Petroleum ITB's training centre at Montrose for drilling and production technology and offshore fire training and the Road Transport ITB's multi-occupational training and educational centres.

A widely acclaimed training innovation, introduced by the EITB, was the group training scheme. This enabled small and medium sized firms, from the engineering and other industries, to join together to provide general and specialist training services for themselves at an economical cost. Grants were made available to assist with meeting the initial setting up costs, to help finance new developments and for the training of training staff. There was also an annual support grant calculated on a *per capita* basis for each establishment in the scheme, with certain limitations based on the group's income. The group had a management committee composed of representatives from the member firms and an ITB adviser. It either appointed a mutually acceptable full-time training officer to manager the scheme or used the services of an approved training organization. This scheme had distinct advantages for firms unable to justify the setting-up of internal training schemes for a limited number of employees.

The above list is, of course, not exhaustive. The ITBs have over the past 20 or more years accumulated a wealth of training knowledge and expertise which has been freely available to firms within their scope. Some have merely required advice, guidance or information, whilst others have taken advantage of the practical help, both internal and external, that the Boards have been able to provide. The larger organizations, which can support professional training teams of their own, may have more to give to the Training Boards than to receive from them. But this must be profitable for the training profession as a whole, because the inputs to the Boards from the country's leading training practitioners can add significantly to their resources, which can then be made available to anyone who may wish to draw on them.

One valid criticism of some Training Boards was that over the years they established a cumbersome bureaucratic system which became something of an irritation to their clients. Retaining a penal system in the form of a training levy, however small, will do little today to induce employers to do more training. All they really need is a high standard of professional help and advice to deal with specific problems as and when they arise. How should it be paid for, if there are no levies and only limited government aid? If firms have asked for a service that is valued, surely they are prepared to pay the market rate for it.

It was recorded on p. 226 that only seven of the original 23 ITBs now remain. The loss of the others has not surprisingly met with mixed reactions. Employers who do not mourn their passing may drift back into complacency in carrying out their training responsibilities. This would be regrettable at a time when training is being seen at the highest level in the country to be of vital importance to our survival as a trading nation. On the other hand, it could be argued that those employers have been shown the way and the removal of training boards will not necessarily result in regression. Let us hope that this is true. Many of the remaining employers will be very sorry to lose their ITBs, because they had built up a profitable relationship with them and had come to rely on their services. These employers should ensure that they make full use of the expertise available in the offices of the Manpower Services Commission, now the Training Commission.[130]

The Commission has done admirable work in providing training and re-training opportunities for both young people and adults, including special facilities for the disabled. The TWI scheme (see p. 132), although now discontinued, was of immense help to employers who wanted to take their first steps in supervisory training during a period when other facilities were in short supply. With the growing and increased sophistication of both internal and external training arrangements for supervisory staff, this basic course has been overtaken by programmes more closely geared to individual needs.

Two major training schemes sponsored by the MSC are the Job Training Scheme and the Youth Training Scheme (YTS) (see Chapter 10). It has been recognized that the level of success of the TOPS scheme in leading to employment after training or re-training was variable and this led to a re-appraisal of its objectives.[133] One result was that TOPS was replaced with the Job Training Scheme, greater attention being given to flexibility and each individual trainee's specific needs.

When the YTS scheme was introduced in September 1983 it was claimed by the government to be 'the single most successful thing we have done in training'. It has attracted much attention at all levels of the community and its reception has been mixed. In the writer's view it was unreasonable to expect too much from the early stages of its operation. The scheme was subject to entirely new management arrangements involving locally appointed managing agents and sponsors. In spite of the difficulties of setting up such a national framework, it was successfully established and well over 300,000 training places were taken up throughout the country in the first year. This number has increased to about 400,000 in the year 1987/88.

There have been criticisms of the programme from those who feel that young people are being used as cheap labour, are not getting the training they need and are not being employed at the end of it. If some employers are not meeting their commitments under the YTS programme, they are most likely to be the ones who would not meet them under any scheme. The YTS can hardly be blamed for that, but closer monitoring which will persuade such employers to face up to their responsibilities should help to reduce the problem. This need raises other difficulties, however. The managing agents who are on the spot are nominally employers who can provide YTS places within their own organizations and/or co-ordinate the scheme over a number of organizations in a particular locality. Inevitably, one person in an organization will be appointed to carry out these responsibilities and that person is likely to be a full-time employee with limited time to allocate to the project. Those who have been so appointed will testify to the excessive burden which is placed on them when they have to seek co-operation not only from their own employers' managers but also from those of other organizations with widely differing interests and commitments. Owing to the sheer magnitude of the programme, it is clear also that the Commission itself is not able to provide the monitoring resources; hence its appointment of managing agents. In order to establish some control over the quality of management of the YTS scheme, all providers will have to hold Approved Training Organization status if they are to continue as managing agents after 1 April 1988.

The educational establishments involved have likewise had their problems in operating their part of the YTS scheme. The programme is far-reaching in the sense that it is designed to cater for all 16-17 year old school leavers, irrespective of their school achievements, abilities, interests etc. Colleges have had some difficulty in producing course material which will hold the interest of such a widely varied group of people. In addition, the college environment does not always commend itself to those whose school achievements are limited.

Having regard to the fact that the YTS scheme embraces young people of all types and of differing needs, it should not be expected to work miracles. The available evidence suggests, however, that the success rate is better than many reports would have us believe. Most employers take the programme seriously, recognizing that it is in their best long-term interests to do so. Some who have taken on trainees reluctantly have been pleasantly surprised at how well they have developed and have been happy to offer them suitable employment or further training. Those who have discharged their trainees at the end of the training period may have been forced into this position by economic factors. Different issues are thereby raised which are outside the scope of this book. The trainees not offered employment have not usually wasted their time for a year, but at the very least have improved their job prospects in the open market by the acquisition of skills and knowledge which they may not otherwise have obtained. In addition to acquiring that competence, they should also have been able to 'learn how to learn'. There are already healthy signs that employers recruiting staff are beginning to discriminate in favour of the young person who has completed a *two* year YTS programme (see next page). They are realizing that there is a payoff for them in taking on someone who not only has some experience of work, but also has vocational and transferable skills, backed up by suitable qualifications. Another attractive feature of the present YTS Scheme for the employer is the encouragement and scope given to the 'enterprising young person' prepared to make and take opportunities.

Bearing in mind the trauma suffered by many young people when entering employment after having spent most of their lives in full-time education, there is merit in their having been given the opportunity to learn about the world of work itself and about the rules, conditions, practices, disciplines etc that apply in it. The transition from school to work is a major turning point in a person's life and does, of course, lay the foundation for future career progress. Those who provide the facilities therefore have to do so with sensitivity and understanding. The standard of training that is given on entry into the world of employment can be critical and among other things demands instructional competence not only in terms of the knowledge and skill to be imparted but also in the ability to create the conditions for learning to take place. Criticisms have been levelled at some who are charged with responsibility for instructing school leavers in the YTS programme that they are not sensitive to the special needs of young people and so introduce a barrier to learning and cause unnecessary stress. The Training Commission responded to the need for guidance in this area by producing a package for the use of YTS tutors and supervisors.[147]

A further problem identified by the Commission[133] in 1984 was that of reconciling the foundation training provided by YTS with the first year of apprenticeship and other initial training schemes of longer duration. One solution suggested was that apprenticeships, which in their traditional form were fast disappearing (see Chapter 7), should be integrated into a YTS programme extended over two years. The decision was implemented in April 1986 to provide all 16 year old entrants with a two year programme of training.

In spite of the efforts made over the past few years to improve the UK's trading performance by training, it would appear to have fallen seriously short of that of other trading nations. A report[148] published in 1984 jointly by the National Economic Development Council and the MSC compared our training and education arrangements unfavourably with those of the USA, West Germany and Japan, and put forward 24 recommendations for change in order to achieve a level of performance which would enable us to compete effectively with these countries. One of the salient points made by the Institute of Manpower Studies, who prepared the report, was that attention should be given both to quality and quantity of training and in particular to the attainment of effective performance at work rather than simply the acquisition of technical skills. Three independent consultants who contributed to the report suggested that the three countries concerned 'overtrained' their workpeople in the interests of making them more receptive to new ideas and methods and more likely to identify and exploit opportunities. By contrast, we in the UK were inclined to train up to the minimum level required for a job to be carried out.[149]

There is little doubt that the major factor in promoting professionalism in training has been the attitude of management. Where managements have recognized its value in contributing towards corporate success, they have taken the trouble to find out what a training professional really looks like, appointed someone of the right calibre and given him the support and resources necessary for him to carry out his responsibilities effectively. In this way, the maximum possible benefit has been derived from training in the organization. Unfortunately, for every management having this insight there are several which do not appreciate what training can do for them. The result is that they may be persuaded to appoint a training officer for quite the wrong reasons and will end up with someone without the necessary qualifications. Sometimes people are moved sideways into training for no better reason than that they have to be found alternative work. Whether or not they are suited to it, or need specialist training for it, is not given any consideration at all. The effect of this kind of policy is to create a situation where the incumbent cannot do justice to the role, the function falls into disrepute for no fault of his, and management decides that training has failed. These are unhappy situations which do nothing to enhance the reputation of the profession.

The preoccupation of some managers and others with the outdated idea that training is something required only by apprentices and craftsmen has proved an irritation to training specialists for a very long time. It is one of the main reasons why employers may appoint training officers who are not capable of pursuing the full range of training activities. It almost becomes a self-fulfilling prophecy. 'Our training department does not know enough about management, so we don't do any management training.' Where the need for management or supervisory training is recognized, it is often sub-contracted. In medium and large businesses, however, there are advantages in dealing with it internally, provided training staff of the right calibre are recruited. The costs of using external resources can be exorbitant, and internal staff are likely to have a much more intimate knowledge of the organization and its needs than sub-contractors can hope to acquire in a limited period of project time.

The areas in which training has probably made the greatest strides are those concerned with methodology and matching the training to the true needs of an organization. Training officers tended in the past to go through a period early in their career when they saw training packages as the answer to most of their requirements. The approach to similar problems was stereotyped, both from the point of view of the material used and also the way in which it was used. In a sense, this may have arisen from inexperience, when the pre-designed package would have been seen as a lifeline, a device requiring the minimum of effort and skill to use. Although there are still some experienced trainers who operate in this way, most have come to realize that the best can only be achieved from training when it is directly related to the needs of the business. One should have no preconceived ideas as to how a training programme should be carried out or what material should be used. These decisions should only be made when it is known what is required in detail. It is then possible to tailor the resources and methods to the specific needs.

Advanced thinking about the conditions needed for effective learning to take place has helped to improve training efficiency. For instance, whilst retention does not automatically follow from simply telling somebody something, there is evidence to show that this approach can be valid where the learning method chosen is appropriate. A good deal of research into instructor style[57] and a systems approach to training has been carried out by the Industrial Training Research Unit (ITRU). The CRAMP system highlights five types of learning: Comprehension, Reflex action, appropriate Attitudes, Memorising and Procedural learning. If the learning methods for particular tasks are used as the basis of the training design, the end result is more likely to be effective in terms of meeting the training objectives.

The systems approach to training is demonstrated by ITRU's recent work on *Training in Fault Finding Skills.*[156] For a very long time, many skills have been acquired by what we have chosen to call 'experience'. Both employers and employees have convinced themselves that those skills could only be developed over a long period, usually several years, of practice. The skilled workers have been able to earn themselves places as 'key' workers, deemed to be irreplaceable because of the inordinately long time it would take for the necessary skills to be learned by someone else. They have been able to hold the employer, and sometimes their colleagues, to ransom by failing or refusing to pass on their skills. ITRU's work has shown that, with systematic analysis of the job and the skills involved, coupled with trainability tests[36] to ensure that selected workers have the basic ability to learn the skills, not only can these problems be overcome but the training periods can be dramatically reduced, often from several years to a few weeks. Important aspects of the approach in this project are: that the training of the specialist fault finder needs to be done alongside that of the operator so that they work in closer collaboration; dependence upon human memory is no longer acceptable; constant updating of skill and knowledge is vital; and everyone involved with the work is expected to think about it at all times in a systems-orientated way.

For those skills where, for example, a concept has to be developed, a group discovery learning approach has been used with some success. Trainees are given realistic tasks and are provided with the facilities and resources to enable them to find and test solutions for themselves. There are clear advantages in adopting this approach for lasting learning, particularly with middle-aged and older trainees and with tasks requiring understanding. It is particularly useful in the training of managers, supervisors and specialists, but can be equally effective with other groups. As stated on p. 106, one of the key ingredients of group training is the sharing of experience and knowledge between participants jointly engaged in problem-solving. Unfortunately, the documented results of participative training are limited due, no doubt, to the difficulty of measurement. The available evidence seems to suggest, however, that whilst success may not be guaranteed by the use of such methods, they are favoured by the majority of training specialists who have had experience of them.[64,67,150]

One area in which the training profession can claim some success is that of trainee motivation. Whilst there may have been confusion and some scepticism about the various theories which have been offered by the behavioural scientists, one thing that has come home to training specialists over the post-war years is that, when providing training opportunities for employees, the factors which motivate them and affect their behaviour cannot be ignored.[54] At one time employees were treated as though they all conformed to the same pattern and could be handled as homogeneous groups. It did not occur to trainers and instructors that varying responses were only partly due to varying abilities. Individuals were not only dissimilar in terms of their interests, knowledge, skills and understanding, but different forces were at work on them which affected their motivation or willingness to put effort into the task. Recognizing that such differences existed and required sensitive handling was a major breakthrough which was of great benefit to the training profession.

As previously suggested, the shortage of suitable means of evaluation has created problems in trying to assess the success or otherwise of training. The areas where this presents the least difficulty are those involving repetitive jobs such as are encountered on a mass- or batch-production line. It is comparatively easy to measure actual output against targeted output and to count the precise number of rejects produced. Quantity and quality are therefore readily ascertained and the effects of any training easily assessed. In factories where formal training for production workers has not been introduced, the thought does not cross anyone's mind that efficiency might be greatly improved by such means. Those who have been persuaded to implement systematic operator training, however, have usually been rewarded in the long term by significantly improved output performance. Sound training has also produced a higher standard of workmanship, resulting in a more acceptable product with fewer rejects. Improved morale can usually be expected to lead to lower absenteeism and labour turnover, although the latter may sometimes increase initially when operators become aware that they can sell their newly acquired skills elsewhere! There is welcome evidence of reduced accident rates since safety training has brought about a growing awareness of the hazards in a job and how they should be avoided.[151]

The recession and high levels of inflation have dealt the training function a heavy blow in recent years. Across-the-board cuts in resources, including staff, have decimated some training departments which were already operating on a shoestring. Ironically in such times there may be a strong argument for increasing rather than decreasing the training strength. If for economic reasons the overall workforce has to be reduced, it is imperative that those who remain are trained to operate as efficiently as possible. This requirement, which affects all departments including management, creates a substantial amount of potential work for training staff. Unfortunately, the need to cut overheads tends to take precedence over all else.

The record of training has therefore been variable, and has perhaps been more greatly influenced by factors outside the profession than within it. Most people who have chosen training as a career, and indeed many who have been drafted into it, are enthusiastic people whose dedication has increased with experience. In general, they have been prepared to put in a good deal of effort to keep pace with developments affecting them and they have been increasing their professional standards steadily. This gradual improvement in work performance for some of them has understandably had an effect on their acceptability and whilst things may not have moved as fast as they would have liked, it has nevertheless been progress in a most difficult period.

What is training's future?

Where does the training profession go from here? Whatever the frustrations that training specialists in the UK have been experiencing during the recession, there is little doubt that they will be able to look forward to better things now that the economy shows signs of improving. It is paradoxical that, at a time when training should have been able to make its maximum contribution towards helping to keep firms in business, it was looked upon as a luxury which could not be afforded. This constraint, however, should not have been seen as a setback but as an opportunity to prepare for the predicted expansion when it came.

The inevitable result of contraction in business during a recession is a disconcerting shortage of skilled people to cope with an upturn when it takes place. This provides a strong argument for carrying out training when there is plenty of time to do it so that employees are fully competent to handle the increased output when it is required. Since this policy is seldom followed, training staff suddenly find themselves greatly overloaded with work and required to produce instant results. They would therefore be wise to prepare themselves for this eventuality so that they are not caught unawares and put in a position where they are unable to cope with the demands. Additional staff will obviously not be forthcoming until after the needs have been demonstrated, but there are other things that training staff can do in advance to help lighten the load. If, for example, the planning of the anticipated training, even to the extent of producing the paperwork, can be carried out some time before the event, this will lessen the burden considerably when the go-ahead is eventually given. There is always a substantial time-lag between taking the initial training action and seeing the results of such action. It is when one has to start from scratch to produce results at short notice that one feels that the task is insurmountable.

There has been considerable debate over the past few years about the need to re-train adults in skills arising from new technology and methods.[103] In the main the discussion has centred around the loss of traditional skills and their replacement by higher-level skills, with all the problems that this entails in terms of employee adjustment to a strange new world. The explosion of information technology has had a major effect on the training scene. Because of the dramatic changes in language, methods of work etc necessary, this creates special difficulties for trainers. Inevitably, the highly technical nature of the subject matter means that the knowledge and expertise of specialists have to be used when establishing training programmes. If a non-technical trainer is responsible for the overall project, he has the problem of processing the information provided by the specialist in such a way that learning is not impeded by mystique, the use of jargon or the trainees' fear of change by reason of their unfamiliarity with the subject.

One of the consequences of introducing more efficient methods of work which has been given less attention is that working hours will become shorter and leisure hours will increase. Since this situation is brought about directly as a result of improved working practices, the responsibility for training employees to be able to cope with their newly acquired leisure time would appear to rest at least partially on the shoulders of the training department. If employees are not fully occupied during these increased leisure hours, there is a risk that their attitudes to work may change. This is an area which requires closer study.

The increasing professionalism of those employed in the training function gives cause for optimism. They continue to acquire new knowledge about business and about training, gradually moving away from the idea that the training officer's job is a purely administrative one. Instead they are becoming much more involved in planning at the corporate level and in ensuring the quality and relevance of the subsequent training activities. The professional institutions have also seen the need to update their qualifications from time to time in order to make them more relevant to the needs of the present and of the future.

There is evidence that the conventional training officer's role is undergoing a radical reassessment in some organizations. ITRU is currently involved in a study which pursues the concept of the 'investigative trainer'.[156] He is seen as an internal consultant with a pro-active role (see pages 78 and 196), being more directly involved with top management than most training officers are accustomed to be and therefore being in a position to influence board decisions where they are likely to have training implications. ITRU is examining the investigative skills required by such a trainer, comparing his role with that of the professional outside consultant or the academic involved in research. It is seeking to identify his investigative training needs, so that he can be helped to equip himself with suitable techniques and skills to enable him to discharge his training consultant responsibilities with competence and flexibility. One large employer in the motor industry has adopted the investigative trainer philosophy, having replaced the former direct trainer role with one involving 'change agents' (see pages 77-8), each of whom has responsibility for a specialized area, such as the training of graduates. The advantages of employing highly trained internal consultants who have the ear of management is clear in terms of lifting training standards in an organization. It is to be expected that more employers, encouraged by an improving economic climate and a return to profitability, will see that there are considerable benefits to be reaped from changing their approach to training in this way.

Thus we can look forward to seeing training specialists adopting a more proactive role. There is a growing awareness of the fact that if training action is simply left to those who are directly responsible for it, eg managers and supervisors, some important needs will be overlooked simply because there are no suitable triggers to stimulate a response. The training manager and his staff will therefore be more inclined than in the past to initiate action themselves by drawing management's attention to these requirements and gearing their own resources to satisfying them. This calls for much greater involvement of training with the management of the business and underlines the need for the development of team work at all levels. Obtaining acceptance of the team work concept requires an appreciation of what prevents people from operating as a team. For example, in some instances it does not even occur to them that there are advantages in working more closely together. They feel perfectly capable of carrying out the requirements of their own job descriptions and may not see the need for active co-operation with others who are supposed to be working towards the same goals. Many of the constraints to sharing knowledge and views for the common good tend, however, to be more personal. For instance, they may feel that sharing their assets with others will have a diluting effect and may in some way undermine their own positions. They may even enjoy a sense of power in being able to guard information that is not readily available to others. Undoubtedly there are some whose personal objectives are more important to them than those of the organization and some, too, who like to have their own way but avoid the conflict by isolating themselves. The fear that their deficiencies may be exposed by their having to bare their souls to a group is often very real. This is a form of insecurity which could largely be overcome by working as a member of a team once the initial barrier is broken down. Another factor which should not be overlooked is the possibility that due to a lack of awareness of the effect they have on other people they do not recognize a need to establish better personal relationships. Since all these constraints to operating as a team are also constraints to getting the job done effectively, there are clear advantages to be gained by promoting team work wherever practicable (see pp. 110-16).

Another change in emphasis in training activities which we can expect to continue over the next few years is the move towards development as distinct from pure training.[71] Training implies preparation to carry out the specific skill requirements of a job, whilst development involves the much wider concept of enabling employees to develop and grow with the organization of which they are part. In other words, training needs are derived from the dynamic work situation, which provides opportunities for the solution of real problems and response to change. Training packages have a limited role to play; solutions have to be specific to the identified problems. The development of a learning rather than an instructional climate is part of the process and we can reasonably expect improvements in attitudes, in application to work and ultimately in work performance to result from this approach. People who are actively involved in the operations of an undertaking, who feel part of it and essential to its success, are more likely to make a worthwhile contribution than those who are treated as mindless machines.

The adoption of a development rather than a pure training approach brings with it the need to monitor the progress of employees throughout their careers with the organization. At one time the aptitude of a new recruit for a particular job was given limited consideration. Some people ended up in the wrong jobs, and nobody saw fit to do anything about it. A good deal of time and money was wasted on training people for, and keeping them in, jobs to which they were not suited. There are heartening signs that training staffs are addressing themselves to this problem. They are having more say in recruitment procedures in an effort to reduce the risks of engaging unsuitable trainees. They are also conscious of the need to keep a constant vigil on training progress, so that they are able to recognize at the earliest possible stage any lack of aptitude for or interest in the proposed job. This attention to the trainee's performance and his demonstration of skills which would be of value elsewhere, enables the training department to consider action necessary to place him in the right job. This is a matter of considerable importance currently, since employment legislation discourages employers from dismissing employees without a very good reason. Allowing an employee to remain for an excessively long time in a job which is unsuitable and then dismissing him because he is not doing it properly is likely to be viewed with some disfavour by an industrial tribunal.

Some training in the past has been abortive because there has been a failure to establish precisely what we do in our jobs. There has been a temptation to accept what we think we do and to derive training needs from such data. Henry Mintzberg[152] has pointed out, however, that what we think we do and what we actually do are two different things. For example, whilst managers will say that their jobs are to plan, organize, co-ordinate and control, these claims are not borne out in practice. Instead, although admittedly they work at a relentless pace, they tend to operate in a reactive or fire-fighting way, responding to situations as and when they arise. The evidence that Mintzberg has put forward to support this contention has influenced some training managers to pay closer attention to identifying the true elements of jobs before attempting to design training programmes for them. This approach is expected to gain ground in the future.

There is no doubt that communication skills[153] have received a good deal of attention from training specialists in recent years. There is unlikely to be a trainer who has not at some time run a programme which incorporates these skills, yet people still seem to be singularly unsuccessful in communicating effectively! Reasons for the popularity of communication training are not hard to identify. Trainees find it satisfying because they can easily relate it to their experience and they do not normally find the subject itself difficult. Trainers sometimes choose it because it is a soft option for them, too; it is relatively simple to design training programmes. Nevertheless, it is of continuing importance since satisfactory communication is at the root of corporate effectiveness. It follows that the subject should be handled in such a way that it really brings about improved performance in communicating and is not simply a pleasant entertainment. One way in which this can be achieved is by integrating it carefully into other training activities and not identifying it as a separate subject. The principles can be incorporated in, for example, case studies, role plays and business games (see pp. 116-21), since these attempt to reproduce real-life situations. It is reasonable to predict that this type of activity will expand in the future and will become more sophisticated with the increased use of computers and video recording equipment.

One way in which training departments can improve their services is by providing assistance to employees in using sources of information for their self-development. Internal libraries under the control of the training department are extremely useful in this respect and the provision of reading lists covering topics of importance is also greatly valued. Prescribed reading as a training method was described on p. 143 and this is likely to be used increasingly, particularly if financial resources should continue to be limited.

There is much to be done in the whole area of employee relations training. Relationships between managers or supervisors and their subordinates often leave a lot to be desired. Too many assumptions are made about what should be expected from employees and too little attention is given to what they are capable of doing, what motivates them and what influences there may be on their lives outside work. Many of the core skills that managers are expected to possess are neglected, because it is taken as read that if they are practising managers they already possess them. Examples are: conducting various kinds of interview, such as performance review, selection, dismissal, redundancy, discipline, grievance; making business presentations to groups at all levels; instruction; delegation; time management; running meetings; organization of work; decision-making. Adequate managerial performance depends on being able to demonstrate effectiveness in such areas. Disputes between managements and trade unions also bring to light serious deficiencies in negotiating skills. At a time when industrial performance is essential for the country's economic recovery, we shall have to pay more attention to training in these vital skills.

Liaison with external bodies, particularly educational and professional establishments, which influence the activities of the training department, will be of growing importance in the future. The combined resources of the education and employment sectors have to be optimized in order to train employees to perform their roles adequately. It is therefore vital that the outputs of these two sources of knowledge and skill should interlock. They should be complementary and not in conflict. Theory learned with one should be put into practice with the other and one should help to update the other. This integration, if it is to work satisfactorily, requires a constant dialogue and understanding between the two parties and there is evidence to suggest that this dialogue is improving all the time.

The factor which is likely to have the greatest impact on the future of training will be the discovery of an effective means of evaluating it. There are hopeful signs that the pressures on training departments to prove their effectiveness will give rise to the development of acceptable methods of measuring their results. Project work and action plans are steps in the right direction, but much remains to be done.

What will be the future of the government-backed training organizations? The Training Commission has shown itself to be committed to the cause of training. Although some may have been critical of it in the past for the way in which its affairs were conducted, there is no doubt that it is gaining in reputation and it is making a determined effort to tackle the real issues, albeit with limited resources. With strong support and encouragement from the government, it has built up a good relationship with employers, trade unions and educational authorities alike. Its general training arrangements are under constant review and, where necessary, changes are made in the light of experience and in discussion with the government and other bodies. It recognizes in particular that, although past and present schemes have been of value, its programmes must measure up to the *current* needs and the expectations of the long-term unemployed.

Early in 1988, in a White Paper *Training for Employment*,[158] the Government outlined its strategy for training the unemployed to enable them to take advantage of the 'growing number of job vacancies' in the UK. In his preface, the Secretary of State for Employment stated, "As this White Paper makes clear, we need nothing less than a revolution in attitudes to training and retraining: a revolution which engages the commitment of employers and employees alike. As a nation we need to accept training through life and make it a reality".

The main features of the new programme, which is as yet unnamed but is due to run from September 1988, will be as follows:

- it will replace the Community Programme, the old and new Job Training Schemes and other training programmes for unemployed adults;
- it will offer up to 12 months full-time training, at least 40% of which will be directed training (or off-the-job learning), the programme being designed to meet the needs of the individual;
- the training provided will range from basic skills, including numeracy and literacy, to craft and technician level;
- anyone who has been unemployed for over 6 months will be eligible. Special arrangements will be made for disabled people, ex-Regulars, women returning to the labour market, people whose first language is not English, ex-offenders, people wanting training in business start-up or other enterprise training and people wanting training in skills needed in high tech industries or skill shortage areas;
- trainees will be referred in the first instance to a 'training agent' for an assessment of individual needs and aptitudes and the preparation of a personal action plan;
- a 'training manager' will deliver each trainee's training programme;
- on completion of the programme, the trainee will receive a record of his/her achievements;
- a new system of payment will ensure that trainees receive a guaranteed allowance in excess of the benefit entitlement;
- trainees will be protected under both equal opportunities and health and safety legislation in the same way as employees.

The Training Commission will be appointing and paying training agents and training managers and will expect them to be capable of delivering high quality training. They will include existing providers and organizations not previously involved with programmes for unemployed adults. The programme will have an annual budget of around £1.4 billion and is expected to have a throughput of 600,000 people per year. It is therefore the largest training programme that the UK has ever had, representing a massive investment which should gladden the heart of every training specialist. It would appear to be a genuine attempt to meet the needs of the country's unemployed and deserves success.

Over the past few years, the Commission has stimulated action in other more specialized areas of need. It has, for example, given considerable help to high tech industries. Together with the Department of Trade and Industry and a number of large employers, it assisted the National Interactive Video Centre[154] in setting up facilities for teachers, trainers etc to use interactive video technology (see Chapter 7). Through the Engineering Industry Training Board, it provided grants for, among other things, courses aimed at conversion from non-electronic to electronic skills. The learning needs of trainers have attracted far greater attention and help is now being provided to improve the delivery of training material.[125] The Open University has carried out considerable research into how students learn, incorporating its findings in the distance-learning methods used in its own programmes. Since 1984 the development of the University's self-funding Open Business College has represented a significant step forward, as has been the introduction of the Scientific and Technological Updating Programme, providing multi-media distance learning courses and self-study packs in the computer field. As a result of the increase in the use of open learning, the Commission plans to introduce a Code of Practice on the subject in the autumn of 1988.

In promoting training, the Commission is anxious to give due recognition to employers who excel in it, particularly in the areas of adult training and foundation training for young people. It has therefore introduced a system of widely acclaimed National Training Awards, the intention being to reward effectiveness in a specific area of training, rather than to acknowledge overall training performance. All the above are encouraging trends which the writer hopes will continue.

Those ITBs which survived the 1981 review[129] were the ones which were seen at the time to be most successful, such as Engineering, Hotel and Catering, and Construction. They are continuing to provide their members with considerable help and guidance, concentrating their efforts on the pressing needs of the day rather than on traditional training programmes. They have long since moved away from the custom of promoting acceptable training practices by imposing sanctions on offenders and now operate more as consultants whose expertise is respected. There would appear to be no good reason to change this.

In the writer's view, the future of the training profession over the next few years is unlikely to be characterized by dramatic innovation. There would appear to be considerable scope for the further development of those approaches which have met with some success and shown promise in the recent past and with the solution of those problems which have so far defied solution. One of the encouraging pointers to training progress is the growing professionalism of training staff, supported by their institutions. This is manifest in their increasing involvement in business planning and the development of better approaches to, and methods of, carrying out training at all levels.

The initiating role of the training department, which fills a serious gap in many organizations, will without doubt gain impetus. It is to be expected, too, that training staff will make a significant contribution to the promotion of team work, on the basis that true organizational success can only come from people working together towards a common objective. To this end, there is likely to be more stress on the concept of employee development as distinct from training in specific skills. This is essential in order to cope adequately with organizational change which is a characteristic of our modern society. Closer monitoring of employee progress will also be necessary to ensure that there are no square pegs in round holes, but everyone is trained to do the job to which he is best suited.

Experience provides us all with a continuous input of knowledge used in our everyday lives. There are still many people who believe that it is the only satisfactory route to acquiring job knowledge and skill. Properly designed training has, however, proved itself to be a means of reaching acceptable job performance more rapidly and more efficiently. If we want employees, from management down to the shop floor, to make an early contribution to the organization's operations, we can no longer afford to leave them to spend many years acquiring their basic skills by experience alone. In the interests of corporate success, which is influenced by economics, to say nothing of workforce morale, we must ensure that the performance of everyone in the organization is optimized at the earliest opportunity. Training's role in this process is a key one.

It has to be conceded that the future of training generally is largely dependent on the economic climate in the country and on the consequent conditions under which the organization is operating. Financial limitations restrict the activities of the function and prevent it from realizing its potential. It is very difficult for training professionals to be patient in circumstances where they are convinced that they could be making a much greater contribution towards efficiency and effectiveness, with the attendant saving in costs.

At the time of writing, there are heartening signs of growing confidence in the country's future. Employment opportunities are increasing, but paradoxically the potential growth of many businesses is limited by the shortage of trained personnel. It is difficult to understand why the skills necessary to sustain the hoped-for upturn in business could not have been more readily anticipated by employers, particularly since the Government, the Training Commission, the employers' associations, the professional institutions *et al* have been warning us constantly of the likely consequences of being caught unprepared. It is to be hoped that the warnings will soon be heeded before it is too late. The opportunities offered in an improving economic climate must certainly not be lost.

Notes and Bibliography

1. Roberts, C R Wynne *Introduction to Work Study* (3rd edition). International Labour Organization, 1979, Currie, R M (revised by Faraday, J E) *Work Study* (4th edition). British Institute of Management, 1977
2. Mayo, Elton *Management and Morale*. Harvard University Press, 1941
3. Maslow, Abraham H 'A theory of human motivation'. *Psychological Review* Vol 50 (1943) pp. 370-96; Maslow, Abraham (ed.) *Motivation and Personality* (2nd edition). Harper and Row, 1987
4. Herzberg, Frederick, Mausner, Bernard and Snyderman, Barbara *The Motivation to Work* (2nd edition). Wiley, 1959; Herzberg, Frederick *Work and the Nature of Man*. T Y Crowell Co, 1966
5. Argyris, Chris *Personality and Organization: the Conflict Between the System and the Individual*. Garland Publishing, 1987
6. McGregor, Douglas M *The Human Side of Enterprise*. McGraw-Hill, 1985
7. Likert, Rensis *New Patterns of Management*. McGraw-Hill, 1961; Likert, Rensis *The Human Organization: its management and value*. McGraw-Hill, 1967
8. Hunt, John W *Managing People at Work*. McGraw-Hill, 1st edition 1979, 2nd edition 1986
9. *Industrial Training Act 1964*. HMSO, 1964; Perry, P J C *The Evolution of British Manpower Policy* from the Statute of Artificers 1563 to the Industrial Training Act 1964). British Association for Commercial & Industrial Education (BACIE), 1976
10. [a] Detailed syllabuses, lists of publications and other information may be obtained from the appropriate Industrial Training Board. Addresses may be found on pages 347-354 of Armstrong, Michael *The Personnel Yearbook 1988* Kogan Page (in assoc. with IPM)
    [b] A report *Trends in Employment and Training of Craftsmen and Craftswomen 1988* is available from the Engineering Industry Training Board
11. *MSC Corporate Plan 1987/1991* Obtainable from the Sales Department, Training Commission Room W1111, Moorfoot,

Sheffield S1 4PQ. A 1988 catalogue of books and training materials marketed by the MSC is also available from this address.

12. Smith, J E *Cash Flow Management* (2nd edition). Woodhead-Faulkner in association with Alex Lawrie Factors, 1980
13. *Reference Book for Employers* (covering Employment Acts and Regulations generally) and *Employment Law* (covering its provisions in more detail). Croner Publications Ltd, Croner House, 173 Kingston Road, New Malden, Surrey KT3 3SS (Both with monthly amendments service.)
14. Institute of Training and Development (formerly Institution of Training Officers), Marlow House, Institute Road, Marlow, Bucks SL7 1BN; for summary of the ITD's services, qualifications and examinations, and a list of approved centres for appropriate courses, see Part 7 (pages 213-221) of *Directory of Trainer Support Services 1988*. Kogan Page (in assoc. with ITD)
15. Institute of Personnel Management, IPM House, 35 Camp Road, Wimbledon, London SW19 4UW; for a summary of the IPM's aims and services see Part 1 (pages 9-12) and for its Codes of Practice Part II (pages 95-122) of Armstrong, Michael *The Personnel Yearbook 1988*. Kogan Page (in assoc. with IPM)
16. Easterby-Smith, Mark *Evaluation of Management Education, Training and Development*. Gower Publishing, 1986; Bramley, Peter *Evaluation of Training: a Practical Guide*. BACIE, 1986; Rae, Leslie *How to Measure Training Effectiveness*. Gower Publishing 1986; Lawson, Ian *Target Setting*. Industrial Society, 1987
17. Megginson, David and Boydell, Tom *A Manager's Guide to Coaching*. BACIE, 1979; Singer E J *Effective Management Coaching* (2nd edition) IPM 1979; Deegan, A *Coaching – a Management Skill for Improving Individual Performance*. Addison-Wesley, 1980; Sagar, Eileen *Effective Delegation Skills*. ITRU 1984; Clutterbuck, David *Everyone needs a Mentor*. IPM 1985; Rae, W Leslie *Coaching for Results*. Industrial Society, 1987
18. Winfield, Ian *Learning to Teach Practical Skills: a Self-Instructional Guide*. Kogan Page, 1979; Training Division MSC *Presenting a Training Session – the Occasional Trainer's Guide to Resources*. MSC, 1982; Rae, W Leslie *The Skills of Training – a Guide for Managers and Practitioners*. Gower Publishing, 1983; Pepper, Alan D *Managing the Training & Development Function* p. 243. Gower Publishing, 1984
19. Dudick, Thos. and Goocki, R *Handbook of Business Planning and Budgeting for Executives with Profit Responsibility*. Van Nostrand Reinhold, 1983; Argenti, John *Corporate Planning*. Institute of Chartered Accountants, 1986; Cox, Bernard and

Fawn, John (eds.) *Corporate Planning in Practice*. Kogan Page, 1987 (in assoc. with Chartered Institute of Management Accountants and the Strategic Planning Society)

20. Humble, John *Management by Objectives in Action*. McGraw-Hill, 1970; Humble, John *Management by Objectives*. Gower Publishing, 1975; Morrisey, George *Management by Objectives and Results for Business and Industry*. Addison-Wesley, 1977; Humble, John *Improving Business Results*. McGraw-Hill, 1982
21. Bramham, John *Practical Manpower Planning* (3rd edition). IPM, 1982; Richards-Carpenter, C *Relating Manpower to an Organization's Objectives*. Institute of Manpower Studies, 1983; Pettman, Barrie O *Manpower Planning Workbook*. (2nd edition) Gower Publishing, 1984; Bennison, Malcolm and Richards-Carpenter, Colin *Relating Manpower to an Organisation's Objectives*. Gower Publishing 1985; Armstrong, Michael *A Handbook of Human Resource Management*. Kogan Page, 1987
22. Burgoyne, John and Stuart, Roger *Management Development – Context and Strategies*. Gower Publishing, 1978; Watson, Charles E *Management Development through Training*. Addison-Wesley, 1979; Woodcock, Mike and Jones John E *Manual of Management Development*. Gower Publishing 1985 (see also ref. 19)
23. Huczynski, Andrzej *Encyclopedia of Management Development Methods*. Gower Publishing, 1983; Taylor, Bernard & Lippitt, Gordon (eds) *Management Development and Training Handbook*. McGraw-Hill, 1983; Mumford, Alan *Handbook of Management Development* (2nd edition). Gower Publishing 1986; Molander, Dr C *Management Development: Key Concepts for Managers and Trainers*. Chartwell-Bratt Ltd, 1986; Margerison, Charles *Management Development Bibliography*. MCB University Press, 1987
24. Johnson, Robert G *The Appraisal Interview Guide*. AMACOM, 1980; Stewart, Valerie and Stewart, Andrew *Practical Performance Appraisal*. Gower Publishing, 1978; Long, Phil *Performance Appraisal Revisited* IPM 1986; Long, Phil *Assessment Centres*. IPM, 1987; Armstrong, Michael *A Handbook of Human Resource Management*. Kogan Page 1987
25. Robinson Kenneth R *Effective Performance Review Interviews*. Institute of Personnel Management, 1983; Lawson, Ian *Appraisal and Appraisal Interviewing*. Notes for managers series, Industrial Society, 1987
26. Blake, Robert R and Mouton, Jane S *Corporate Excellence through Grid Organization Development*. Gulf Publishing Company, 1968; Blake, Robert R and Mouton, Jane S *Consultation – a Handbook for Individual and Organization Development*. Addison-Wesley, 1983
27. Hague, Hawdon *Executive Self-Development: Real Learning in Real Situations*. Macmillan, 1974; Hague, Hawdon *Helping*

Managers to Help Themselves. Context, 1979; Jaap, T and Hampshire, Sheila *How to Realize your Potential* IPM 1981; Woodcock, Mike and Francis, Dave *The Unblocked Manager*. Gower Publishing, 1982; Francis, Dave and Woodcock, Mike *Fifty Activities for Self-Development*. Gower Publishing, 1982; Armstrong, Michael *How to be a Better Manager*. Kogan Page, 1983; *Self-Development for Women Managers* MSC Report, 1985; Barrington, Harry *Learning about Management*. McGraw Hill 1985; Boydell, Tom *Management Self-Development: a guide for Managers*. ILO Publications, 1986; Armstrong, Michael *A Handbook of Management Techniques*. Kogan Page, 1986; Lockett, John *Be the Most Effective Manager in Your Business*. Thorsons, 1987; Honey, Peter *Improve your People Skills*. IPM, 1988

28. Jones, Dr J A G *Training Intervention Strategies*. Paper published by Industrial Training Service Ltd, 1981 (See also Ref. 79)
29. Boydell, T H *A Guide to the Identification of Training Needs*. BACIE, 1976; Turrell, M *Training Analysis*. Trans-Atlantic Philadelphia, 1980; an action pack including the booklet *People – the Key to Success* and a video *Successful People* obtainable from NEDO books, Millbank Tower, Millbank, London SW1P 4QX
30. Boydell, T H *Guide to Job Analysis*. BACIE, 1970; *How to Use Job Analysis for Profitable Training*. Food, Drink & Tobacco Industry Training Board; McCormick, E *Job Analysis: Methods and Applications*. AMACOM, 1979; Gael, S *Job Analysis: a Guide to Assessing Work Activities*. Jossey-Bass, 1983
31. Webber, Ross *A Time and Management*. Moffat Publishing, 1981; Timpe, A Dale *Management of Time*. Facts on File (US), 1987; Adair, John *How to Manage Your Time*. Talbot Adair, 1987
32. MSC Training Studies *Task Analysis, Learning and the Nature of Transfer*. 1983; Desberg, Peter and Taylor, Judson H *Essentials of Task Analysis*. University Press of America, 1987
33. MSC *Glossary of Training Terms*. (3rd edition) HMSO, 1981
34. Singleton, W T *Introduction to Ergonomics*. World Health Organization, 1972; Oborne, D J *Ergonomics at Work*. Wiley, 1987; Oborne, D J *Applied Ergonomics Handbook*. Butterworth, 1987
35. Sargent, Andrew *Delegation*. Notes for managers series, Industrial Society; Jenks, James M and Kelly, John M *Don't Do. Delegate!* Kogan Page, 1987
36. (a) *Catalogue of Occupational Tests, Training Courses and Consultancy Services* is obtainable from NFER/Nelson Publishing, Darville House, 2 Oxford Road East, Windsor, Berks SL4 1DF (includes tests formerly published by the National Institute of Industrial Psychology); Part 5 (page 161) of *Directory of Trainer Support Services 1988*. Kogan Page (in assoc. with ITD)

(b) The Test Agency Ltd, Cournswood House, North Dean, High Wycombe, Bucks HP14 4NW

(c) Trainability tests (with particular application to adult re-training) and tests to identify skill transferability are produced by the Industrial Training Research Unit, 71, Bridge Street, Cambridge CB2 1UR

(d) *EITS test catalogue* is obtainable from Educational and Industrial Test Services Ltd, 83 High Street, Hemel Hempstead, Herts HP1 3AH

37. Anastasi, Anne *Psychological Testing* (5th edition). Collier Macmillan International Series, 1982; Toplis, John, Dulewicz, Vic and Fletcher, Clive *Psychological Testing – a Practical Guide.* IPM, 1987

38. Information about Occupational Personality Questionnaires (OPQ), Occupational Testing courses and training in Assessment Centres, Interviewing Skills and Personality Assessment is obtainable from Saville & Holdsworth Ltd, The Old Post House, 81 High Street, Esher, Surrey KT10 9QA

39. Cooper, C L (ed.) *Improving Interpersonal Relations.* Gower Publishing, 1981; Phillips, K and Fraser, T *The Management of Interpersonal Skills Training.* Gower Publishing, 1982; Rae, Leslie *The Skills of Human Relations Training.* Gower Publishing, 1985; Binstead, D *Developments in Interpersonal Skills Training.* Gower Publishing, 1986; Nelson-Jones, Richard *Human Relationship Skills.* Holt, Rinehart and Winston, 1986; Honey, Peter *Improve Your People Skills.* IPM, 1988; a list of Management Training Centres in the UK is given in Part V (pages 355-377) of Armstrong, Michael *The Personnel Yearbook 1988.* Kogan Page (in assoc. with IPM) and also in Part 2 (pages 104-115) of *Directory of Trainer Support Services 1988.* Kogan Page (in assoc. with ITD)

40. Grummitt, Janis *A Guide to Interviewing Skills.* Industrial Society, 1980; Hackett, Penny *Interview Skills Training – Practice Packs for Trainers* (2nd edition). Institute of Personnel Management, 1981; Bolton, G M *Interviewing for Selection Decisions.* NFER-Nelson Publishing, 1983; Stewart, Dorothy *Handbook of Management Skills.* Gower Publishing, 1987

41. Board, Robert de *Counselling People at Work: an Introduction for Managers.* Gower Publishing, 1983; *Counselling News for Managers.* Magazine published by the Centre for Professional Employment Counselling (CEPEC), Sundridge Park Management Centre, Plaistow Lane, Bromley, Kent BR1 3JW; Megranahan, Mike *Counselling: a Practical Guide for Employers.* IPM, 1988; *Counselling at Work* – video package provided for group training or self-instruction by NACAB Vision, Myddleton House, 115/123 Pentonville Road, London N1 9LZ

42. Robinson, Kenneth R *The Do's and Don'ts of Making Business Presentations*. Cambridge Management Training, 1983
43. Lists of external courses for managers are to be found in
    (a) The National Training Index – an updating service on subscription from 6 Hanover Street, London W1R 9HH
    (b) *Management Training Directory* (9th edition). 1988 – edited by Allan Wood and published by Alan Armstrong & Associates
44. Robinson, Kenneth R *101 Accounting Definitions for the Non-Accountant*. Cambridge Management Training, 1985
45. *The Training of Clerks – Booklet No. TR8*. Engineering Industry Training Board, 1969
46. An example of a recommended training programme for graduate engineers is to be found in the EITB's booklet No. TR22 *The Training of Graduates in Engineering 1983*; Morris, Robert and Vosburgh, Richard *Career Development for Engineers and Scientists*. Van Nostrand Reinhold, 1987
47. Ottaway, Richard N *Change Agents at Work*. Greenwood, 1979; Pepper, Alan D *Managing the Training and Development Function*. Gower Publishing, 1984
48. Towers, Brian (ed.) *A Handbook of Industrial Relations Practice*. Kogan Page, 1987
49. *Employment Protection Act 1975* HMSO, 1975; Advisory Conciliation and Arbitration Service (ACAS) *Code of Practice No. 2 (Disclosure of Information to Trade Unions for Collective Bargaining Purposes)*. HMSO, 1977; Page, G Terry *An Employer's Guide to Disclosure of Information*. Kogan Page, 1978; Thomason, George *A Textbook of Industrial Relations Management*. Institute of Personnel Management, 1984
50. ACAS *Code of Practice No. 1 (Disciplinary Practice and Procedures in Employment)*. HMSO, 1977; ACAS *Discipline at Work – the ACAS Advisory Handbook*. 1987. Intended to complement the above code and available from any ACAS office (Headquarters: Clifton House, 83-117 Euston Road, London NW1 2RB)
51. Rogers, Carl R *Freedom to Learn for the 80s* (2nd edition). Charles E Merrill, 1983
52. Bass, Bernard M and Vaughan, James A *Training in Industry – the Management of Learning*. Tavistock Publications, 1966; Berger, M L and P J *Group Training Techniques*. Gower Publishing 1972
53. MSC leaflet *Learn How to Learn* 1983, details obtainable from Sales Office, Room W1111 Training Commission, Moorfoot, Sheffield S1 4PQ; Mumford, Alan *Learning to Learn for Managers*. Journal of European Industrial Training Vol 10 No 2, 1986
54. Simpson, William A *Motivation*. Notes for managers series, Industrial Society; Robinson, Kenneth R *A Practical Approach to Employee Motivation*. Cambridge Management Training, 1984;

Martin, Peter and Nicholls, John *Creating a Committed Workforce.* IPM, 1987; Garnett, John *The Work Challenge.* Industrial Society, 1987

55. Georgopoulos, Basil S, Mahoney, Gerald M and Jones, Nyle W 'A path-goal approach to productivity'. *Journal of Applied Psychology* Vol 41 (1957) pp. 345-53
56. Biddle, Derek and Evenden, Robin *Human Aspects of Management.* IPM, 1980; Argyris, Chris *Reasoning, Learning and Action: Individual and Organization.* Jossey-Bass, 1982; Fiedler, Fred Edward and Garcia, Joseph E *New Approaches to Effective Leadership: Cognitive Resources and Organizational Performance.* Wiley, 1987; Reddin W J *How to Make Your Management Style More Effective.* McGraw-Hill, 1987
57. Industrial Training Research Unit *What's in a Style?* ITRU research paper TR3. This and other publications, workbooks etc obtainable direct from ITRU at the address given in ref. 36(c)
58. Brown, George *Lecturing and Explaining.* Methuen, 1978; Gibbs, Graham etc *Fifty-three Interesting Things to Do in Your Lectures.* Technical and Educational Services, 1987
59. Taylor, H M and Mears, A G *Right Way to Conduct Meetings, Conferences and Discussions* (8th edition). Paperfronts, 1983; Seekings, David *How to Organise Effective Conferences and Meetings* (3rd edition). Kogan Page, 1986; Janner, Greville *Complete Speechmaker* (3rd edition). Hutchinson, 1986; a conference checklist is provided in Part V (pages 378-381) of Armstrong, Michael *The Personnel Yearbook 1988.* Kogan Page (in assoc. with IPM); for a list of UK conference venues see Part 5 (pages 162-191) *Directory of Trainer Support Services 1988.* Kogan Page (in assoc. with ITD)
60. Munson, Lawrence S *How to Conduct Training Seminars.* McGraw-Hill, 1984
61. Sattler, W M and Miller, N E *Discussion and Conference.* Prentice-Hall, 1968; Janner, Greville *On Meetings.* Wildwood House, 1987 (See also Ref. 62)
62. Debenham, A I S *Training Officer's Guide to Discussion Leading.* BACIE, 1969
63. Francis, Dave *Fifty Activities for Improving Corporate Communication.* Gower Publishing, 1987
64. Adair, John *Training for Leadership.* Gower Publishing, 1978; Kilman, Ralph 'An organic-adaptive organization – the MAPS method'. *Personnel*, May-June 1974 pp. 35-47; Delbecq, André L et al *Group Techniques for Programme Planning: A Guide to Nominal Group and Delphi Processes.* Green Briar Press, 1986; Rackham, Neil and Morgan, Terry *Behaviour Analysis and Training (BOAC project).* McGraw-Hill, 1977; Babington-Smith, B *Training in Small Groups – a Study of Five Methods* (revised

edition). Pergamon Press, 1979; Woodcock, Mike *Team Development Manual*. Gower Publishing, 1979; Adair, John *Effective Teambuilding*. Gower Publishing, 1986. See also references 105 and 106

65. Belbin, R Meredith *Management Teams*. Heinemann, 1984; Margerison, Charles and McCann, Dick *How to lead a Winning Team*. MCB University Press, 1987; Cooke, Anne *Women and Training – Developing a Major Resource*. MCB University Press, 1987
66. Suessmuth, Patrick 'Training small groups – how to structure them for better results'. *Training*, June 1976; Suessmuth, Patrick *Ideas for Training Managers and Supervisors: useful suggestions, activities and instruments*. University Associates, 1978
67. Mangham, Iain 'Building an effective work team'. *Training and Development Journal*, 1971
68. Anthony, William P *Participative Management*. Addison-Wesley, 1978
69. Information on work restructuring may be obtained from: Technical & Efficiency Organization Department, N V Philips Gloeilampenfabrieken, Eindhoven, Holland; Christopher and Christopher *Job Enrichment: How Far Have We Come?* University Press of America, 1983
70. Lawrence, P R and Lorsch, J W *Developing Organizations: Diagnosis and Action*. McGraw-Hill, 1969; Woodcock, Mike and Francis, Dave *Organisation Development Through Teambuilding*. Gower Publishing, 1981; Saunders, Graham *The Committed Organisation*. Gower Publishing, 1984 (See also ref. 8)
71. *Code for Continuous Development: People and Practice*. IPM. October 1984
72. Drucker, Peter F *Management Cases*. Heinemann, 1978; Page, G Terry *Personnel and Training Management Yearbook and Directory 1980* Section 22. Kogan Page, 1979; Easton, Geoff *Learning from case studies*. Prentice-Hall, 1982; May, Sheila *Case Studies in Business*. Pitman, 1984; Laird, Dugan *Approaches to Training and Development* (2nd edition). Addison-Wesley, 1985
73. Reese, W L (ed.) *Dictionary of Philosophy and Religion*. Harvester Press, 1980
74. Maier, Norman R F, Solem, Allen R and Maier, Ayesha A *The Role Play Technique*. University Associates, 1975; van Ments, Morry *The Effective Use of Role-Play: a Handbook for Teachers and Trainers*. Kogan Page, 1983
75. IPM (NCTD) and Peter Dye Associates *IMPPACT! Improving the Management of People, Performance and Company Trading*. IPM, Nov 1987; Christopher, Elizabeth and Smith, Larry *Leadership Training through Gaming*. Kogan Page, 1987; Part 5 (page 161) of *Directory of Trainer Support Services 1988*. Kogan Page (in assoc.

with ITD); Elgood, Chris *Handbook of Management Games* (4th edition). Gower Publishing, 1988.

76. Rawlinson, T. Geoffrey *Creative Thinking and Brainstorming*. Gower Publishing, 1983; Timpe, A Dale *Creativity*. Facts on File, 1987
77. (a) A summary of the value engineering technique and a useful reading list are given in the Engineering Industry Training Board's booklet *Courses for Managers – Value Engineering*, produced with the assistance of Value Control Ltd. Obtainable from: EITB, 369 Euston Road, London NW1 3AR.
    (b) Value Control Ltd, Drayton Holloway, nr Tring, Herts HP23 4LB are consultants in value engineering and associated techniques
78. (a) The address of ERGOM (European Research Group on Management) is: Predikherenberg 55, 3200 Kessel-LO, Belgium
    (b) Adair, John, Ayres, Richard, Debenham, Ian and Després, David (eds). *A Handbook of Management Training Exercises* (available in three separate volumes). BACIE, 1978, 1980 and 1987
79. Argyris, Chris *Intervention Theory and Method: Behavioural Science View*. Addison-Wesley, 1971; Kenney, John and Reid, Margaret *Training Interventions*. IPM, 1986 (See also ref. 28)
80. Foxon, Trevor and Peck, Trevor *Supervisors: their Selection, Training and Development*. Notes for managers series, Industrial Society; Bittel, L and Madison, J *The Complete Guide to Supervisory Training and Development*. Addison-Wesley, 1987
81. Rackham, Neil *Developing Interactive Skills*. Wellens Publishing 1971 (See also refs. 39, 64)
82. Blumberg, Arthur *Sensitivity Training: Processes, Problems and Applications*. Syracuse University (Continuing Education Centre), 1971; Argyle, Michael *The Psychology of Interpersonal Behaviour*. Penguin Books, 1983
83. Blake, Robert R and Mouton, Jane S *New Managerial Grid*. Gulf Publishing, 1978; Blake, Robert R and Mouton, Jane S *The Managerial Grid III* (3rd edition) Gulf Publishing, 1984
84. Berger, M L and P J *Group Training Techniques* (Chapter 3 'Managerial Grid Training – an application in ICI Pharmaceuticals Division' by George Clark). Gower Publishing, 1972
85. Harris, Thomas *I'm OK – You're OK*. Pan Books, 1973; Jongeward, Dorothy (*et al*) *Everybody Wins: Transactional Analysis Applied to Organizations*. Addison-Wesley, 1976; Barker, Dave M *TA and Training – the theory and use of Transactional Analysis in Organisations*. Gower Publishing, 1979; Berne, Eric *Games People Play: Psychology of Human Relationships*. Penguin Books, 1980
86. Carby, Keith and Thakur, Manab *Transactional Analysis at Work*. IPM Information Report 23, 1976

87. Lists of producers of audio-visual hardware, including film projectors and videotape recorders may be found in Part 5 (pages 159-160) of *Directory of Trainer Support Services 1988*. Kogan Page (in assoc. with ITD); for films, videos and interactive videos, Johannsen, H (ed.) *Know your Training Films: Directory and Reviews* (2nd edition). Management Update, 1987; training films suppliers are given in Part 2 (pages 128-140) *Directory of Trainer Support Services 1988* (as above)
88. In-tray exercises are produced by
    (a) Daedel Training Ltd, Peak House, 66 Croydon Road, Beckenham, Kent BR3 4AA
    (b) a student pack (16-18 years) is available from Hobsons Publishing plc (on behalf of the Careers Research and Advisory Centre), Bateman Street, Cambridge CB2 1LZ
89. Russell, Peter *The TM Technique*. Routledge & Kegan Paul, 1978
90. Vernon, Peter J (ed.) *A Series of Case Histories of the Use of Programmed Learning*. National Committee for A-V Aids in Education (US). 1969; Day, Harry *Self-Instruction – an Approach to Staff Training*. HMSO, 1984; Bell, Chris *PLET Programmed Learning and Educational Technology*. The quarterly Journal of the Association for Education and Training Technology (AETT). Kogan Page
91. Further information may be obtained from the Open University, Walton Hall, Milton Keynes, Bucks MK7 6AA
92. Government White Paper *A New Training Initiative – a Programme for Action*. MSC, 1981
93. MSC consultative document *An 'Open Tech' Programme*. MSC, May 1981
94. Information about available open-learning materials may be obtained from MARIS-NET (Ely) Ltd, Bank House, 1 St Mary's Street, Ely, Cambridgeshire CB7 4ER; Lewis, R (ed.) *Open Learning in Action* (O.L.Guide 1). Council for Educational Technology, 1986; Bennett, Roger *Through the Open Door – Today's Revolution in Open Access and Distance Learning*. MCB University Press, 1986; Airey, F and Goodman, M N *A Survey of Distance Education in Industry Training*. Harbridge Consulting Group, 1986; *Ensuring Quality in Open Learning – A Handbook for Action* MSC (MC39) Nov 1987; a list of open learning material suppliers is provided in Part 2 (pages 128-140) of *Directory of Trainer Support Services 1988*. Kogan Page (in assoc. with ITD); *Open Learning Directory 1988/89* MSC (MC37) Apr 1988; the office of the Open College is at St Mary's House, London Road, Sheffield S2 4LA
95. *Induction – Notes for Managers No. 21*. Industrial Society, 1973; Fowler, Alan E *Getting Off to a Good Start: Successful Employee Induction*. Institute of Personnel Management, 1983

96. Belbin, Eunice, Belbin, R Meredith *Problems in Adult Re-Training* Heinemann, 1972 (The authors are now Directors of Employment Development Unit Ltd, 7a Rose Crescent, Cambridge CB2 3LL – researching cost effective ways of creating employment); Miller, Kentalle and Miller, Isobel *Retraining and Tradition: Skilled Worker in an Era of Change*. Beekman Publishers, 1975; a report on adult re-training *Developing Skilled Learners*. MSC, 1988

97. Kniveton, Bromley and Towers, Brian *Training for Negotiating*. Business Books, 1978; Brewster, Chris and Connock, Stephen *Industrial Relations Training for Managers*. Kogan Page 1980; Le Poole, Samfrits *Never Take No for an Answer* – a guide to successful negotiation. Kogan Page, 1987

98. Dean, Christopher and Whitlock, Quentin *A Handbook of Computer-Based Training*. Kogan Page 1984

99. Jenkin, J M *Computer-Based Training – A Guide for Trainers and Managers*. MSC 1983; *Introduction to Computer Based Training*. A multi-media pack for trainers, resulting from an MSC funded survey by the Open University, 1985. Available from the OU (see ref. 91).

100. Kearsley, Greg *Computer-Based Training – a Guide to Selection and Implementation*. Addison-Wesley, 1983. Note: this book also includes a very detailed bibliography; Lewis, Robert *Computer-Based Training*. Parthenon Publications, 1987

101. Parsloe, Eric (ed.) *Interactive Video*. Sigma Technical Press, 1984. Note: This book also includes an excellent glossary of terms

102. O'Neill, Gerard *Interactive Video in Training*. Parthenon Publications, 1987

103. *Impact of New Technology on Skills in Manufacturing and Services*. MSC (RD28); Blaazer, Caroline *Managing Information Technology*. Industrial Society, 1987

104. Boydell, T H and Pedler, Mike (eds) *Management Self-Development: Concepts and Practice*. Gower Publishing, 1981

105. Pedler, Mike (ed.) *Action Learning in Practice*. Gower Publishing, 1983; Barrington, Harry A *Learning about Management*. McGraw-Hill, 1984; Mumford, Alan (ed.) *Action Learning*. MCB University Press, 1987

106. Revens, Reginald W *Action Learning – New Techniques for Management*. Blond & Briggs, 1980; Revans, Reginald W *The Origins and Growth of Action Learning*. Chartwell Bratt Ltd, 1982

107. A report on 'EEC employment and company law: recent developments and prospects' by Dr Michael Gold (editor of *European Industrial Relations Review*) is given in section 2.1 of the *Personnel and Training Databook 1985*. Kogan Page. It includes a concise summary of the Draft Fifth and Vredeling Directives

108. Jennings, C, McCarthy, W E J, Undy, R *Managers and Industrial Relations – the Identification of Training Needs*. MSC, 1983. Obtainable from Research Secretary, Templeton College, Oxford Centre for Management Studies, Kennington, Oxford OX1 5NY
109. Employment Relations Ltd, 62 Hills Road, Cambridge CB2 1LA
110. 'The use of repertory grid methods' by Mark Easterby-Smith is to be found in Chapter 26 of Taylor, Bernard & Lippitt, Gordon *Management Development and Training Handbook*. McGraw-Hill, 1983; Stewart, Valerie, Stewart, Andrew & Fonda, Nickie *Business Applications of Repertory Grid*. McGraw-Hill, 1981
111. One such association is the Academy of Graphology, 3 Queen Elm Square, London SW2 6ED. Enquiries concerning its activities and publications may be made to the Research Secretary, Mrs V Sharma, 47 Monks Walk, Buntingford, Herts SG9 9EE (home address)
112. Information about computer-assisted graphology may be obtained from Character Analysis, 13 Burgess Field, Chelmer Village, Chelmsford CM2 6TR
113. A statement, 'Standards and routes to registration', designed to switch emphasis from time serving to the attainment of standards, knowledge and skills, was issued in 1985 by the Engineering Council, Canberra house, Maltravers Street, London WC2R 3ER
114. Briggs, L J & Wager, W W *Handbook of Procedures for the Design of Instruction* (2nd edition). Educational Technology Publications, 1981
115. Millar, Colin *Organization and Methods*. Cassell, 1983; Anderson, R G *Organization and Methods* (2nd edition). Trans-Atlantic Philadelphia, 1980; Cemach, Harry P *Work Study in the Office* (6th edition). Anbar Publications, 1986
116. *Reviewing the Effectiveness of Training*. Food, Drink & Tobacco Industry Training Board, 1972 (See also ref. 33)
117. Frost, Michael J *How to Use Cost Benefit Analysis in Project Appraisal*. Gower Publishing, 1975
118. *Survey of Training Costs* (new series no. 1). Industrial Society, 1985
119. Hall, N *Cost-Benefit Analysis in Industrial Training*. Manchester monograph 6, University of Manchester, 1976; Kearsley, Greg *Costs, Benefits and Productivity in Training Systems*. Addison-Wesley, 1982; Kearsley, Greg *Training and Technology*. Addison-Wesley, 1984
120. Rackham, Neil *Development and Evaluation of Supervisory Training*. Research Report 71/1, Air Transport & Travel Industry Training Board, March 1971
121. Philips, Jack J *Handbook of Training Evaluation and Measurement Methods*. Gulf Publishing, 1983
122. Farnsworth, Terry *Developing Executive Talent*. McGraw-Hill,

1975; a list of management consultants and training consultants may be found in Part 2 (pages 59-98) of *Directory of Trainer Support Services 1988*. Kogan Page (in assoc. with ITD)

123. Rodger, Alec, Morgan, Terry and Guest, David *The Industrial Training Officer – His Background and His Work*. IPM, 1971

124. Birkenbihl, Michael *Train the Trainer*. Chartwell Bratt, 1984 (See also ref. 125 below)

125. (a) *Training of Trainers – First Report of Training of Trainers Committee*. HMSO (MSC), 1978; *Direct Trainers – Second Report of Training of Trainers Committee*. HMSO (MSC), 1980; *Decisions about Training: a Guide to Reviewing Training Arrangements*. MSC, 1983; a paper on *Developing Trainers: MSC support for training of trainers and staff development*. MSC, 1987

(b) Industrial Training Research Unit *The Role and Tasks of Tutors in Open Learning Systems*. 1984/5 Report by ITRU – see ref. 36(c); practical material for trainers *CRAMP: – Linking Learning and Training*. ITRU package; *Trainer's Guide to Materials and Resources in Adult Training* (a bibliography of materials available). BACIE, 1986; Industrial Training Service Ltd and ITRU *Deciding Designing Delivering: The competencies of staff involved in computer based training*. MSC(MC13) 1986; ITRU *Tutor Competencies for Open Learning*. MSC(MC27) 1986. The Training Commission has also produced publications investigating ways in which information technology can be applied to training (MC1, MC15, MC34 & CS01). All its publications are obtainable from: The Sales Manager, Training Commission PP2, Freepost, P.O. Box 161, Bradford BD9 4BR. Information from: The Sales Office, Training Commission, Room W1111, Moorfoot, Sheffield S1 4PQ; Mathias, Haydn, Budgett, Robin and Rushby, Nick (eds.) *Designing New Systems and Technologies for Learning*. Kogan Page, 1988

126. Powell, L S *A Guide to the Use of Visual Aids* (3rd edition). BACIE, 1970; Otto, Calvin P and Glaser, Rollin O *The Management of Training: a Handbook for Training Directors*. Addison-Wesley, 1970; Kearsley, Greg *Training and Technology*. Addison-Wesley, 1984

127. Pearson, Sonia and Coulthard, Derek *Personnel Procedures and Records* (4th edition). Industrial Society (in assoc. with Gower Publishing), 1987

128. Johnson, P S 'The economic evaluation of operator training'. *Industrial Relations Journal*, September 1970 pp. 61-70; Garbutt, Douglas *How to Budget and Control Cash*. Gower Publishing, 1985; The Planning Exchange *Paying for Training – a PICKUP*

guide. Department of Education and Science, 1987. Obtainable from the Planning Exchange, 186 Bath Street, Glasgow G2 4HG; Deloitte, Haskins and Sells report *The Funding of Vocational Education and Training*. MSC 1987 (See also Ref. 44)

129. MSC report *A Framework for the Future – A Sector-by-Sector Review of Industrial and Commercial Training*. MSC, July 1981
130. Information on the Commission's activities is available from any of its Regional or Area Offices. Addresses may be found in Part 2 Section 9 of Armstrong, Michael (consultant ed.) *The Personnel Yearbook 1988*. Kogan Page (in assoc. with IPM)
131. *MSC Manpower Review* (Section 5 – The Commission's Plans 1980-84). MSC, May 1980
132. *MSC Training for Skills – A Programme for Action*. MSC, December 1977
133. (a) *MSC Corporate Plan 1984-1988*. MSC, May 1984
   (b) The Commission produces a bi-monthly newsletter *Focus on Adult Training; Training Bibliography* – texts on the UK's vocational education and training system. BACIE, 1985; Cooper and Lybrand *A Challenge to Complacency – a report on Adult Training*. MSC. 1986
134. Department of Employment and Department of Education and Science *Training for Jobs*. HMSO, 1984
135. The Department of Education and Science publishes an occasional bulletin, *PICKUP in Progress*, which gives details of the PICKUP programme and how it is being implemented; a report *A Partnership in Learning*, arising from a research project commissioned by PICKUP, has also been produced by the Department, whose publications are available from the Adult Training Promotions Unit, Room 2/14, DES, Elizabeth House, York Road, London SE1 7PH
136. MSC consultative document *Towards an Adult Training Strategy*. MSC, 1983
137. *IPM Digest* p. 7. Institute of Personnel Management, January 1985
138. (a) Lists of schools and careers services in a particular area may be obtained from the Education Officer of the appropriate local authority. Colleges of further and higher education and private colleges are given in Part 2 (pages 116-127) of *Directory of Trainer Support Services 1988*. Kogan Page (in assoc. with ITD)
   (b) Names and addresses of polytechnics and universities in the UK are listed in Armstrong, Michael (consultant ed.) *The Personnel Yearbook 1988*, Kogan Page (in assoc. with IPM)
139. Names and addresses of business schools and management training centres may be found on pages 344-345 and 355-377 respectively of Armstrong, Michael (consultant ed.) *The Personnel Yearbook*

1988. Kogan Page (in assoc. with IPM); UK business schools are also listed in *Directory of Trainer Support Services 1988*. Kogan Page (in assoc. with ITD)

140. A list of professional, qualifying and advisory bodies and their addresses is given in Part 6 (pages 195-209) *Directory of Trainer Support Services 1988*. Kogan Page (in assoc. with ITD)
141. Confederation of British Industry, Centre Point, 103 New Oxford Street, London WC1A 1DU
142. Trades Union Congress, Congress House, Great Russell Street, London WC1B 3LS
143. A list of employers' associations may be found in *Directory of Employers' Associations, Trade Unions, Joint Organizations, etc.* HMSO for department of Employment, 1977, plus three-monthly amendments
144. A list of British chambers of commerce may be found in the *Reference Book for Exporters* (with amendment service). Croner Publications (see ref. 13)
145. A list of technical, academic, educational and professional qualifications may be found in *British Qualifications 1988* (18th edition). Kogan Page
146. The 'Economic Progress Report' is printed by HMSO and is obtainable from Economic Progress Report (Distribution), Central Office of Information, Hercules Road, London SE1 7DU. An index of main statistical sources which are also of value to training staff is published in Section 5.7 of the *Personnel and Training Data-book 1984*. Kogan Page
147. *Introductory Programme for YTS Tutors and Supervisors*. A training pack commissioned by the MSC from the Centre for Learning and Development and obtainable from Guildford Educational Services Ltd, 276 High Street, Guildford GU1 3JL
148. Report *Competence and Competition: Training and Education in the Federal Republic of Germany, the United States and Japan 1984*. Obtainable from NEDC Books, Millbank Tower, Millbank, London SW1P 4QX
149. Hayes, Chris, Anderson, Alan and Fonda, Nickie 'International competition and the role of competence'. *Personnel Management* journal September 1984, pp. 36-38
150. Campbell, John P (*et al*) *Manageral Behaviour, Performance and Effectiveness*. McGraw-Hill, 1970; Smith, Peter B *Group Processes and Personal Change*. Harper & Row, 1980; Rees, R *Group Working Lifts Morale and Output*, Works Management, 1984
151. Evidence that sound operator (and other) training reduces accidents can be made available by British Safety Council, National Safety Centre, 62-64 Chancellor's Road, London W6 9RS
152. Mintzberg, Henry *The Nature of Managerial Work*. Harper & Row, 1973

153. Leavitt, Harold J *Readings in Managerial Psychology* (3rd edition). University of Chicago Press, 1980; Newman, Ruth G (*et al*) *Communicating in Business Today*. D C Heath, 1987; Thayer, Lee *Communication and Communication Systems: in Organization, Management and Interpersonal Relations*. University Press of America, 1987

154. The National Interactive Video Centre, 24/32 Stephenson Way, London NWE1 2HD produces case studies, maintains a register of current research, runs seminars and provides hands-on experience of IV equipment on its premises.

155. (a) The National Training Awards scheme, first introduced in 1987, is run by the NTA Office of the Training Commission. Details are available from Freefone National Training Awards or by post from Freepost, Training Commission, Moorfoot, Sheffield S1 4PQ
(b) *National Training Awards* – a report on the first year's results by Max Burgess and Keith Lathrope. Obtainable from NTA Distribution Office, 7 Rutland Way, Sheffield S3 8DG
(c) Comment on first year's entries by Keith Lathrope. Personnel Management, March 1988, page 6

156. Information on the research projects *Training in Fault Finding Skills – a Systems Approach* and *The Investigative Trainer* is obtainable from ITRU. (See ref. 36(c))

157. The address of the headquarters of the National Council for Vocational Qualifications (NCVQ) is 222 Euston Road, London NW1 2BZ

158. Government White Paper *Training for Employment* (Cmnd 316). HMSO, 1988. Copies obtainable from HMSO, or details from the MSC, Room E414, Moorfoot, Sheffield S1 4PQ

Index

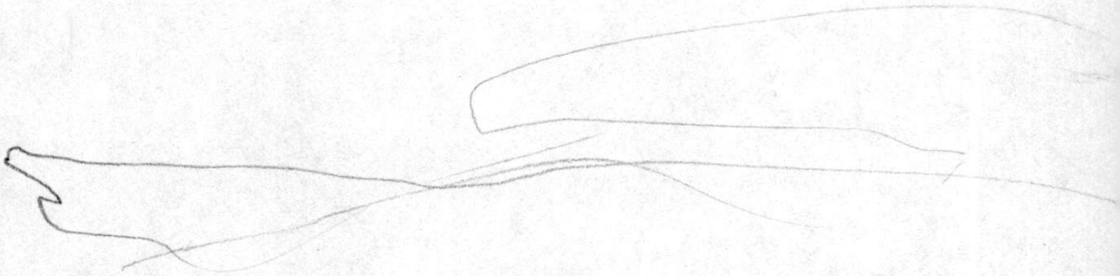

Fri 27th AM HRM II
Mon 13th AM – ACC
tues AM 14th – E.D
Wed AM – M.M.P I
PM French